The
EVERLASTING FLAME

The
EVERLASTING FLAME

Zoroastrianism in History and Imagination

Edited by Sarah Stewart

with
Firoza Punthakey Mistree · Ursula Sims-Williams
Almut Hintze · Pheroza J. Godrej

SOAS
University of London

in collaboration with

I.B. TAURIS
LONDON · NEW YORK

Published on the occasion of the exhibition

**The Everlasting Flame:
Zoroastrianism in History and Imagination**

Brunei Gallery · SOAS · University of London
11 October–14 December 2013

Patron: **Zubin Mehta**

Curated by

**Sarah Stewart · Firoza Punthakey Mistree
Ursula Sims-Williams · Almut Hintze · Pheroza J. Godrej**

Exhibition designed by Morris Associates

Sponsored by

The Zoroastrian Trust Funds of Europe · Aequa Foundation

Cyrus Poonawalla principal sponsor (India) · TATA Enterprises

Farrokh K. Kavarana · Vahid Alaghband · Zarir Cama

California Zoroastrian Center · The Farhangi Foundation · Dr Abtin Sassanfar
The Incorporated Zoroastrian Charity Funds of Hong Kong, Canton and Macao
Iran Heritage Foundation · British Institute of Persian Studies
Soudavar Memorial Foundation · Mr Pallonji Mistry
The Bombay Parsi Punchayet · Erach Roshan Sadri Foundation
Ms Vika Irani · Vahid Kooros

Dedicated to the memory of
Mobed Faridoon B. Zartoshty
and
Mobed Mehraban J. Zartoshty

First published in 2013 by I.B.Tauris & Co Ltd
6 Salem Road, London W2 4BU • 175 Fifth Avenue, New York NY 10010
www.ibtauris.com

Published in association SOAS, University of London
© 2013 SOAS, University of London

Distributed in the United States and Canada exclusively
by Palgrave Macmillan, 175 Fifth Avenue, New York NY 10010

ISBN 978-1-78076-809-0 (hardback) • ISBN 978-1-78076-810-6 (paperback)

A full CIP record for this book is available from the British Library
A full CIP record is available from the Library of Congress
Library of Congress Catalog Card Number: available

Designed by E&P Design • Printed and bound in Italy by Printer Trento

Frontispiece: Dhunbai Jamsetji Tata (1861–71)
Artist: P. B. Hatte • 1906 • Oil on canvas • 69.2 x 59.1 cm • Collection: Hameed Haroon

Chapter openers (Essays and Catalogue): *Tanchoi* Sari
Early 20th century • Woven *tanchoi* silk • Private collection (see also page 195)

page 258: Zoroaster, founder of the seven liberal arts
c.1475–80 • Ink on parchment • British Library Cotton Augustus V, f. 25v

CONTENTS

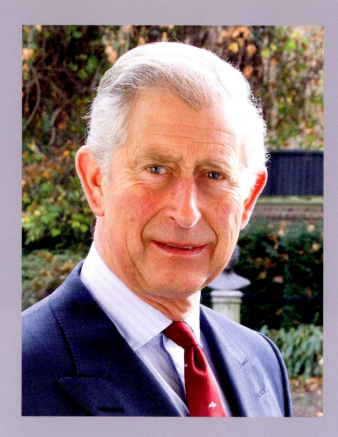

CLARENCE HOUSE

When I was invited to write the Foreword for the catalogue accompanying a new exhibition narrating the visual history of Zoroastrianism, I could not help but reflect on the apposite timing of what is – I am told – the first such exhibition in the United Kingdom.

For millennia, Zoroastrianism has had a profound yet often undervalued influence on cultures and societies across the world. Travelling from ancient Persia to the west coast of India, Zoroastrian philosophy has enriched the development of numerous art forms – from illuminated sacred manuscripts to *tanchoi* silk weaving.

Zoroastrianism's influence on the teachings of Judaism, Christianity and Islam has been well documented. But what is perhaps less well known is the way in which the message at the very heart of Zoroastrianism - "good thoughts, good words and good deeds" – continues to offer an integrated response to the challenges of the twenty-first century, where communities so often struggle to live together in harmony. In an increasingly secular world, it seems to me to be <u>vitally</u> important that sacred wisdom accumulated over thousands of years is preserved for future generations.

I could not be more delighted, therefore, that the School of Oriental and African Studies has mounted this important exhibition. It will, I hope, be a source of education and inspiration for all who visit it and a fitting tribute to an ancient Faith which reveres the illuminated mind.

ACKNOWLEDGEMENTS

SOAS, University of London would like to thank all those whose generosity has made this exhibition and catalogue possible

Without the generosity of our lenders, both public institutions and private individuals, this exhibition could never have realised its ambitious vision. They are listed on page 251 and SOAS is very grateful to them all.

We would particularly like to thank the following people for their support and collaboration: The Nour Foundation and Professor Nasser D. Khalili, Professor Michael Rogers and Ms Nahla Nassar, The Chester Beatty Library, The National Museum of India, Dr Venu Vasudevan and Dr Jayshree Sharma, Chhatrapati Shivaji Maharaj Vastu Sangrahalaya and Mr Sabyasachi Mukherjee, Bombay Parsi Punchayet – F. D. Alpaiwalla Museum and Mrs Nivedeta Mehta, Tata Central Archives and Ms Freny Shroff, the Institute of Archaeology in Samarkand and Dr Berdimuradov, the Afrasiab Museum in Samarkand and Dr Mustafakulov, Mr Fereydoun Ave, Ms Janet Rady, Mrs Fatema Soudavar Farmanfarmaian and Mr Vahid Kooros.

An exhibition of this nature would not be possible without the help and encouragement of many people throughout the world whose support we would like to acknowledge.

In India
Dr Shernaz Cama of UNESCO Parzor, Mr Muncherji Cama, Mr Sam Chothia, Mrs Bapsy Dastur, Mr Yazdi H. Desai, Mr Noshir Gobhai, Mrs Pheroza Godrej, Mr Farooq Issa, Mr Rumi Majoo, Mr Dinshaw Mehta, Mr Khojeste Mistree, Mrs Firoza Punthakey Mistree, Kaiyan Mistree, and Tashan Mistree Byramji, Mr Jimmy Mistry, Mr Sarosh Patel and his team at Effects Tech Sets, Mrs Perin Pudumjee, Mr Homi Ranina, Mr Anupam Sah, Ms Sudha Seshadri, Mr Hamza Taher of Daudbhoy M. Tayebally and Khuzaima Badani of Khozem Glass and their teams.

The priests who have helped us procure many of the Fire Temple items, photographs and footage of ritual ceremonies: Ervad Asphandiar Dadachanji, Ervad Hormuz Dadachanji, Ervad Behram Dordi, Ervad Ramiyar Karanjia, Ervad Porus Katrak, Ervad Rohinton Pavri and Ervad Faredoonji Turel.

In Pakistan
Mr Hameed Haroon, Mrs Franey Irani, Mrs Aban Marker Kabraji and Mrs Nilufer Patel.

In the United Arab Emirates
Mrs Hutoxi Kandawalla.

In Hong Kong
Mr Neville Shroff of The Incorporated Zoroastrian Charity Funds of Hong Kong, Canton and Macao.

In the United States
Dr Ardeshir Anoshiravani, Mrs Shida Anoshiravani, Mrs Dolly Dastur, Ms Azita Dehmobed, Mr Ramin Farhangi, Mrs Roshan Rivetna, Dr Jenny Rose.

In London
Mr David Barnett, Ms Shahin Bekhradnia, Lord Karan Bilimoria, Mr John Borsberry, Mr Andrew Campbell-Tiech, Mr Christopher Clark, Mr Rusi Dalal, Mrs Roshan Dalal, Mrs Lesley Eden, Mrs Shernaz Engineer, Ms Liliya Evtimova, Mrs Poppy Gordon Lennox, Mr Anwar Hasan, Mr David Landsman, Mr Dorab Mistry, Mr Charles Peyton, Ms Marianne Pilloux, Mrs Ursula Sims-Williams, Mr Bahtiyor Turaev, Lord Michael Williams of Baglan, the World Zoroastrian Organisation.

Students of SOAS past and present
Alexandra Buhler, Anabel Inge, Rosheen Kabraji, Farida Seddon, Burzine Waghmar.

At SOAS
Naaznin Adatia, Anna Contadini, Mike Haddon, John Hollingworth, Louise Hosking, George Jenkins, Sian Jones, Fiona McWilliams, Katie Nugent, Vincenzo Paci, Richard Poulson, Katie Price, Glenn Ratcliffe, Vesna Siljanovska, Natasha Williams, Jane Wood, Valentina Zanardi, Cosimo Zene.

CONTRIBUTORS
TO THE CATALOGUE

We are also grateful to all those who have contributed to the catalogue.

British Museum
Ladan Akbarnia (LA)
John Curtis (JC)
Vesta Sarkhosh Curtis (VC)
St John Simpson (St JS)

British Library
Ursula Sims-Williams (USW)

SOAS
Alexandra Buhler (AB)
François de Blois (FB)
Almut Hintze (AH)
Nicholas Sims-Williams (NSW)
Sarah Stewart (SS)
Burzine Waghmar (BW)

Harvard University
Yishai Kiel (YK)
Prods Oktor Skjærvø (POS)

Collège de France
Frantz Grenet (FG)

Zoroastrian Studies
Firoza Punthakey Mistree (FPM)

Claremont University
Jenny Rose (JR)

The State Hermitage Museum
Mariam Dandamaeva (MD)
L. Yu. Kulakova (LYK)
Pavel Lurje (PL)

Unesco Parzor
Shernaz Cama (SC)

FOREWORD

Professor Paul Webley
Director and Principal of SOAS

Zoroastrianism is one of the oldest religions of the world. Its physical reach extended far beyond the boundaries of what we now refer to as Central Asia and Iran. Its metaphysical influence is apparent in the philosophies and religions that appear to have eclipsed it. But appearances can be deceptive.

This unique exhibition and book bring together in visual form the many strands of Zoroastrian beliefs and practices as they have developed over the last 3,000 years. The visitor is taken on a journey through time, alighting at intervals to inspect artefacts, texts and paintings from worlds both familiar and yet very different from our own.

The subtitle, 'Zoroastrianism in History and Imagination', is well chosen. Never before has London – or Europe for that matter – seen in one place rock reliefs from Persepolis, Persian miniatures and illustrated manuscripts depicting hell's inferno, let alone a fire temple, a tower of silence or a Parsi salon. Yet for me, it is in the smaller treasures that the history of a people is brought to life. The testament to past sensuality demonstrated by the 'amorous couple' from ancient Elam is, in its own way, as revealing of a culture as any marvel of ancient engineering.

I am proud that SOAS, with its long history of collaboration with the oldest Zoroastrian diaspora outside Iran and India, is hosting this exhibition. At SOAS we value and promote engagement with diasporic communities in the UK and beyond through our research, teaching and outreach programmes. These are complemented by the facility of a world-class venue for the arts that SOAS has in the Brunei Gallery.

SOAS has an unrivalled position within the academic world as guardian of specialised knowledge in the arts and cultures of the Middle East, Asia and Africa. Zoroastrianism has been taught at SOAS since 1929. Professor Mary Boyce, whose seminal works rekindled academic interest in the English speaking world, taught Zoroastrianism from 1947 until 1982. Many distinguished scholars have followed in her footsteps.

Yet neither this exhibition, nor the continuation of Zoroastrian scholarship at SOAS, would have been possible without the help and support of a large number of people and organisations.

In 2011, SOAS received a substantial donation from the Zoroastrian Trust Funds of Europe, which led to the establishment of the Zartoshty Chair in Zoroastrian Studies held by Professor Almut Hintze. It is fitting that this volume is dedicated to Mobeds Mehraban and Faridoon Zartoshty. SOAS is also indebted to the Zoroastrian Trust Funds of Europe and its President, Mr Malcolm M. Deboo, for securing the core funding for this exhibition as well as sponsoring its catalogue. We are also profoundly grateful to the Aequa Foundation.

Without the support of Dr Cyrus Poonawalla in India we would not have the spectacular installations made by Indian craftsmen that so enhance the exhibition. We would like to thank TATA Enterprises for its generous sponsorship. Also, Mr Farrokh Kavarana, Mr Zarir Cama and Mr Vahid Alaghband are warmly thanked for their contributions.

SOAS would like to thank Mr and Mrs Mistree for their dedication to this project. The knowledge and expertise, not to mention the time, that Mrs Firoza Punthakey Mistree has devoted to the exhibition goes well beyond her remit as curator. We have also benefited greatly from the advice and support of Mrs Pheroza Godrej in Mumbai. Mr Ramin Farhangi garnered valuable support from the United States. We appreciate the help given by our advisors to the exhibition, especially Professor Frantz Grenet who guided us towards obtaining significant loans from Central Asia and Dr Jenny Rose who applied her expertise to imperial Iran, the ancient world and the Zoroastrian diaspora. The exhibition is enriched by the translations of Avestan texts by Professor Almut Hintze. We thank Dr John Curtis for his advice on the narrative text for the British Museum artefacts.

We are delighted to have the institutional collaboration of the British Library as well as the loans from their important collection of Zoroastrian manuscripts. The catalogue has been produced in an exceptionally short period of time and we are grateful to Ursula Sims-Williams of the British Library for the time she has devoted to editing and proofreading as well as her contributions to its content. We also thank Iradj Bagherzade and our editor, David Hawkins, at I.B.Tauris, and Ian Parfitt for his layout and design.

The demands of an exhibition of this nature have been challenging and it is a tribute to the curators that it has come to fruition. They have been fortunate in having the experience and administrative competence of Poppy Gordon Lennox. John Hollingworth in the Brunei Gallery as well members of SOAS and LMEI staff have all contributed to the smooth running of various aspects of the exhibition.

Without the expertise, talent and tireless energy of Colin Morris and his team at Morris Associates the scale and scope of this exhibition could not have been achieved.

And last but not least, this exhibition would not have happened without the vision, commitment and energy of the curator, Dr Sarah Stewart. The exhibition was for some years just a gleam in Sarah's eyes – now it is a reality thanks to the clarity of her thinking and her absolutely astonishing work-rate, and we should all be very grateful to her.

INTRODUCTION

Sarah Stewart

SOAS, University of London

Contemporary Zoroastrianism derives its authority from three principal sources: the Iranian tradition that gave birth to the religion, the Parsi tradition established in India after Iran became a Muslim land, and the western, predominantly academic, tradition that emerged when Zoroastrian religious texts became a focus of Oriental Studies in the late eighteenth and nineteenth centuries. An account of one tradition cannot fail but to draw on the other two since all have become interwoven in the past three hundred years. *The Everlasting Flame* combines these three traditions to present a visual narrative of the history of Zoroastrianism. In the first part of the book, scholars from various fields including archaeology, history, language and religion have contributed essays that complement the narration, which mirrors the exhibition, in the second part of the book. In ten sections that bring together artefacts, texts, paintings and textiles, this tells the story of a rich and complex religion, its peoples and their culture.

Although it was perhaps conceived as a universal doctrine for mankind, Zoroastrianism developed predominantly as an ethnic religion among Iranian communities. Various factors combined to preserve this state of exclusivity, not least of which was the Arab conquest of Iran in the seventh century CE. Gradually, Zoroastrianism became a minority religion in its homeland. For those who resisted conversion to Islam, and also for those who migrated to India over a century later, Zoroastrian customs and traditions were cherished. In the last two hundred years Zoroastrians, both Parsi and Irani, have migrated to other parts of the world, in particular North America, and also to Great Britain, Australasia and the Middle East. To a large extent the Iranian, Indian and diasporic Zoroastrian populations have maintained their identity through religious practice, popular culture, conservation of community wealth and intermarriage.

A key to understanding the development of the Zoroastrian religion is the fact that its religious texts were in oral transmission for many hundreds of years before being committed to writing. This oral tradition, made all the more important by the absence of any contemporary account of the early phases of the religion, has shaped the way in which Zoroastrians have understood their faith, and has influenced the perceptions of others who have come into contact with Zoroastrianism at various times throughout its long history. It is only in the latter part of the twentieth century that scholars began to study the ancient texts of the Avesta, or Zoroastrian religious book, through the prism of an oral rather than a literary tradition. The small corpus of Avestan texts that survived the exigencies of Zoroastrian history was subject to many redactions, translations and interpretations. The 'primary' source has thus come a long way from its original composition. For example, the ancient *Yashts*, hymns addressed to divinities of the Zoroastrian pantheon, represent an accumulation of ideas and events, both actual and mythological. Characteristic of these oral texts is a lack of temporality – they are set outside any historical timeline – and also literary structures and devices that were designed to act as mnemonics, like the repetition of verses and the exaggeration of the deeds of protagonists, such as gods, heroes and kings.

The Gathas belong to an ancient Indo-Iranian tradition of wisdom poetry and consist of rhetorical questions addressed by Zarathustra to the god and source of revelation who spoke to him, namely Ahura Mazda, 'the Wise Lord'. The remaining texts, in Young Avestan, were allowed to evolve and represent a number of historic levels. Whilst we cannot know the way in which these texts were understood by ancient peoples we can safely assume that their exegesis and transmission is likely to have been solely the preserve of priests from the time the Avestan language ceased to be comprehensible to the laity.

It is thought that such religious texts as survived the Persian conquests of Alexander of Macedon were transmitted orally until the compilation of the Sasanian Avesta possibly sometime in the sixth century CE. The prolific output of Zoroastrian religious literature in the ninth century CE formed the basis of what is sometimes referred to in western terminology as the classical tradition. Religious texts were compiled, mainly by priests, with the purpose of reinforcing doctrine and belief while at the same time discouraging people from converting to Islam.

The paucity of material available for the early period of Zoroastrianism, the relatively late arrival of the Avesta into the world of scholarship in the eighteenth century, the allusive nature of its ancient texts and the lack of theological development after the ninth century in Iran are all factors that have given rise to a multiplicity of theories about the origins and nature of Zoroastrianism. In consequence, Zoroastrians and non-Zoroastrians, scholars, priests and lay-people continue to debate the origins of the Avestan language, the genesis of the religion and the purport of its doctrines, the date, birthplace and even the very existence of Zarathustra. The Gathas have been scrutinised for answers to such questions as whether or not Zarathustra advocated the abandonment of the narcotic *haoma* and the practice of animal sacrifice; whether the religion is essentially monotheistic or dualistic – terms incidentally that are best understood within the context of the Abrahamic religions. The practice of *khvaetvadatha* (MP *khvedodah*) or next-of-kin marriage and the rigorous purity laws prescribed in Younger Avesta and Pahlavi texts are issues that have generated discussion and sometimes polarised debate. One of the outcomes has been to 'return' to (i.e. to seek authority in), the teachings of Zarathustra. In Iran this is termed *Gatha puyan* or 'return to the Gatha'.

This book does not seek to answer these questions, but it does provide context. This is achieved by bringing together in the first part the most recent research on many of these subjects. In the second part, the juxtaposition of texts and images, commentary and analysis offers the reader the same journey through the history of Zoroastrianism that the visitor experiences in the exhibition.

In the introductory catalogue section Jenny Rose gives us a view of the ancient world and its urban civilisations from Mesopotamia to the Indus valley. This is a world of movement and flux made visible to us primarily through the work of archaeologists and philologists who have attempted to locate the ancestors of the Avestan-speaking peoples, the Indo-Europeans or Proto-Indo-Europeans. Our artefacts from Luristan support J.P. Mallory's contention that: 'If we must have concrete legacies, then the best claim is that of horse domestication and the social consequences this revolution in transportation and warfare brought to the world'.[1] It is to the advent of the latter that Mary Boyce attributes Zarathustra's doctrine regarding the fundamental opposition of good and evil.

The second section of the catalogue deals with the sacred texts of Zoroastrianism, with examples selected from the British Library's unique collection of Zoroastrian manuscripts, curated by Ursula Sims-Williams. Certain Avestan manuscripts explain the main components of Zoroastrian religious thought, as well as the most important Zoroastrian priestly ceremony, the Yasna. Found within is the idea of retribution for good and bad deeds, the earliest references to the dichotomy between good and evil and the creation of the universe, together with the concept of the Divine Immortals, *Amesha Spentas*. This section, written by Almut Hintze, introduces the Younger Avestan text of the *Videvdad*, explains the significance of the *Yasna Haptanghaiti* liturgy and proceeds to outline Zoroastrian exegetical literature and Pahlavi books. In the essay that accompanies this section, Hintze gives a comprehensive account

1. Mallory (1989): 270

of the various possibilities concerning the origins of the religion, its languages and movement of its peoples. Entitled 'Words without context' the chapter explains why it is that the Older Avesta cannot be located in space and time and gives an overview of the prehistoric Indo-Iranian culture from which the religion of the Avesta emerged. The scope of this chapter allows us to appreciate the major innovation of the Avestan religion, namely the rejection of the Indo-Iranian gods, the *daevas*, and worship of Ahura Mazda.

The third section focuses on the Silk Road, Central Asia and China, where archaeologists have produced a wealth of material regarding Zoroastrian practices far away from the Iranian heartland with which it is normally associated. Frantz Grenet writes about the significance of Zoroastrian funerary practices in both Sogdiana and Chorasmia, as well as among expatriate Sogdian communities in China. As he observes, the regional practice of depositing bones in ossuaries has enabled a more comprehensive study than has been possible in Iran where this custom was not followed. Depictions of Zoroastrian rituals including a sacred fire and priests wearing the *padam* (mouth covering) are, in some cases, combined with Zoroastrian motifs showing the weighing of the soul to determine its good and bad deeds and thus its eschatological future. In the funerary monuments in China there are instances of a fusion of ideas where Chinese motifs have been adapted to reflect Zoroastrian beliefs.

Also from China is one of the treasures of the British Library collection, the *Ashem Vohu* prayer, which pre-dates any other written Zoroastrian text by some four centuries. A Bactrian document addressed to the god Mihr, translated by Nicholas Sims-Williams is concerned with collection of taxes payable by the god himself. Although not religious in content, this is typical of a worldview that is found in the ancient *Yashts*, where there is no distinction drawn between

the celestial and terrestrial worlds and gods and men move effortlessly between them.

The section on the Judaeo-Christian World contains some of the rarest of the British Library's collection of texts concerning Zoroastrianism. None of these have been exhibited before. It is this part of the story that deals with some of the links between Zoroastrianism and Judaism and shows the way it came to be imagined in the world of medieval Christianity. The interaction between Jewish scribes during the Talmudic period in Babylon and Zoroastrian priests in the Sasanian capital of Ctesiphon is discussed by Prods Oktor Skjærvø with reference to the Babylonian Talmud and the Zoroastrian law book, the *Videvdad*. Anke Joisten-Pruschke's essay complements this section with an account of the relations between Jews and Zoroastrians during the Achaemenid, Parthian and Sasanian periods. We learn about the interest paid to Zoroastrianism by the Platonic Academy in Athens in the third and fourth centuries BCE from various seventeenth-century accounts based on classical sources. The figure of Zoroaster (which is the Greek form of Zarathustra's name) aroused curiosity in medieval Christendom, where he became associated with magic. Two outstanding fifteenth-century manuscripts from the British Library are the Italian work *Il Tesoro*, which attributes to Zoroaster the discovery of magic, and one that once belonged to Henry VIII of England where, in addition to magic, he is described as the founder of the seven liberal arts. As far as we know, these early scholars had no recourse to written sources or knowledge of Avestan, relying completely on the somewhat 'creative' descriptions of the Classical world.

Zoroastrianism as the religion of imperial Iran is a topic covered by Philip Kreyenbroek in chapter 5. The implications of the oral transmission of texts are discussed here, with reference to the Achaemenids. Whilst the transmission of core texts and rituals was largely consistent, there must also have been local variations. Artefacts, coins and stone reliefs from the Alpaiwalla Museum in Mumbai and from the British Museum give substance to the imperial splendour of the Achaemenid and Sasanian dynasties in the section by Jenny Rose. The lion and bull motif of Mesopotamian origin, and the winged symbol originating in ancient Egypt became associated with Zoroastrianism. The king's sacred fire is also a common motif depicted on the reverse of coins. The significance of the Sasanian period in the history of Zoroastrianism is marked by the invention of the Avestan alphabet and the compilation of the Great Sasanian Avesta.

From the peak of its glory as the state religion of a powerful empire, the Zoroastrian narrative moves to that of the religion of a conquered minority. This has some fascinating ramifications. The output of religious literature in the ninth century provides insights into the theological developments that were occurring within Zoroastrianism at the time, motivated, perhaps, by the need to explain, consolidate and persuade. Albert de Jong's article gives a new perspective to this period, contending for the intellectual inclusion rather than exclusion of Zoroastrians in the new world of Islamic Iran. The Persian texts of the *Arda Viraf Nameh* and their juxtaposition with the *Mi 'raj Nameh* and the *Divina Commedia* are not intended to demonstrate continuities, or point to the origins of ideas. Rather they are intended to give an insight into the value system by which notions of reward/retribution were applied to the everyday lives of Zoroastrians, Christians and Muslims. In the Persian version of the Pahlavi text of the *Arda Viraz Namag* we see that the reference to the marriage of Arda Viraf to his seven sisters has been omitted. This is an early example, perhaps, of changing sensibilities. Whereas the Pahlavi literature extolled the practice of *khvedodah*, or next-of-kin marriage, in time it became understood to refer only to marriage between first cousins.

The growth of Persian literature, in particular the epic *Shahnameh* of Ferdowsi is shown within the context of pre-Islamic Iran. The dualistic imagery of the kings and heroes of Iran perpetually at war with a non-Iranian foe, usually the Turanians, or barbarians from the north, is strongly reminiscent of the *Yashts*. The main theme of the *Yashts*, invocation of the gods, is but a minor subject in the epic whose purpose was to provide a chronology of events and to reinforce a sense of Iranian identity. This part of the catalogue proceeds to show the impoverished state and diminished population that had become Zoroastrian Iran by the sixteenth century under Safavid rule. Contact with the Parsis in India during the mid to late eighteenth century began to reverse this situation with the revival of Zoroastrian fortunes in Iran.

The next section traces the legendary journey of the Zoroastrians from Iran to India according to a text that has come down to us as the late-sixteenth-century poem *Qesseh-ye Sanjan*, ('Story of Sanjan'). Alan Williams shows how this poem, which is highly traditional and possibly composed from much older material is a religious myth of community memory rather than a merely historical document. The story accounts for the loss of Iran and its sovereignty to Islam, and celebrates the Zoroastrian rebirth as a community in India, at the centre of which is the enthronement of the Fire of Iranshah, literally translated as 'The King of Iran'. Ursula Sims-Williams gives an insight into the relatively unexplored world of Persian literary culture in India, as well as the different interpretations of the Zoroastrian religion afforded by such texts as the *Dabestan-e Mazaheb*.

Travellers' accounts of the religion of the Parsis take us to the next section, the 'Parsi Salon', that gives a visual account of the rapid growth of the Parsi community in Bombay during the colonial period. Defence of their religion in the face of missionary zeal was to have a profound effect on the development of Parsi identity. For some it became necessary to seek a rational explanation in line with the European Enlightenment for aspects of Zoroastrian religious practice – for example the strict purity laws, which were interpreted according to western scientific notions of hygiene. For others it meant a break from traditional ideas, which resulted in what has become known as the Reform movement. The extraordinary success of Parsi entrepreneurs and their affiliation to European culture is depicted in the many paintings, furnishings and exquisite textiles described by Firoza Punthakey Mistree. Her essay makes the connection between this flowering of ideas and the material wealth derived from the China trade.

At the heart of the story is the Zoroastrian fire temple. This takes us back to Almut Hintze's account of the ritual texts and the significance of the central priestly act of worship, the Yasna. But it also demonstrates the fusion of ritual and devotional life. In the fire temple we see the way in which the symbol of Zoroastrianism, the fire, serves to underpin doctrine, ritual and worship. It is also fire that cements the two contexts of Iran and India together, as described in the *Qesseh-ye Sanjan*, through the establishment of the Iranshah on Indian soil.

The subject of the modern diaspora could fill an entire exhibition and it is to be regretted that here we have room for only a glimpse of the various Zoroastrian communities around the world. Yet the narrative provided by Jenny Rose does give a strong sense of the many ways in which both Parsis and Iranis have adapted their lives to different host communities.

The future of the religion is in the hands of young Zoroastrians and our postscript for them is to be found in the small collection of paintings and sculptures provided by the Iranian Zoroastrian artist, Fereydoun Ave. Here is a thoroughly modern collection through which is presented the doctrine of the seven creations together with excerpts from the ninth-century Pahlavi book of the *Bundahishn*.

NOTE ON TRANSLITERATION

The chapters in this volume draw on a large number of sources in different languages (Avestan, Middle Persian, Persian and Parsi Gujarati) for which different transliteration systems are normally used. The I.B.Tauris house style has been adopted here but it has not been possible to achieve complete consistency.

MAP OF THE ANCIENT WORLD

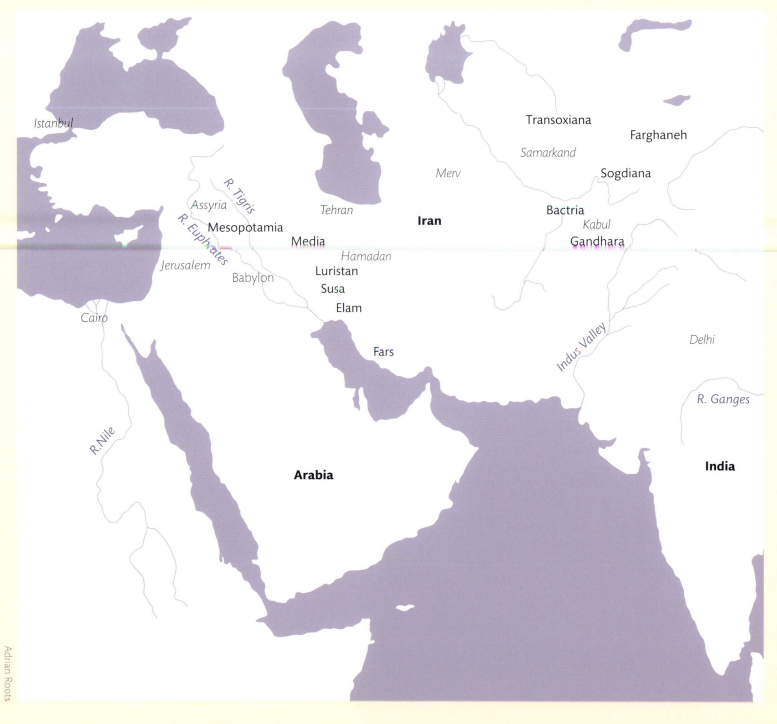

Istanbul

Transoxiana

Farghaneh

Samarkand

Merv

Sogdiana

R. Tigris

Assyria

Tehran

Iran

Bactria

Kabul

R. Euphrates

Mesopotamia

Media

Gandhara

Jerusalem

Hamadan

Babylon

Luristan

Susa

Cairo

Elam

Indus Valley

Delhi

Fars

R. Ganges

R.Nile

Arabia

India

Adrian Roots

ESSAYS

WORDS WITHOUT CONTEXT
the Gathas between two worlds

Almut Hintze

SOAS, University of London

THE OLDER AND YOUNGER AVESTA IN SPACE AND TIME

Nowadays Iran is known for being home to Shi'a Islam. However, long before the arrival of Islam in the seventh century, the region had been the centre of one of the most influential religious traditions, Zoroastrianism. Throughout the more than 1,000 years of Iran's imperial history, extending from Achaemenid (559–330 BCE) through Parthian times (247 BCE–224 CE) to the downfall of the Zoroastrian state at the end of the Sasanian period (224–651 CE), Zoroastrianism was a major religious and cultural force in the Near and Middle East. For instance, coming within its sphere of influence, post-exilic Judaism gradually developed an eschatology and concept of evil that converge with Zoroastrianism and fed first into Christianity and later Islam.

The focus of Zoroastrianism is worship of the god Ahura Mazda, usually rendered as 'Wise Lord' ('Ohrmazd' in Middle Persian). He is the maker of the world, which is therefore worthy of worship (*yazata*) both in its spiritual and material manifestations. At the same time, Zoroastrians reject and scorn the destructive force (*angra mainyu*, 'Ahriman' in Middle Persian) that, coming from outside, counteracts Ahura Mazda's life-giving creative force (*spenta mainyu*) by invading the perfect world and inflicting on it deceit and death. According to Zoroastrian religious teachings, Ahura Mazda revealed the Mazda-worshipping, or Mazdayasnian, religion to the man Zarathustra, who in turn passed it on to humankind. His followers formally worship Ahura Mazda and his creations in prayers and in priestly and lay rituals in which they recite texts composed in the language of Zarathustra: Avestan. The belief that Avestan was Zarathustra's language derives from the tradition, already found in the Avesta, which attributes to him 17 hymns composed in five different metres and known as 'the five Gathas of Zarathustra'.

The Gathas have been handed down in the oral tradition of the Mazda-worshippers at the centre of their most important ritual, the Yasna (Y), or 'worship', which consists of 72 sections and is also the core of all other major priestly rituals (Fig. 1). The Gathas, in turn, are arranged around an equally archaic liturgy in seven sections, the *Yasna Haptanghaiti* (YH). This composite centre of the Yasna, consisting of about 9,500 words in total, constitutes what scholars call the Older Avesta. It is composed in a more archaic language than that of the Younger Avesta, which is much greater in volume and comprised of invocations, hymns and purity laws.[1] The comparatively advanced stage of development of both the language and religious system of the Younger Avesta suggests that considerable time had elapsed since the composition of the Older Avesta. Moreover, the Younger Avestan liturgical texts suggest that when they were composed, the Older Avesta not only already existed but did so with the same internal arrangement and central importance for the Yasna Haptanghaiti ritual as it has in its present form. Numerous quotations and adaptations from both the Gathas and the *Yasna Haptanghaiti* in the Younger Avesta reveal that the Older Avesta, especially the *Yasna Haptanghaiti*, served as its compositional model, which must have been a fixed text.[2] These texts were composed at different times, presumably between 1000 and 400 BCE. The Gathas and the *Yasna Haptanghaiti* must be several centuries older and constitute the oldest extant witness not only to the Zoroastrian religion but also to any Iranian language.

The Older Avesta, however, represents words without any context. There are no geographical names that could fix the texts in space or correlate them with archaeological monuments. Moreover, since Avestan displays no phonological features characteristic of Eastern Iranian languages from later periods, it cannot be associated with any particular known dialect. All that is certain is that it is different from the Persian idioms of southwestern Iran.[3] The Gathas and *Yasna Haptanghaiti* thus stand as archaic literary compositions between the prehistoric Indo-Iranian and Proto-Iranian periods and the historical Younger Avestan age.

The Younger Avesta, by contrast, mentions identifiable places from southern Central Asia, such as Sogdia, Margiana and Bactria, and the Indo-Iranian borderlands. Moreover, places such as Lake Kansaoya (the modern Lake Hamun) and the River Haetumant (the modern River Helmand in Sistan) play significant roles in epic and theological Avestan imagery. Some of the beliefs, such as the birth of the 'victorious' Saoshyant, or world saviour, are especially connected with the land of Sistan.[4] Cult practices involving excessive blood-spilling while killing animals, burning the juniper plant and bodily convulsions by the Daeva-worshipping Vyamburas (*Yasht* 14.54–6) are similar to those observed in the early nineteenth century among the 'Kafiris' in Nuristan in north-eastern Afghanistan. They are still attested among the Kalash Kafirs and other peoples in the Hindu Kush.[5]

The earliest Zoroastrian sources with absolute dates come from the Achaemenid period in the form both of royal inscriptions and other written documents and of reports by foreign observers, in particular the Greek historian Herodotus.[6] Most of the surviving evidence for the religion during the subsequent Seleucid and Parthian periods also consists of foreign reports by Greek and Roman authors in addition to numismatic, epigraphic and archaeological sources. The largest body of Zoroastrian religious literature that has survived dates from Sasanian and early Islamic times and is composed in the Middle Persian, or Pahlavi, language.[7] However, much of this, such as the *Bundahishn*, entails reworkings of older, Avestan material.

INDO-IRANIAN ORIGINS

Zoroastrianism is rooted in the prehistoric Indo-Iranian culture of the second and third millennia

BCE and shares a common heritage with the closely related Vedic language and culture of ancient India. Indo-Iranian, in turn, is a branch of the Indo-European language family to which groups such as Celtic, Italic, Germanic, Baltic, Slavic, Albanian, Greek, Armenian, Anatolian, Tocharian and their modern descendants also belong. The location of the homeland of the Indo-European peoples has been subject to an extensive and ongoing debate. According to a currently widely accepted model, the Proto-Indo-Europeans emerged around 4500 BCE 'out of local communities in the forest-steppe of the Ukraine and south Russia'.[8] Markers of Indo-European culture include the domesticated horse and light horse-drawn vehicle with spoked wheels, used in warfare and chariot races. The Proto-Indo-Iranians presumably split off in the third millennium BCE and moved east-wards towards the Greater Ural region, where they are usually associated with the Bronze Age Andronovo culture of the Eurasian steppe. They lived as nomadic pastoralists with a tribal-based economy and three social classes (priest, warrior and stockbreeder), their domestic animals including cows, sheep, horses and dogs. The horse-drawn, spoked-wheel chariot, driven by a charioteer and mounted by a warrior, was used for war and racing, for which there was a prize at stake (Fig. 2).

Archaeological evidence from the Tobol river area suggests that Andronovo people lived temporarily in clusters of a few timber-built dwellings but then moved on to new sites, owing to degradation of the grazing grounds and human and animal diseases and epidemics resulting from poor hygiene.[9]

According to a currently widely accepted hypothesis, the later Indo-Aryans were the first to leave the northern steppes in the late third millennium BCE. A group migrated westwards and eventually settled in northern Mesopotamia to form an upper class in the non-Indo-European Hurrian kingdom of the Mitanni. It is from there that the earliest historical evidence for any Indo-Iranian language comes, both in the form of divine names in a 1380 BCE treaty between the Mitanni and Hittite kings and also in Indo-Aryan words in other Hittite documents, particularly a text by the Mitanni Kikkuli relating to horse training. Other groups moved south of the northern steppes and passed through the more highly developed non-Indo-European oasis civilizations of Bactria and Margiana, called Oxus culture or the Bactria-Margiana Archaeological Complex (BMAC), which dates from around 2400 to 1600 BCE.[10] Having emerged in Margiana out of the Namazga V culture and spread to Bactria, the BMAC is characterized by urban settlements with agriculture and large-scale irrigation systems (Fig. 3).

The BMAC now plays an important role in discussions of the archaeology of the early Indo-Iranians. One of the key problems of identifying Indo-Iranian expansion into today's Iranian lands, Pakistan or India has been that these regions provide no evidence of any Andronovo material with which the Indo-Iranians are associated. Thus there appears to be no archaeological support for what linguistic and literary sources imply, namely that the regions of Greater Iran and north-western India, inhabited by non-Indo-European peoples, were penetrated by Indo-Iranians, or, in archaeological terms, people of the Andronovo culture of the northern steppe. What we do find, however, are large amounts of typical Andronovo steppe artefacts on BMAC sites, and subsequently intrusive BMAC material in Iran, Afghanistan and Pakistan.[11] It has, therefore, been suggested that the southward-moving Indo-Iranians passed through a 'membrane', as it were, of urban BMAC civilization. Undergoing a process of acculturation and bilingualism, they adopted the material culture of the Oxus civilization while retaining their own language. On the model of contemporary relationships between the settled agriculturalist Tajiks and the semi-nomadic Uzbeks, it has been suggested that the acculturation of the steppe population took place by regular seasonal contact with those settled in the oases. In this process, the non-Indo-European language of the urban BMAC civilization enriched the lexicon of the Indo-Iranians with, for instance, terms for certain animals and for building. Such words, which are found in both Iranian and Indo-Aryan but have no Indo-European etymology, include the word for 'camel' (*ushtra-*), for 'donkey' (*khara-*, probably of Mesopotamian origin) and for 'brick' (Vedic *ishtaka-*, AV. *ishtya-*, OP *ishti-*, from a Central Asian word **isht*).[12] The subsequent expansion of the BMAC can then be correlated with further movements of transformed Indo-Iranians. Such migrations are probably not to be conceived as 'invasions' but rather as periodic infiltrations of ethnic and linguistic groups in search of new grazing grounds. It is very likely that the people of the BMAC were in contact with the Indus civilization, whose northernmost outpost, Shortughai, is located in eastern Bactria. The BMAC ended around 1700 BCE with its so-called 'collapse' but continued in an impoverished form at Tureng Tepe until about 1600 BCE.

Profound cultural changes in Central Asia resulted in the culture called Yaz I, dated c. 1500–1000 BCE. The people of this early Iron Age period tended to live on newly founded sites in a rather rural society.

Most of their pottery is handmade and some is painted with red or black geometrical designs. Remains of grinding stones and grain point to a sedentary population with a mixed economy of agriculture and stockbreeding.[13] While there is evidence for some overlap of Oxus civilization technology, there are also far-reaching links, including to western Turkmenistan and the Andronovo culture of the northern steppes.[14] The fact that no graves were found in the area after 1500 BCE until the arrival of the Greeks in the Hellenistic period has been interpreted as indicating that the dead were disposed of by means of exposure.[15] Since a good deal of evidence suggests that the custom of exposing the dead was practised by Iranians, one could argue that the Yaz I culture might be Iranian but not necessarily Zoroastrian. However, in non-Zoroastrian cultures, exposure of bodies is just one means of disposing of the dead, and there are always burials as well. What is striking in the Yaz I culture is that there is not a single burial in the area, pointing to an ideological basis for exposing the dead, perhaps the one that the Avesta prescribes: that burials defile one of Ahura Mazda's creations, the earth, and so are not permissible.

ZOROASTRIAN COSMOLOGY AND ESCHATOLOGY

As stated above, the focus of the Mazdayasnian religion is the worship of Ahura Mazda. While the title *ahura-*, 'lord', corresponds to the Vedic *asura-* and is inherited from Indo-Iranian,[16] this is probably not so in the case of the divine name *mazda-* because there is no Vedic deity called **medha-*, 'wise one'.[17] The earliest evidence for the divine name *ahura-mazda-* is widely thought to be found in the collocation *as-sa-ra ma-za-ash* in the neo-Assyrian cuneiform tablet K252, col. 9, line 23 (Cat. 7). Although this document comes from the library of Assurbanipal (668–*c.*630 BCE), it could be a copy of a middle-Assyrian text from the second millennium BCE.

The retention of the intervocalic -s- in the form *as-sa-ra*, if the latter represents Iranian *ahura-*, would favour the earlier date.[18]

A characteristic innovation of the religion of the Avesta is that the worship of Ahura Mazda is coupled with the rejection of the Indo-Iranian gods, the Daevas. Not only in the Zoroastrian texts but also in all Iranian languages, the Indo-Iranian and ultimately Indo-European word for god, **deiwo-*,[19] has changed its meaning from 'deity' to 'demon'. This development is traceable as a gradual process, since in the oldest texts, the Gathas, *daeva* still means 'god', albeit a false one who should not be worshipped, while in the Younger Avesta a *daeva* has become a 'demon'. The Gathas represent the Daevas as having been produced by the destructive force of 'Bad Thought' (Cat. 17):

> [*Yasna* 32.3] But you, (false) gods (*daeva*), all of you are
> offspring from Bad Thought,
> and (so also is the one) who greatly worships you.
> (Seed) from Deceit and Pretension (are),
> moreover, the repeated actions for which you are
> known in the seventh part of the earth.

The downgrading of the gods of earlier generations and their subordination to another power forms part of a belief system that divides everything into good and evil. These two distinct groups are mutually exclusive, diametrically opposed to one another and described in the Gathas as 'life-giving' (*spanyah-*) and 'destructive' (*angra*) respectively (Cat. 15):

> [*Yasna* 45.2] I shall tell forth the two forces (which were)
> at the beginning of life.
> The life-giving of these two will speak to the destructive
> one in the following way:
> Neither our thoughts go together, nor our pronouncements
> nor our minds,
> neither our choices nor our words nor our deeds,
> neither our beliefs nor our souls.

The spiritual creation

In the Pahlavi *Bundahishn*, which is a more coherent account based on the Avesta, Ohrmazd, with whom the 'life-giving force' had by then merged, resided on high in eternal light, omniscience and goodness, while Ahriman, the 'destructive force', existed below in eternal darkness, deception and destruction.[20] They were completely disconnected, separated from one another by the Void. Ohrmazd, being all-knowing, was aware of the existence of the destructive force, and in order to prevent it from invading and destroying his light, he produced out of his own essence of light many qualities, his spiritual creation, which he needed for the battle against his adversary. The idea that Ohrmazd produced the spiritual creation out of himself is also found both in the Gathas, according to which 'through birth' Ahura Mazda is the 'father' of the 'life-giving force', of 'truth' and of 'right-mindedness', and in the Younger Avesta, where he is presented as the father of the 'Life-giving Immortals', the Amesha Spentas.

According to the Pahlavi account, Ahriman then crawled to the edge of his darkness and, looking across the Void, beheld the beautiful spiritual creation of Ohrmzad and was immediately seized by the desire to destroy it. However, as he was unable to achieve any destruction without an 'army', he returned to his darkness and miscreated out of his own essence of darkness many *dew*s, which is the Middle Persian form of the Avestan *daeva*, his evil spiritual counter-creation. That the *dew*s were the products of the destructive force agrees with the Gathic passage in *Yasna* 32.3, quoted above, which declares the Daevas, the 'false gods', to be the off-spring of 'Bad Thought'.

Ohrmazd, aware of Ahriman's activities, offered peace and immortality on condition that Ahriman worshipped him and his creations. But Ahriman refused, convinced that he would prevail. Ohrmazd therefore proposed to limit the time of conflict to 9,000 years, knowing that the first 3,000 years would go according to his own will, the second to both his and Ahriman's will, but that at the end of the third triad his foe would be rendered powerless. Once he had obtained Ahriman's consent, Ohrmazd chanted the holiest of all Zoroastrian prayers, the *Ahuna Vairya*. The Avestan source of this idea is attested in *Yasna* 19.1–4, according to which Ahura Mazda chanted this prayer after having made his spiritual creation but before the material one. The Pahlavi account goes on to say that, since the *Ahuna Vairya* encapsulates all the knowledge of the Avesta,

Ahriman saw his own and the *dews'* destruction, the resurrection of the dead and the final perfection of Ohrmazd's creations. Shocked by this, he fell back into his darkness and lay prostrate and unconscious for 3,000 years.

The material creation

During the period of Ahriman's unconsciousness, Ohrmazd made the material world out of the spiritual one, on which it depends for its existence. The link between the spiritual and the tangible and visible is highlighted by the well-known systematic correspondences between the material and spiritual creations, according to which, for instance, cattle correspond to good thought (*vohu manah*), fire to truth (*asha*), earth to right-mindedness (*armaiti*), water to wholeness (*haurvatat*) and plants to immortality (*ameretatat*). Ohrmazd made one exemplar of each of his creations in two stages: first, the material item in a spiritual state and then the same in a material one. The stone sky surrounded the world like an egg shell. The lower half of the oval-shaped cosmos was filled with water on which the flat earth floated carrying one plant, one animal, represented by a cow (*gaw*), and one human being, represented by a man (*Gayomard*). The atmosphere filling the upper part accommodated, in ascending order, the stars, moon and, finally, the sun. In the sphere above the sun was the three-tiered space of Ohrmazd's spiritual world: 'endless light' (AV. *anagra raocah*), 'best life' (AV. *vahishta ahu*) and the 'House of Welcome' (AV. *garo demana*), Ohrmazd's own abode.[21]

The attack and the re-creation of the material world

Awaking from his stupor to the perfect material world in the year 6000, Ahriman, by nature destructive, could only attack. Although no coherent narrative of this myth is preserved in the Avesta, certain Avestan terms only make sense within the general framework of such a myth. The story goes that Ahriman, attacking from outside, bored a hole into the bottom half of the stone sky. He rushed upwards through the water, which he polluted, crawled on to the earth and killed the plant, animal and human being. Then he stormed the sky, hoping to invade Ohrmazd's heavenly abode of the 'House of Welcome'. However, while he was doing so, he was stopped by Ohrmazd's soldiers and generals, including the *spentamainyava* stars (that is, the Milky Way), and was unable to penetrate their defensive line. These stars form the sky's protective zone, which in the Middle Persian texts is compared to a *kusti*, the sacred belt worn by Zoroastrians. Ahriman was thus prevented from invading the celestial spheres and pushed back on to the earth.

However, he had already wrought havoc on the earth and killed Ohrmazd's original, 'sole-created' specimens of plant, animal and human being. But since the material creations had first been created in spiritual form, Ohrmazd was able to purify their seed by means of the respective prototypes (*ewenag*), preserved in heavenly zones that were impenetrable to Ahriman. Taking the blueprint of each of his creations up to the evil-free celestial regions, he purified the water in the 'stars holding the seed of the water' (Avestan *staro afshcithra*), the earth in the 'stars holding the seed of the earth' (AV. *staro zemascithra*), the plant in the 'stars holding the seed of the plant' (AV. *staro urvaro. cithra*), the animal in the 'moon holding the seed of the animal' (AV. *mah gaocithra*) and the human being in the sun. Subsequently, Ohrmazd remade the material creation, but this time *en masse*: 282 animal species, male and female, and the first human couple, a man and a woman.[22]

Ohrmazd's re-creation of the material world inserted his creatures into a world that was already afflicted by the destructive force, Ahriman, against whose aggression (AV. *draoman-*) they had no defence. According to the Avesta, the Daevas rushed around on the earth unhindered and openly gave vent to their lust. Moreover, they attacked human beings and raped women (YT 19.80).[23]

FIG. 4

Yasht 19.84–92
Ff. 270v–271r of
manuscript F1,
a codex of the
Niyayishn and *Yashts*

Dastur Dr K. M.
JamaspAsa

Zarathustra and the defeat of Angra Mainyu and his minions

The unrestrained rule of the Daevas came to an end at the birth of Zarathustra. Realizing their defeat, the Daevas recognise that Zarathustra is their arch-enemy (vd 19.46). He has control over them by means of the *Ahuna Vairya* prayer (yt 19.81).

Zarathustra restrains the Daevas by means of the very prayer that Ahura Mazda recited before making the material world (see page 6). He received the Mazdayasnian religion from Ahura Mazda as the weapon against the Daevas to be passed on to humankind. By worshipping Ahura Mazda and scorning the Daevas,[24] Zarathustra's followers strengthen Ahura Mazda and simultaneously weaken the Daevas and their chief, Angra Mainyu. They thus contribute towards Ahura Mazda's victory and the final defeat of Evil, achieved in 'perfection' or Frashegird (av. *frashokereti*) at the end of the 9,000 years.[25] In the Avesta, the most detailed account of these eschatological events is found in the *Zamyad Yasht*

(*Yasht* 19, Fig. 4). A posthumous son of Zarathustra will emerge from Lake Kansaoya (= Hamun) in Sistan. His name, Astvatereta, is based on the Gathic expression 'truth may be corporeal' in *Yasna* 43.16, and he is described as the 'victorious one' of the *saoshyant*s. The Avestan term *saoshyant* literally means 'the one who will be strong', in the sense that this person will overcome the Daevas and Angra Mainyu. Astvatereta will advance with his comrades, brandishing the weapon that various heroes of Iran's national history bore before him when they slew dragons and other enemies. He will resurrect the dead with his gaze and make the material world incorruptible and undying. In a great final battle, Ahura Mazda's good forces, such as 'Good Thought', will defeat the evil ones, such as 'Bad Thought', and finally the originator of the Daevas, Angra Mainyu, will withdraw, powerless.

Finally, the Pahlavi texts describe a universal judgement in which all resurrected bodies have to pass through a stream of molten metal and be purified, the evil ones experiencing great pain. At that point, the bodies will be reunited with their respective souls and each person will be reinstated in perfection in body and soul.

Individual judgement

In the meantime, the souls have been waiting in either the 'House of Welcome' or in Angra Mainyu's 'House of Deceit', depending on the outcome of each individual judgement. The Avestan *Hadokht Nask* (h) gives detailed parallel accounts of the different fates awaiting the truthful and deceitful ones respectively.[26] Once a person has died, the soul of the truthful one sits in an orderly fashion by the head of its dead body, while that of the deceitful one scuttles about near the head. The soul of the truthful person recites two lines from the *Ushtavaiti* Gatha in correct Old Avestan (h 2.2–6). But the Old Avestan language of the line from the *Kemnamaeza* Gatha, *Yasna* 46.1, which the soul of the deceitful person recites in h 2.20, is corrupt.

It not only displays Young Avestan language features, but also interpolation of the name of Ahura Mazda, whom the deceitful soul had refused to worship in life, yet invokes at this stage, and destroys the metre of the Gathic stanza. This situation goes on for three days and nights, after which the soul has to move on. The truthful one seems to be passing through flowers and enjoying lovely perfumes and southerly breezes, but the deceitful one passes over frozen grounds, foul stench and cold, northern winds. At this point, their respective *daena* appears to the soul. That of the truthful person is described in great detail as a beautiful maiden. The soul engages in a dialogue with her and the *daena* identifies herself not as a maiden but as the person's good deeds done while alive. One would expect the description of the bad *daena* to be in analogous but negative terms. Unfortunately, however, all Avestan manuscripts abbreviate at this point. As a result, the description of the bad *daena* survives neither here nor elsewhere in the Avesta, though it is found in the Pahlavi accounts, which are described in greater detail by Sarah Stewart in this volume.

The emphasis of the Zoroastrian tradition on the worship of Ahura Mazda and the vehement opposition to that of the Daevas has produced a number of elaborate scenarios of reward and punishment with regard to an individual's allegiance during life. After death, a person will reap the fruits of his or her good or bad thoughts, words and, especially, deeds. Zoroastrian literature has produced a genre of other-worldly journeys at which glimpses are gained as to what happens after death and the nature of reward and retribution. The accounts of the punishments in Hell serve as a warning to people living on earth. Such accounts, while at times abounding with entertaining detail, have grown on the bedrock of the Zoroastrian principle that only the worship of Ahura Mazda guarantees a good life both on earth and in the hereafter.

ZOROASTRIANISM AS AN IMPERIAL RELIGION
under the Achaemenids and Sasanians

Philip G. Kreyenbroek
University of Goettingen

Zoroastrianism developed as a descendant and new branch of the ancient religion that the ancestors of the Iranian tribes had once shared with those of the northern Indians. Zoroastrianism must therefore have had many elements in common with the religions of other Iranian peoples, such as those of western Iran. Important new developments in the Zoroastrian worldview included the centrality of the opposition of good and evil; the belief that the world is a theatre of war in which the two forces of good and evil would fight one another; the need for each human individual to choose between those forces; the existence of Heaven and Hell after death; and the belief that the world as we know it will come to an end once evil has been fully overcome.

It is widely thought that Zarathustra lived some time before 1000 BCE, possibly somewhere to the north-east of modern Iran. If this is so, then more than five centuries passed before the first contemporary written evidence of Zoroastrian beliefs in the inscriptions of the Achaemenids (559–330 BCE) appeared in Pars in the south-western part of Iran. It is true that most of the religious texts of Zoroastrianism in the Avestan language must have existed before this time, but they were transmitted orally,[1] and it is unlikely that they were committed to writing until the Sasanian period (224–c.650 CE), the second imperial era of Zoroastrianism. During the first centuries of its existence, Zoroastrianism probably developed as a religion of relatively small communities, first in eastern and south-eastern parts of the Iranian world and later spreading to the south-west and west. It is only at the time of the second Achaemenid ruler Darius I (521–486 BCE), that we find written evidence reflecting a system of beliefs that can best be understood as deriving from the teachings of Zarathustra.[2] Although there was no question of imposing its teachings on most of the non-Iranian peoples under Achaemenid rule, this was the time when Zoroastrianism emerged into the light of history as an 'imperial faith', that is, as the mode of worship favoured by the court of a major empire. This first imperial period came to an end with the conquest of Iran by Alexander the Great in 330 BCE. Zoroastrianism continued to be the religion of the Iranian population afterwards, and was presumably the religion of the Arsacid kings (247 BCE–226 CE), about whom relatively little is known. It is not until the Sasanian period, however, that we again find a close and explicit connection between imperial power and the Zoroastrian 'church'. Therefore we shall here be concerned solely with the development of Zoroastrianism under the Achaemenid and Sasanian dynasties.

THE ACHAEMENIDS

As far as the Zoroastrianization of Achaemenid Iran is concerned, we should avoid imagining this process as one of 'conversion' as the word is generally understood in our time: with representatives of an established, fully developed and theologically mature religion setting out to convert non-believers. In Iran, the very fact that Zarathustra is not mentioned in the royal inscriptions suggests that people's perceptions of 'religion' differed fundamentally from ours. It is important to note, moreover, that the Persians – the Iranian-speaking population of the south-western part of Iran now known as Pars – were relatively recent arrivals who were still in the process of adapting their religion and culture to the conditions of the new homeland when the Achaemenids came to power. When the Iranian tribes established themselves in Pars perhaps less than two centuries before this time,[3] they brought their own religious traditions with them, but they were also confronted with the much greater sophistication of the civilization of the Elamites (which had developed as an 'imperial' culture in the region since c.2700 BCE).[4] As a result of the contact between these two cultures, their respective religious traditions appear to have been in the process of coalescing.[5] Significantly, this shows that they were both *capable* of doing so, that is, that their understanding of 'religion', unlike ours, did not prevent them from reshaping their religious traditions in significant ways when this was felt to be appropriate. While most modern Western believers feel bound by the traditional parameters of their religious traditions and are often disinclined to accept innovations, the Persians of early Achaemenid times were evidently prepared to adopt such beliefs and practices as they thought most likely to help them achieve the goals for which they turned to religion. When the court of Darius decided to promote the Zoroastrian cult, therefore, it may have regarded this merely as a particularly satisfactory way of serving the gods, rather than a campaign to bring light to the heathen.

The advent of Zoroastrianism on the Persian scene meant that yet another way of dealing with the divine was added to the newly emerging 'Elamo-Persian' tradition. In sources from the time of Darius I, we find references to Elamite priests (*shatin*) and Iranian ones (*magush*) who, more or less indiscriminately, worshipped both Elamite and ancient Persian gods. As a third category of priests, these texts begin to mention 'those who make the fire grow' (*athravakhsh*), that is, presumably Zoroastrian priests, in whose rituals fire played a particularly prominent role. Moreover, we already see a tendency emerging there for *magush* to adopt the title of *atravakhsh*.[6] This suggests that as Zoroastrianism gained popularity in western Iran, local priests began to perform rituals in the Zoroastrian manner, with their liturgy in the Avestan language. Avestan differs considerably from Old Persian, the language of Achaemenid Pars, and was to remain the 'sacred', liturgical language of Zoroastrianism. No adequate way existed as yet to write down texts in that language so that they could be read from the page. Therefore western Iranian priests who did not have an active command of Avestan needed to learn the liturgy and related texts by heart. This in turn led to the first 'fixation' of most Avestan texts,[7] which until then had probably been transmitted relatively freely. The lack of written sources, combined with the need to memorize the liturgy *verbatim*, allows us to deduce that there must have been an unbroken tradition of teaching and exegesis, probably extending from early Zoroastrian times, through the Achaemenid period, down to the Sasanian era and beyond. As the natural languages of western Iran developed away from the 'Old Iranian' stage (to which Old Persian and Avestan both belong), Avestan became increasingly incomprehensible and was thought of as a mysterious, sacred language.

Transmission of religious teaching took place largely in the form of questions and answers. This implies that the Zoroastrian tradition was open to development, since the questions asked by the public must have changed along with cultural development. Zoroastrian teaching, then, was probably prone to developing new insights as well as divergent local forms. We are given some indications of this by the extant sources of the time of Darius I. On the one hand, we have a large number of clay tablets dating from the earlier part of Darius' reign which show that the court sponsored certain religious cults, including Zoroastrianism, in the Iranian heartlands. This material suggests that, at this time, the cult of Ahura Mazda (i.e. Zoroastrianism) still had limited numbers of followers compared to that of the great Elamite god Humban. Still, the Achaemenid court clearly favoured this new 'religion', and its worldview informs our second major group of sources, the royal inscriptions (Fig. 5).[8]

The inscriptions of Darius I clearly aimed to show the population that the king was the legitimate ruler of the land, who was righteous according to Zoroastrian teaching as it was understood in Pars at this early stage. Apart from the fact that the texts extol the worship of the wholly Zoroastrian god Ahura Mazda,[9] the stark opposition between good and evil, which is typical of Zoroastrian teaching, is a key factor in the worldview projected there. The king was divinely

Old Persian cognate, *drauga*, had the more restricted meaning 'lie, untruth'. It is no coincidence, then, that not only Gaumata, but *all* Darius' opponents are depicted in the inscriptions as liars.

At the same time, this narrative shows that the early Persians understood certain aspects of the Zoroastrian message in the light of their own language and culture. The inscriptions, then, help us understand the Zoroastrianization of western Iran in this early phase. But the acceptance of Zoroastrian teachings and practices appears to have been a gradual process. Certain elements were quickly accepted, but the Persians held fast to their traditional beliefs in other areas. Certain Zoroastrian observances, moreover, coalesced with local ones, effectively introducing new forms of ritual into Zoroastrianism.[10]

chosen because he worshipped Ahura Mazda and because he was righteous. Moreover, his opponents are consistently depicted as liars. The figure whom Darius overthrew, for instance, was generally thought to have been Cyrus' son Bardiya (Greek: Smerdis). But the inscriptions tell us that Bardiya had secretly been killed by his brother Cambyses and his place was deceitfully taken by a *magush* named Gaumata, while Cambyses had 'died by his own hand' in Egypt. A great deal of energy must have gone into the dissemination of this account, an Aramaic version of which was brought to Egypt by Persian soldiers, and which is also repeated by the Greek historian Herodotus (*c.* 484–425 BCE). In reality, it is difficult to imagine that a murder and an impersonation at this august level could have taken place unnoticed. It is more plausible to regard this account as an attempt to portray Cambyses as guilty of both fratricide and suicide, which clearly marks him as a follower of evil and thus unworthy of the kingship, while the impostor 'Bardiya/Gaumata' was obviously a follower of evil because he lied. While the Avestan opposite of 'right order' was *druh*, 'chaos, evil', its

The new status of Zoroastrianism as an 'imperial' faith demanded trappings which until then had not formed part of its tradition. Herodotus tells us that ancient Persians found the notion that a god lived in a temple ridiculous, but we see that the prestige other empires derived from their splendid temples led the Zoroastrians of Achaemenid times to experiment with such fixed places of worship. It seems doubtful, moreover, that the earlier Zoroastrian tradition possessed a well-developed religious iconography, let alone one that was adequate for the needs of an empire. In fact, many Achaemenid symbols that came to be regarded as Zoroastrian are of non-Zoroastrian provenance. The 'lion and bull motif', for instance, where the lion defeats the bull, is of ancient Meso-potamian origin and cannot be interpreted on the basis of the usual symbolism of Zoroastrianism, where the bull represents the Zoroastrian religion while the lion is a creation of the evil spirit. Similarly, the 'winged symbol', whose precise significance in Zoroastrian iconography has divided scholars, originates in ancient Egypt and was later adopted by the cultures of Mesopotamia before it reached Iran.

ZOROASTRIANISM BETWEEN THE MAJOR IMPERIAL PERIODS

The defeat of the Achaemenid Empire by Alexander the Great (330 BCE) put an end to the imperial infrastructure that linked local Zoroastrian communities together, so that regional priestly organizations and local traditions developed independently. The fall of the Achaemenid Empire further required an adaptation of Zoroastrian teaching in order to explain why God had allowed a pious Zoroastrian dynasty to be overthrown by a non-Iranian invader. The resulting theological explanation had significant implications for Zoroastrianism and gave rise to 'millennialist' ideas in several other religions in the Middle East. The new teaching claimed that it was ordained that after every good and virtuous era, a period of unrighteous rule would follow, until at the end of a 1,000-year period a saviour would come to restore righteousness on earth. After three such millennia, evil would be fully defeated and the world would be perfect.

Apart from such adaptations to the events of history, the religious lives of Zoroastrian communities seem to have remained relatively unaffected by the Hellenist culture that became dominant in the Middle East after Alexander's victory, and remained so for several centuries.

The Parthian Arsacids, who restored Iranian rule after the Hellenist period, were clearly Zoroastrians, but we can only guess to what extent their religious life resembled that of the later Persian Sasanians. The Parthians called themselves 'friends of Greek culture' (*phil-hellènoi*) and appear to have taken a pluralist view of both culture and religion. The dearth of extant source material for this dynasty means that we cannot go beyond educated guesses, but it seems clear that the Arsacids, though Zoroastrians, did little to promote Zoroastrianism as an 'imperial' religion.

THE SASANIANS

Under the Sasanians, on the other hand, we find the notion that 'religion and sovereignty are twins',[11] indicating that Zoroastrianism had entered its second imperial phase. The early Sasanians sought to legitimize their power through religious propaganda, claiming that the incursion of 'Alexander the Accursed' and the rule of his successors had caused the Zoroastrian faith to become degenerate and that only their dynasty could restore it to its pristine form. These propagandistic claims had far-reaching consequences for the development of Zoroastrianism under Sasanian rule.

First of all, a king claiming to be a restorer of the true religion of the forefathers needs the support of the priesthood. Perhaps because of this, we see a strengthening of the Zoroastrian priesthood and 'church' under the Sasanians. Complex hierarchies developed of both 'learned' and 'administrative' priests. The former concerned themselves with teaching and exegesis, while the latter were the leaders of the 'church', headed by the high priest of the state, followed by those of the provinces, the regions and the cities with their adjacent lands. The role of such administrative priests included the leadership of the complex religious organization of the time, and they also had functions similar to those of modern-day judges and solicitors. The Greek author and traveller Agathias (sixth century CE) tells us that 'nothing receives the stamp of legality in the eyes of the Persians unless it is ratified by the Magi'.[12]

Secondly, the idea of restoring a religion to its 'true' form implies that an ideal, single form of that religion exists and merely needs to be defined anew. This implicit assumption, which characterizes early Sasanian propaganda, can be seen as the beginning of a new preoccupation with an ideal, 'true' form of the religion, in contradistinction to the range of local forms of Zoroastrian religious life that had developed over the centuries.

Another factor that strengthened the need to define the nature of Zoroastrianism as a single, unified religion was the rivalry of two new religions: Manichaeism and Christianity. King Shapur I (241–72 CE), the second Sasanian monarch, welcomed to his court the non-Zoroastrian prophet Mani, to whom he accorded many privileges. Mani (d. *c.* 277 CE) claimed to receive divine revelations through his non-material alter ego or 'twin'. His religion was strongly influenced by Christian teaching, perhaps combined with Zoroastrian elements, and had a pronounced Gnostic character. Mani taught that God had given the same message to all previous prophets, but the message had become distorted over time because it had only been transmitted orally. His own message would be

written down in the languages of its various communities, including Middle Persian and Parthian.

The initial success of Manichaeism and later Christianity in Iran posed a real threat to Zoroastrianism. Under the Achaemenids, Zoroastrianism had taken for granted the existence of different religions, as one would that of different languages, and it had dealt with the challenges of Hellenism by keeping itself to itself. Now, however, it was forced to confront the threat presented by two new 'scriptural' religions: more or less unified systems of belief and practice claiming to be based on a recent revelation that had been written down without distortion and thus represented pure divine truth. Both of these highly proselytizing religions claimed to be intended for all mankind. These claims clearly challenged Sasanian Zoroastrianism, the authority of which was based on an age-old tradition in an arcane language, and which existed in many different forms and had always been regarded as a religion intended primarily for Iranians.

The terms of the religious debates of the age were obviously dictated by the postulates of Manichaeism and Christianity, and contributed to a change in the mental image Zoroastrians had of their religion, from a system of co-existing priestly traditions ultimately deriving from ancient wisdom (not unlike modern Hinduism) to that of a single 'church' whose teachings were based on divine revelation and guarded by a hierarchy of powerful priests, backed by the authority of the state. These changes initially affected people's perception of the religion more directly than its realities, but they influenced later developments and inform the Middle Persian books on which our understanding of Zoroastrianism is largely based.

Mani's great opponent was the Zoroastrian high priest Kirder, who led the church from the time of Shapur I until that of Narse (293–302 CE). He eventually brought about the defeat of Manichaeism in Iran. Kirder, who acquired extraordinary powers, portrays Zoroastrianism in his inscriptions as a single and unified system of religious practices and beliefs. He also strengthened the power of the Zoroastrian priesthood. He describes the results of his activities as follows: (1) the number of rituals increased throughout the land; (2) many state-sponsored sacred fires were founded; (3) the priesthood was made prosperous; (4) charters were sealed for the foundation of many temple fires and the funding of their priests; and (5) all testaments and other official documents henceforth needed Kirder's seal (i.e., in practice, that of an administrative priest under Kirder's authority). When Shapur I conquered the lands around Iran,

Kirder ensured that the Zoroastrian priests and fires there were not harmed. He 'put in order' the affairs of these priests and caused the Zoroastrian religion and the righteous priests to be much respected. On the other hand, he 'punished and reprimanded' heretics and 'those who did not follow the proper exegesis in matters of religion and ritual' (Fig. 6).

The arbiter of the 'righteousness' or otherwise of these foreign Zoroastrian priests was obviously Kirder himself, which implies that, as far as was practicable, Kirder's version of Zoroastrianism was imposed on communities whose original beliefs and practices may have been very different. This ambitious high priest, in other words, directed all of his energies towards the establishment of a Zoroastrian church, based on a single 'true' interpretation of Zoroastrianism: his own.

While in the pre-Sasanian period the authority of the Zoroastrian priesthood had presumably gone unchallenged, Kirder evidently found it necessary to prove his authority – and that of his view of Zoroastrianism – by describing his journey to Heaven and Hell, implying direct contact with the divine. After Kirder, we see that the question of the authority of Zoroastrian teaching continues to preoccupy Sasanian Zoroastrianism. One of Kirder's successors, Adurbad i Mahraspandan, is said to have demonstrated the truth of his teaching by undergoing an ordeal by molten metal. After Adurbad's time we see the emergence of authoritative lineages (*cashtag*) based on the teachings of great priestly teachers.

Together with the rivalry of scriptural religions such as Manichaeism and Christianity, this new preoccupation with authority increased the sense that Zoroastrianism needed written scriptures. While traditional systems of writing had so far been incapable of representing the complex sound system of the Avestan language, a new alphabet was now invented which allowed the written codification of the Avestan texts. We learn that an authoritative written compilation of sacred

FIG. 7

Cave and watercourse at Hajiabad

photograph
© Mieke Kreyenbroek

persists down to the present day, turning traditional Zoroastrianism into a religion that is much concerned with ritual and observance, while its lay followers are dependent on priests for information on its teachings.

RELIGIOUS MONUMENTS AND ARTEFACTS

Many Achaemenid reliefs, including those of Persepolis, Behistun and Naqsh-e Rostam, and several Sasanian ones such as those of Naqsh-e Rostam, Naqsh-e Rajab and Taq-e Bostan, reflect the strong links between church and state in those imperial eras. Like the Achaemenid and Sasanian inscriptions, such images were commissioned by the court and reflect an 'official' version of Zoroastrianism. For a long time it was believed that these sources adequately reflected the religious realities of the Achaemenid and Sasanian eras as a whole. More recently, however, the discovery of new archaeological and ethnographic data has proved beyond doubt that at the popular level Zoroastrian religious life was much more varied than is suggested by the official sources.

A case in point is the recent discovery of a cave near Veshnave in central Iran, which contains a basin into which water flows from the rock.[14] Offerings have been found in the water of this basin, ranging from the remains of a food offering from Achaemenid times or earlier, via a wealth of ornaments thought to have belonged to women, to an early post-Sasanian coin. The cave is only accessible by means of a very low and narrow corridor, through which one must crawl on all fours, which would have vitiated the state of ritual purity priests need in order to officiate. It therefore seems that this was a shrine where the waters were worshipped, perhaps particularly by women, without the prominent presence of priests. References to such a cult of water are found in the Avestan parts of the *Nerangestan*, but the Middle Persian translation of these passages suggests that such practices were no

texts was accepted by religious leaders during the time of Khosrow I (531–78 CE). Possibly following Christian terminology, the resulting sacred book was given the name *abestag*, 'testament'. Only a limited number of copies of this text existed in Sasanian times, however, and the priesthood continued to rely largely on oral transmission.

Khosrow I further had to deal with the aftermath of the reforms of his father Kavad I (488–531 CE), which were connected with the rebellion of Mazdak,[13] a Zoroastrian priest who based his egalitarian teachings on the exegesis of the Avesta (*zand*). When this movement, which had evidently become hugely popular, was defeated, the king forbade the laity to attend sessions of 'priestly studies' (*herbedestan*), which they had hitherto been allowed to attend so as to acquire some knowledge of the teachings of their faith. This state of affairs continued after the Islamic conquest of the mid-seventh century CE, which put an end to the second imperial phase of Zoroastrianism. It largely longer approved by priests.[15] Classical sources confirm, however, that the cult of water was far more important in early Zoroastrianism than the Middle Persian texts lead us to believe.

In the light of this incontrovertible evidence that a Zoroastrian water cult existed, the significance of other material evidence must now be re-examined. Thus the city of Bishapur in the south-west of Iran, which was built by Shapur I, contains what appears to be a sanctuary at whose centre is a large basin into which water flowed from outside, and around which believers may have made solemn circumambulations. At Niyasar in central Iran, we find a cave with a man-made system of corridors leading to a cave-like space next to a waterfall. At Hajiabad, near the famous site of Naqsh-e Rostam in Pars, there is a cave-like hollow in the mountain, next to which was once a big water-fall. Manmade steps lead up to the highest point in the cave, where we find the now defaced image of what may have been a female figure. The fact that Shapur I had an inscription placed at Hajiabad suggests that the site was much visited. It may therefore have had religious connotations (Fig. 7).

While many pre-Islamic monuments and artefacts were clearly informed by Zoroastrianism, there were other sources of inspiration. As we saw earlier, many Achaemenid symbols are of non-Iranian origin. As to Sasanian art, Zoroastrianism probably played a similar role to that of Christianity in Europe: it was important, but many spheres of life had no obvious connection with it. The hunting scenes we find on many Sasanian artefacts, for example, indicate nothing more than a love of hunting.

THE IMPERIAL HERITAGE

After the defeat of the Sasanian Empire, Zoroastrianism continued to be the religion of the majority of Iranians for about two centuries.

However, the administrative structures and hierarchies of the Sasanian church disintegrated, the imperial infrastructure was no longer there and Zoroastrian communities gradually became too poor to support an elaborate priesthood. In the course of the ninth century CE, Islam became the main religion of the land, and many fire temples were transformed into mosques. The leadership of the Zoroastrian community came to rest in the hands of a group of priests who belonged to a single tradition. Members of this lineage were responsible for writing the Middle Persian religious books in the redactions known to us in the ninth and tenth centuries. Thus they defined the way the religion was passed on in the following centuries, creating the impression that Zoroastrianism had always been a more or less unified tradition, dominated by priests and largely orthopractic in character.

In summary, during its first imperial phase, under the Achaemenids, Zoroastrianism was profoundly transformed as the older tradition was adapted to the religious heritage of the western Iranian population. This probably resulted in the emergence of different local forms of Zoroastrianism, a tendency that was strengthened when local priesthoods became more independent after the fall of the Achaemenid dynasty. Against the background of this variety of Zoroastrian cults, the Sasanians, using their enormous power to promote the development of the religion, sought to represent Zoroastrianism as being essentially a unified, coherent faith. The fall of this last Zoroastrian empire resulted in the final codification of the later religious writings on Zoroastrianism by members of a single priestly lineage, which further strengthened the notion that Zoroastrianism had always been a uniform tradition. Recent discoveries of archaeological and ethnographic data show, however, that for a long time the Zoroastrian tradition had in fact been both richer and more complex.

ZOROASTRIAN FUNERARY PRACTICES
in Sogdiana and Chorasmia and among expatriate Sogdian communities in China

Frantz Grenet

Collège de France, Paris

The archaeological evidence for the continuity and transformation of Zoroastrianism comes from temples, images of deities and ceremonies in monumental arts, mobile objects and, last but not least, funerary practices. The latter are especially important for modern research as they were strictly codified in the Avesta and its commentaries; in addition, they alone provide information on the religious practices of the common folk. There have been far better studies in Central Asia than in Iran, partly because the regional custom of depositing bones in mobile ossuaries has left a greater quantity of tangible remains, and partly because of the large-scale archaeological explorations initiated in the Soviet period. Our knowledge of Sogdian funerary practices has been recently supplemented by the discovery of several rich tombs of Sogdian traders in northern China.

TEXTUAL EVIDENCE

The most detailed textual evidence consists of two testimonies from foreign travellers, very different in time and origin.[1] The first, by Onesicritus, a companion of Alexander, is about Bactria, the country neighbouring Sogdiana to the south, and was transmitted by Strabo (XI.11.3): 'Those who had become helpless because of old age or sickness are thrown out alive as preys to dogs kept expressly for this purpose, which in their native tongue are called "undertakers", and while the outskirts of the walls of the metropolis of Bactria look clean, yet most of their inside part (i.e. the slope) is full of human bones.' The reference to gerontocide has sometimes led people to dismiss this testimony altogether as Greek propaganda; indeed, such practices are unattested otherwise among Iranian peoples (except, according to some authors, among Scythians and Caspian nomads), but a hasty disposal of sick soldiers, linked to the fear of demonic pollution through the dead body, is mentioned in connection with Sasanian Iran (Agathias, *Histories* 2.23) and

might have led to more extreme precautions at times. As for the use of human-eating dogs, it is confirmed in strikingly similar terms by Wei Jie, a Chinese envoy at Samarkand in 607 CE: 'Outside the capital, living apart, more than two hundred families specialize in taking care of funerals. These people have built in an isolated place an enclosure in which they rear dogs. Whenever somebody dies, they go and take his corpse, place it in the enclosure, and have its flesh devoured by the dogs. After that one gathers the bones to bury them; they use no coffin, neither inner nor outer.'[2]

EXPOSURE OF THE DEAD

Exposure as a means of disposing of a body is in accordance with the Zoroastrian prescription as stated in the *Videvdad*, the abandonment of the bones on the spot, apparently practised in Achaemenid Bactria, being one of the admitted variants (*Videvdad* 6.51). As this procedure leaves little tangible remains, archaeological confirmation is very scant for these early periods, the evidence being in a sense negative – the absence of any grave with furnishings (except for intruders from the steppes), which on the contrary had been very common in the Bronze Age. In the only cemetery where several tombs belonging to the sedentary population in the early Iron Age have been studied, Dzharkutan in southern Sogdiana, some skeletons showed traces of preliminary exposure and were gathered in pits.[3] At about the time of Alexander's conquest, a potter's kiln near Samarkand had been reused as a *dakhma* (place of exposure) and contained dog bones together with human ones, as prescribed in the *Videvdad*.[4] Such structures, designed to concentrate the impurities, were to be destroyed periodically, which probably explains why only three other specimens are known in the whole of Central Asia: at Erkurgan in Sogdiana (a large tower structure from the Hellenistic period); at Durmen-tepe, also in Sogdiana (a small tower structure of the seventh

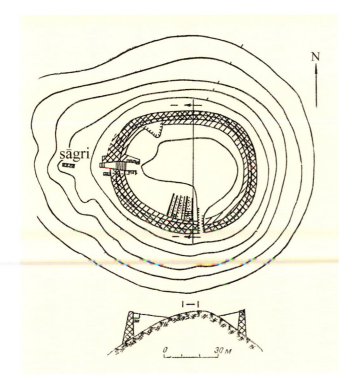

FIG. 8
Dakhma at Chil'pyk
c. 4th–8th century CE
photograph
© F. Grenet, F. Ory

and eighth centuries serving the needs of one family); and at Chil'pyk in Chorasmia. This latter specimen is especially interesting: it consists of a rock spur surrounded by a wall, very much like the seventeenth-century *dakhma* at Kerman, and used by a whole region from the fourth century until the Islamic conquest. It has two features that will later reappear in the *dakhma*s of Gujarat, namely a *sagri*, room for a permanent fire in front of the entrance stairway, and *pavi*s, compartments for the laying of the corpses exposed to vultures (Fig. 8).[5] The Mugh contract V-8, from the archive documents found on Mt. Mugh, to the east of Panjikent, most likely concerns the sale of a half of a bipartite *dakhma* (the Sogdian word is *eskese*, of unclear etymology), erected in a marsh, and where the lamentation (*khshevan*) has to be performed after the body has been laid.[6] In Bactria, though two documents from the kingdom of Rob mention a *dakhma* (*laxmigo*),[7] no such structure has yet been

discovered. The archaeological documentation here shows no clear evidence of Zoroastrianism; what we have are, from the Hellenistic period onwards, mausoleums with multiple vaults where corpses were deposited, and subsequently much evidence of the influence of successive waves of nomadic invaders, in the shape of individual tombs dug in the soil, and in the form of personal ornaments and offerings accompanying the full body.

On the contrary, from the fifth century CE onwards in Sogdiana and one or two centuries earlier in Chorasmia (as well as in Margiana, the border province of the Sasanian Empire), archaeology has evidenced a sequence of practices showing concern for the preservation of the bones and some ritual, iconographic and sometimes even epigraphic references to Zoroastrianism. Perhaps already in the Achaemenid period, Chorasmians had begun

FIG. 9
Reconstruction of the *naus* at Panjikent
5th–8th century CE

V. A. Nil'sen, *Stanovlenie feodal'noi arkhitektury Srednei Azii*, V–VIII vv, Tashkent, 1966, fig. 30

quite similar to those of ossuaries from Palestine in the Roman period, one cannot exclude the possibility that this custom came to Central Asia with the diaspora and was eventually adopted by Zoroastrians, but evidence of intermediary stages is still lacking. The most common material is baked clay, to which Chorasmia adds plaster, less frequently stone. The standard length of an ossuary is approximately 50–60 cm, corresponding to the length of the femur, the longest human bone; the shape is either rectangular or oval, with a pyramidal or hemispherical roof. The opening is cut either on the side or in the roof and can be closed again.

MAUSOLEUMS

The ossuaries were usually deposited in small free-standing family mausoleums, built of mud brick and vaulted (Fig. 9). They are called *naus* by archaeologists (according to the word used in Arab sources), while in Chorasmian they are *frawartik*, and in Sogdian *frawart-kate* 'Fravashis' house'. In some cases, abandoned buildings or ramparts were reused as mausoleums. Funerary pits and *naus* always lay outside the inhabited part of the city. Though exposure in a *dakhma* was known (see above), traces of excarnation by birds or dogs are rarely reported on bones found in archaeological excavations, and it appears that the canonical practice was used only in places deemed suitable. More often, the bodies were left to decompose naturally on brick benches inside the mausoleum, a mode of disposal which preserved the essential respect due to the divine earth. Bones were subsequently gathered and put into jars or ossuaries, which in turn were deposited in the mausoleum, together with the bodies of people recently deceased. In some cases, pits dug out of any building received the ossuaries, or just the bare bones (this seems to be the situation described at Samarkand by the Chinese envoy, see page 18, unless he considered that ossuaries could not be called 'coffins').

to gather pre-excarnated bones in jars and in ceramic ossuaries, some of them anthropomorphic, but this early chronology now appears questionable.[8] Around the period of Sasanian expansion, casket-shaped types were commonplace in Margiana, Sogdiana and Chorasmia (the only country for which we know the local name of these objects: *tabankuk*, literally 'little chest', while the Pahlavi name was *astodan*, literally 'ossuary'). However, the practice of using transportable ossuaries can hardly be linked, at least directly, with Sasanian influence because in Iran such objects are very rarely reported and most known ossuaries are rock-hewn cavities. In Margiana casket ossuaries are documented first in a Jewish cemetery in Merv[9] and, as some shapes and designs appear

Mausoleums remained accessible so as to allow families to lay food offerings at the time of the Fravardigan, the festival for the dead at the end of the year; this custom is mentioned by Biruni with reference to the Zoroastrians who inhabited Sogdiana and Chorasmia in his time,[10] and is confirmed by archaeological discoveries. Among modern Zoroastrians who until recently did not use individual tombs but left the bones in the collective pit of the *dakhma*, offerings and fumigations were carried out in houses.

THE SYMBOLIC MESSAGE OF OSSUARIES

Many ossuaries have perforations, which are likely to have a ritual significance: according to the Pahlavi treatise *Dadestan i denig* 17.3–4: 'in order that light may come to it a hole is made in it' (the context implied is the moment of resurrection). Some specimens also have drill holes around the roof, whose function can be explained thanks to a Chorasmian silver dish showing an ossuary fitted with four movable supports for a baldaquin when it was displayed for a funerary or commemorative ceremony (such a ceremony is attested in a royal context by Chinese accounts of Sogdiana).

Some ossuaries are just plain containers, but many carry incised geometrical or vegetal designs that probably allude to the Sun and Paradise. The top knob of the movable roof can take the shape of a bird or a ram's head, probably symbols of fortune (*khwarrah*) and the ascending soul respectively. A few specimens show more elaborate scenes. In Sogdiana, these motifs were stamped and thus indicate serial production; in Chorasmia, they were painted on request on the plaster. The repertoire is quite varied.

On an ossuary from the vicinity of Shahr-i Sabz (Sogdiana), a pair of fertility gods, Nana and Tir, are depicted holding astral symbols and accompanied by

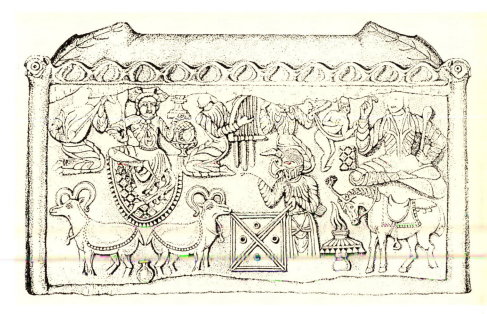

FIG. 10
Ossuary from Sivaz
c. 7th century CE
© F. Grenet

the musicians of Paradise.[11] On several ossuaries from Sogdiana and the Sogdian colonies in Semirechie, a bipartite composition shows, in the lower part, two priests solemnizing the service of the *chaharom*, the 'fourth (day)', which is the moment when the soul crosses the Chinvat Bridge to meet its judges, and in the upper part (sometimes not preserved when it was placed on the roof of the ossuary) scenes related to Paradise. A good example is the ossuary from Mulla-Kurgan (Cat. 36). As everywhere, the Zoroastrian priests are immediately recognizable by the *padam*, the mouth covering that prevents the pollution of the sacred fire, still used by Zoroastrian priests today when they officiate. A variant of this type is the ossuary from Sivaz near Shahr-i Sabz (Fig. 10), where a lone priest is depicted along with four types of offering (*dron*, i.e. sacrificial bread, wine, sheep, horse) and the paradisiac scene is focused on the symbolic dressing of the naked soul, while Ardvahisht, master of fire and Paradise, is enthroned on the left. The exhibition includes still another variant, the ossuary from Yumalaktepa, also near Shahr-i Sabz, which depicts the weighing of the soul (Cat. 35).

FIG. 11
Ossuary from Tok-kala
8th century CE

A. V. Gudkova, *Tok-kala*, Tashkent, 1964, fig. 28

Frequently depicted on ossuaries, in Sogdiana as well as in Chorasmia, are funerary lamentations. Some mourners tear their hair, stab their faces and cut their ears, as on the specimen from Tok-kala in Chorasmia, reproduced in Fig. 11 (the widow is clothed in black while the deceased, clothed in white, is also lamenting). They are plausibly professional mourners, also shown on some individual terracotta statuettes, which might have been used as substitutes for actual mourners when they were considered too costly. Lamentations were probably performed just as the body was deposited in the *dakhma* (they are mentioned in this connection by the Mugh funerary contract, see page 19). They are repeatedly prohibited in Pahlavi treatises (see, for example, *Arda Viraz Namag* 16: the souls for which people have lamented are forced to cross a river that grows in proportion to the tears). Nevertheless, in the cemetery of Tok-kala, ossuaries depicting scenes of lamentation are found side by side with others that

bear Zoroastrian blessings: 'Year 706. Month Fravardin, day Fravardin. This ossuary belongs to the soul of Srawyok son of Tishyan. May their souls rest in eternal Paradise!'[12] Violent lamentations were also part of the composite cult of the goddess Nana, where they echoed the Babylonian cult of Ishtar lamenting her lover Tammuz.

One series of Sogdian ossuaries, all found in the small Miankal region to the west of Samarkand, has a more elaborate theological content because, according to the interpretation proposed by the present author, they depict the six Amesha Spentas solemnizing the final Yasna at the time of Resurrection, each being associated with a specific attribute. On the variant included in the exhibition (Cats 38, 39, 40 and 41), which can be graphically reconstructed (Fig. 12), the short side shows Amurdad, guardian of plants, and Ardvahisht, guardian of fire, with a fire holder and shovel in hand. On the long side, from left to right, we can recognize Hordad, protectress of waters, holding the pestle and *haoma* twigs, which are used to purify this element (water); then Shahrevar, guardian of metals, presenting the mountains that are going to melt at the time of the Last Judgement (in other variants, he is clad in armour, which shows his association with the warrior estate); Vahman follows, making a gesture of blessing, his association with the moon and cattle illustrated by his crown made of crescents and the libation spoon used to pour animal fat; the series ends with Spandarmad, guardian of earth, holding an ossuary as she presents the bones to Ohrmazd upon the Resurrection (as stated in *Bundahishn* 34.5: 'At that time I shall demand the bones to the Spirit of the Earth').[13]

SOGDIAN FUNERARY MONUMENTS IN NORTHERN CHINA

Since the 1990s, knowledge of Sogdian funerary practices and beliefs was unexpectedly enriched

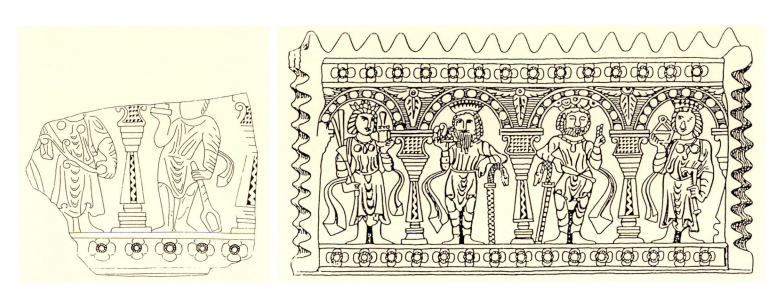

FIG. 12

Ossuaries from Biya-Nayman
7th century CE; graphic reconstruction of the main type

© F. Grenet

thanks to the appearance, in the antique market and in archaeological excavations, of funerary reliefs of Sogdian merchants buried in China. Previously only one such stone monument had been known since the 1920s: the tomb from Anyang, now dispersed between four museums. At present, six tombs safely attributable to Sogdians are known, plus two others from Kansu, which are thematically related to the Sogdian tombs but might have belonged to non-Zoroastrian representatives of other Central Asian peoples. In addition, three bases of funerary beds belong to the same collection.[14] All date from the last third of the sixth century, and a link has been suggested with the persecution of Buddhism in China that started in 569, which might have 'freed up talented stone carvers for non-Buddhist work' commissioned by the richest Sogdian merchants.[15] In fact, three of the tomb owners are identified by funerary inscriptions that give them the title *sabao*, a Chinese administrative function designating the leader of a community of Western migrants and derived from the Sogdian word *sartpaw*, 'caravan leader'.

The underground tomb chambers conform perfectly with the Chinese rich tombs of that period: each consists of a *dromos*, an antechamber and a vaulted funerary chamber, the body lying on a stone bench (ceramic ossuaries of a Sogdian type, however, are known among Sogdian colonists in Xinjiang). The only visible concession to Zoroastrian precepts is the absence of wooden coffins, wood being considered in Zoroastrian texts as a conductor of impurity.

In most tombs, a majority of the panels illustrate the social activities of the deceased in a rather conventional way. Trade is very discreetly alluded to, with one exception: the tomb of Wirkak. The focus is always on the aristocratic way of life, expressed in hunting and banqueting with fellow Sogdians, with other Central Asian peoples, with northern Indians (probably Gandharis or Kashmiris), or with Turks.

At the same time, the wife is always shown dressed as a Chinese lady, sharing a Chinese pavilion with her husband.

Few motifs go beyond these recurring themes, but among them are those related to the divine world. The images that indicate most directly a Zoroastrian milieu are those of priests, immediately recognizable by the *padam* and the *barsom*s (ritual twigs). Two motifs common in Chinese funerary art have been adapted in accordance with Zoroastrian beliefs. One is the riderless saddled horse, in China a symbol of the social status of the deceased, but in Central Asian Zoroastrianism a sacrificial animal consecrated to the god Mithra, judge of the dead. It appears as such in Sogdiana itself on the Sivaz ossuary (Fig. 10), and also in the 'Ambassadors painting' at Samarkand as an element of the New Year procession to the mausoleum of the royal ancestors (Cat. 26). It probably has the same meaning in the funerary cortege shown on the long sides of the Anyang and Miho gates, while on the reliefs of the sarcophagus of Yu Hong, Mithra himself appears to welcome the sacrificial horse.[16] Another reworked motif is the 'bird-priest', a fantastic creature combining the face and arms of a priest with *padam*, and the body of a cock; they appear most often in pairs, tending a fire altar, in privileged places such as the lintel of the door of the funerary chamber or the base of the funerary couch – like on the Victoria and Albert base (Cat. 42). The motif derives from Indian *kinnara*s and Chinese 'Vermillion Birds', also a funerary symbol, but the models were transformed in order to express the presence of the god Srosh in the fire ritual (according to *Videvdad* 18.14, the cock is Srosh's *sraoshavarez*, assistant priest).[17] His presence in all Sogdian Chinese graves belonging to Zoroastrians, as well as his absence in the two graves suspected to be non-Zoroastrian, can be explained by the fact that the soul is placed under Srosh's direct protection during the three days after the death, after which he helps it to cross the Chinvat Bridge.

The funerals themselves are shown in only one set of reliefs, now kept at the Miho Museum in Japan. On one panel (Fig. 13), members of the family meditate on a rocky landscape, probably the place where the corpse was abandoned to animals; at the top, the family is shown again, together with mourners, while a priest solemnizes the office of the *chaharom*. To the right, one can see the rump of two camels between rails; in front, two women are standing, one holding a piece of cloth. This somewhat enigmatic scene can be explained with the help of the already discussed Sivaz ossuary (Fig. 10), for they show two successive phases of the same ritual, involving the *sedra*, the piece of cloth woven by women of the family for the sake of the departed. On the Miho relief, a woman is holding the *sedra* towards the Chinvat Bridge; on the Sivaz ossuary, the soul, now in Paradise, is being wrapped in the *sedra*, held on one side by a god (presumably Vahman, according to the Pahlavi version of *Sih-rozag* 1.2), on the other side by a kneeling female figure, presumably the widow symbolically sharing in the action.[18]

The crossing of the Chinvat Bridge itself is depicted on a fragmentary ossuary from Samarkand now in the Tashkent Historical Museum, and with a profusion of detail on the eastern wall of the sarcophagus of the *sabao* Wirkak, found in regular excavations at Xi'an, capital of the Northern Zhou dynasty (Fig. 14).[19] The lower part begins at the entrance to a long bridge guarded by two dogs emerging from behind rocks. Two Zoroastrian priests are standing at the entrance. Among the crowd crossing the bridge are four human figures (a couple and two children) who have almost reached the other side. Behind them, walking past two flaming balls, are a couple of horses, a donkey, a cow, a sheep, two camels and a bird. The bridge crosses tormented waters, from which emerge the heads of two horrid creatures. The lower structure of the bridge itself is supported by posts with monster-headed capitals. On the far left of the scene, the bridge reaches a rocky shore, over which flies a legion of winged creatures. The upper part of the scene must also be 'read' from right to left. A two-armed god holding a trident in his right hand is seated above three bulls and surrounded by a halo flanked by two attendants holding a billowing scarf. Underneath, a couple sit together, facing three crowned figures. The woman wears a Chinese garment and holds a cup in her right hand, whereas the man, wearing Western clothes and a hat, holds a tray or a cylindrical object. A crowned winged figure stands in front of the couple. Behind her, to the left, two similarly crowned ladies holding a cup and a flower emerge from behind a mountain range. These mountains form a natural boundary between the upper and lower parts of the scene.

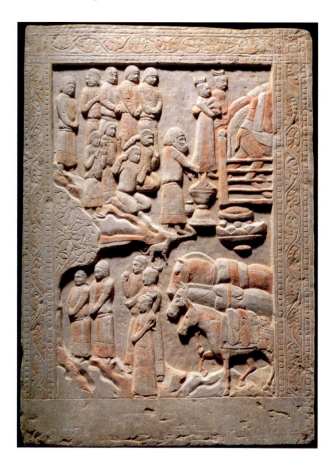

FIG. 13
Panel with funerary scene from the Miho couch
c. 570–580 CE
photograph
© F. Grenet

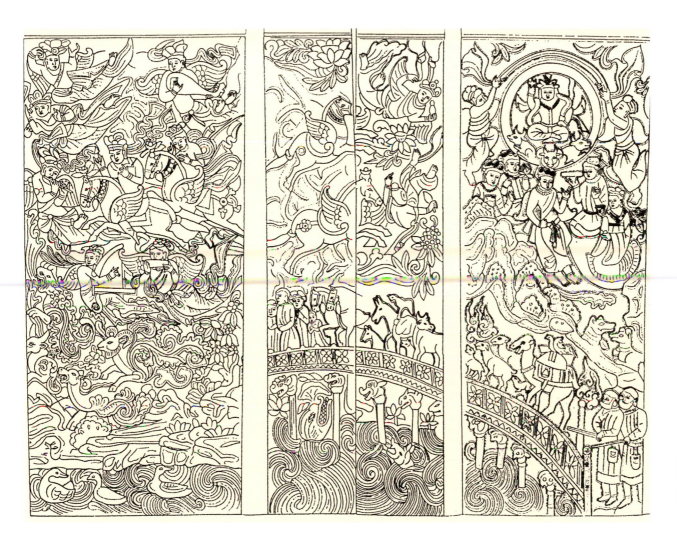

FIG. 14
Eastern face of the sarcophagus of Wirkak
579 CE
© Yang Junkai

The scene continues with an image of four winged horses: two of them flying to the right, the others heading left. The horses on the left are mounted by a couple, preceded to the far left by musicians playing their instruments, and an escort of hybrid creatures with elaborate tails, dashing towards the rocky shore.

Most details of this scene, though not all, can be interpreted by reference to Zoroastrian texts describing the journey of the soul after death, the most straightforward parallels being found in the ninth-century

Pahlavi treatises *Bundahishn* and *Selections of Zadspram*.

The bridge that occupies two-thirds of the lower part of the scene is the Chinvat Bridge crossing over the pit of Hell, the latter being symbolized by the monstrous heads emerging from the swirls or carrying the posts. Two details are particularly relevant to the identification of the bridge: the two dogs that can be seen from behind the rocks above the entrance are mentioned in the Avesta as guardians of the bridge;

the flames burning in two places over the initial section of the bridge are those that help the soul to cross in the darkness (*Selections of Zadspram* 30.52: 'The fire form leads across the Chinvat Bridge … and then there stands the likeness of a mountain over which the soul ascends' (in the image under discussion, the bridge is set in front of rocks).

Some other details of the lower part of the scene are not directly described in the Pahlavi texts just quoted, but they appear to be at least consistent with their contents. The two Zoroastrian priests stand before the entrance of the bridge but are not walking on it; they appear to have solemnized the *chaharom* ceremony and, so to speak, 'dispatched' the souls towards the bridge. The deceased Wirkak and his wife have just crossed above the head of

the larger monster with its mouth turned upwards, which shows that they have successfully passed the test of the bridge and are no longer under the threat of falling into Hell. They are followed by a variety of animals. This echoes a statement in *Zadspram* (30.57) concerning the creatures of Paradise: 'The form of the beneficent animal will turn to many kinds of the five classes: on land the quadrupeds, in the water the fishes, in the air the bird form, which will rejoice the soul by their pleasant voice.' The fact that one of the camels crossing the bridge is laden with wares probably reflects the particular concerns of a Sogdian merchant on his deathbed.

The upper part of the first panel on the right shows the next stage in the ascent to Heaven. The scene is presided over by a god whose iconographic features

FIG. 15
Yu Hong couch
593 CE
© F. Grenet, F. Ory

(bulls, trident) are those of Shiva, but with two unusual variations: the god has one head instead of three, and a billowing scarf is held over his halo by two flying attendants. In Sogdiana, the iconography of Shiva was transferred to the Iranian god Vayu, god of the atmosphere (in Sogdian Weshparkar, 'Vayu who acts in the superior region'); his specific function as an atmospheric Iranian god is marked here by the addition of the scarf, a symbol of the blowing wind. According to the *Bundahishn* 30.23, the 'Good Way', distinct from the 'bad' one which takes the soul away from the body, plays a decisive role just after the crossing of the bridge: 'On the summit of Mount Harborz the Good Way takes [the soul] by his hand, he brings it to his own place, and as he has received this soul he hands it over.' In Pahlavi texts the theme of the encounter with the atmospheric Way sometimes overlaps with that of the Den, the embodiment of the deceased's own faith, coming in a scented breeze. In the present case, it appears that the Den is depicted just under the Way as a winged lady with her right hand passed under the belt (*kustig*), which is by itself a symbol of the Zoroastrian faith. With her left hand she makes a welcoming gesture, or perhaps she is going to receive from Wirkak the roll inscribed with his good actions in life. She is followed by two other maidens, without wings, who hold respectively flowers and a cup, objects which a Sogdian description transmitted in a Manichean text ascribes to the Daena herself. The middle and left thirds of the upper part of the scene are filled with celestial musicians and four winged horses with astral symbols on their heads. Two are mounted by the deceased couple with crowns on their heads, and the horses are paired as those of Mithra's quadriga in various depictions of this god. The notion here expressed is clearly that of 'the station of the Sun which is the radiant Paradise' (*Bundahishn* 30.26).[20]

A different version of the couple enjoying their existence in Paradise is illustrated on a relief from the tomb of the *sabao* Yu Hong (Fig. 15). The deceased, who is said in his epitaph to have travelled widely in Western countries, and his wife are seated together in front of a pavilion. This is common on Chinese funerary reliefs, whether Sogdian or not, but in this particular case some details indicate the Zoroastrian Paradise: the crowns, the musicians (the Iranian name for Paradise, *garodman*, means 'house of the song of praise'), the haloed female attendants, one of whom has wings, which according to Sogdian conventions identify her as a heavenly creature.

Clearly, such works could be commissioned only in a milieu well instructed by Zoroastrian priests who had access to texts very similar to those used in Sasanian and post-Sasanian Iran.

JEWISH AND CHRISTIAN RELATIONS WITH ZOROASTRIANISM

Anke Joisten-Pruschke

University of Goettingen

At the time of the great Persian empires of the Achaemenids, Parthians and Sasanians, there were many ethnic groups in imperial territories besides the various Iranian-speaking ones. They had their own languages, cultures and religions. One such group was the Jews, who had lived there from neo-Babylonian times onwards. The Christian mission throughout the Iranian lands led to an increasing presence of Christians under the Parthians and their successors, the Sasanians.

In Parthian and Sasanian times, towns were melting pots of cultures, languages and religions. Under the Parthians, ancient Babylonian cities such as Uruk, Babylon and Kish – to name but a few – saw a revival of their Babylonian cults.[1] In fact, Babylonian culture survived in the Mesopotamian region until well into the Sasanian period.[2] In the west of the Parthian and Sasanian realms, there were also Greek cities, whose structures were based upon the Hippodamian plan, and so-called 'round-cities', where Zoroastrians, Jews, Christians, Mandeans and adherents of Gnostic groups lived.[3] To the east of these realms, the populations of cities included Manicheans and Buddhists. As the use of trade and travel routes for private purposes demonstrably increased, encounters between peoples of different beliefs, for example, in caravanserais and at the cities' markets, led to interchanges in the sphere of religion that were independent from institutions and/or religious officials. While encounters between official representatives of the various religions – or rather, their statements about each other – are often well documented, we have no documentary evidence for the everyday contacts between people of different beliefs in the great Persian empires. Generally speaking, such encounters and their effects in the private and religious spheres should not be underestimated, for they could influence popular culture and change religious ideas. We will give examples of such encounters in the following pages.[4]

ACHAEMENID PERIOD (559–330 BCE)

In 597 BCE Jerusalem was conquered by the neo-Babylonian King Nebuchadnezzar II, the Temple of Solomon was destroyed and a part of the population of Judaea – predominantly the elite – was forcibly moved to Babylonia and resettled there. In exile, the Jews could keep their faith and identity. Various sources also demonstrate that some of them had careers at court or in the military.[5] When the Achaemenids conquered Babylon (539 BCE) and incorporated it into their empire, the Jews of Mesopotamia became subjects of the Achaemenid Empire. As the empire's borders expanded westwards as far as Egypt, the region of Judaea/Israel, the homeland of the Jews, came under Achaemenid rule. Until the defeat of the Achaemenids by Alexander the Great (330 BCE), the Jews remained subjects of that dynasty and part of the population of the Achaemenid Empire.

The temple of Jerusalem, which had been destroyed by Nebuchadnezzar II, was reconstructed with the permission of King Cyrus, and the temple's treasure was returned. In addition, the Jews of Mesopotamia were given permission to return to their homeland.[6] Their number was not very large, and there were already considerable Jewish communities in Babylonia in Achaemenid times. The Bible portrays Cyrus in a very positive way; indeed Deutero-Isaiah calls Cyrus a 'Messiah' (IS. 45.1) – an exceptional honour, as Cyrus was a gentile who was not related to the House of David.

The encounter between Zoroastrians and Jews can be imagined if we examine the military colony on the island of Elephantine (Jeb) in the Nile, not far from Aswan. The colony plays a central role here, because of the discovery of a collection of papyri[7] which offer important insights into the private lives of its multicultural and multi-religious inhabitants. Pilgrim[8] was able to identify individual living quarters found in archaeological excavations with houses referred to in the archives,[9] by evaluating the results of the excavation of the living quarters[10] and analysing the information in the documents about the relative positions of the houses and their location with respect to the Jewish temple of Elephantine and the grounds of the temple of the Egyptian god Khnum (Fig. 16).

The city plan shown is very informative. Next to the living quarters of the Jew Mibtahiah lived the Egyptian Espemet, the Khwarezmian Dargamana, the Jews Hosea, Jezaniah and Konaiah, and the Aramean Hazzul. The living quarters of Jehoishmalie are next to an Aramaic sanctuary, to the dwelling of the Jew Anani and to that of the Egyptian Hor (a gardener of the god Khnum), as well as to the accommodation of the brothers Pahi/Pahe and Pemet/Pamet, who operated the ferry near the cataracts. South of this housing complex was the temple of the Jews of Elephantine, and between these two complexes ran the royal road. The eastern part of the plan is occupied by the temple grounds of the god Khnum. If one looks at the size of the living quarters, it is clear how small they were and how cramped the space that the inhabitants had to share. It was almost impossible to avoid one another. Counting only the owners of the dwellings within this small area, we find five to six nationalities who spoke at least four languages (Aramaic, Egyptian, Babylonian and Khwarezmian) and followed a number of religions (Aramean gods, Egyptian religion, Babylonian religion, Judaism and Zoroastrianism). Strikingly, only very few disputes and court cases are referred to in the papyri.

It was characteristic of Achaemenid policy to grant their provinces and satrapies local autonomy, allowing the greatest possible freedom for all cultural, religious and economic structures and 'to interfere as little as possible in the traditional and social structures of their province'.[11] When Persian sovereignty was endangered by upheaval or conflict, however, this local autonomy could immediately be curtailed. In

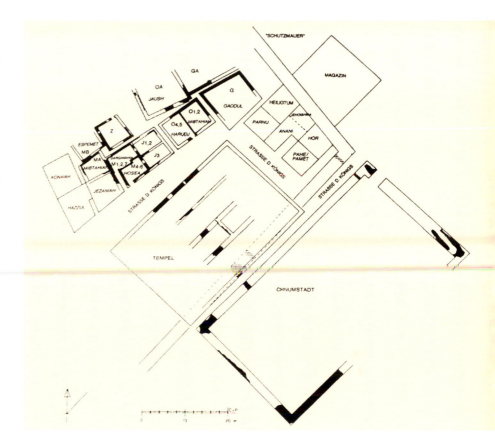

the sphere of religious observance, moreover, radical interventions could be made into the practices of a non-Zoroastrian religion if the sensibilities of the Persian governor were offended. This occurred on the island of Elephantine in 410 BCE, when an uprising took place in which the Jewish temple of Elephantine was destroyed. The Jews described the occurrence as follows: '(Military) divisions of the Egyptians rebelled. We did not leave our post (i.e. we have done our work) and nothing was found that was destroyed by us (the king) in the 14th year of Darius, when our Lord Arsames went to the king. This is the crime which the priests of the god Khnub [Khnum] (committed) in the fortress Jeb (i.e. Elephantine), together with Vidranga who was the Frataraka (governor) there. They gave him silver

FIG. 16

Living quarters of Elephantine

from C. von Pilgrim, 'Textzeugnis und archäologischer Befund: Zur Topographie von Elephantine in der 27. Dynastie', in H. Guksch and D. Polz (eds), *Stationen, Festschrift für Rainer Stadelmann* (Mainz, 1998): 485–97.

and goods …'[12] Concerning the destruction of their temple, they wrote: 'Afterwards, Naphaina led the Egyptians (there) with the other troops. They came to the fortress of Jeb with their weapons, entered this temple, razed it to the ground and smashed the columns of stone they had there. (Also) they destroyed the portals of stone, five in number, built of square blocks of stone, which they had in this temple, and their perpendicular doors, and the locks, that these bronze doors had, and the roof of cedar wood, all together with wooden things and the other things that were there, all was burned by fire. The vessels of gold and silver and whatever was in (this) temple, they took it all and appropriated it.'[13]

The destruction of the temple of the god Yahweh hit a vital nerve in the Jewish community. From now on, its main concern was to gain permission for the reconstruction of the temple, so they petitioned the satrap Arsames and high priest at Jerusalem. They did not receive an answer from either. Three years later (407 BCE), they sent another petition, this time addressed to the official responsible for their ethnic group, Bagohi the governor of Judah, asking him to support the reconstruction of their temple. Eventually they did receive permission to rebuild, but with the following proviso: 'Sacrifices of food and sacrifices of incense they will offer on this altar'[14] – the implication being that burnt offerings were excluded. It is generally assumed that the reason for forbidding burnt offerings was the consideration in which the Persians held the priests of the god Khnum, for whom the sacrifice of a ram was sacrilege. The thought of their sacred animal – the ram – being burnt on the altar of foreigners would have been an affront. However, since the Egyptians were suspected of having taken part in the rebellion, this assumption is unlikely. Some researchers[15] in fields other than Iranian studies assume that the Zoroastrians generally rejected the sacrifice of small animals. Such arguments ignore the fact that Zoroastrians, as part of the Yasna ritual, practised animal sacrifice.[16]

Why, then, did the Persians forbid the Jews of Elephantine to make burnt offerings? The obvious reason is that for the Jewish burnt offering, the animal was killed and the priest received the skin and a piece of the meat. The rest of the animal was completely burnt. The Zoroastrians, on the other hand, offered the fat of the sacrificial animal as *zaothra* to the fire, but it would be unthinkable to bring an entire carcass (which would have been considered polluting) in direct contact with the fire.[17] The assumption that this was indeed the reason is further strengthened by the fact that Papyrus Sachau 10.6 explicitly states: 'It is a Mazdayasnian who is set over the province.'[18] Preserving the purity of the fire was a fundamental element of the Zoroastrian cult. Direct contact between fire and dead flesh would lead to the pollution of the fire, necessitating a complicated sequence of rituals to restore its purity.[19] Banning burnt offerings in the newly built Jewish temple of Elephantine, therefore, was a rational decision in view of the religion of the ruling dynasty, and illustrates the boundaries of Achaemenid religious tolerance.

PARTHIAN PERIOD (250/238 BCE–224 CE)

During the Parthian period, there were large Jewish communities in Mesopotamia.[20] The settlement of Jewish communities in the regions east of Mesopotamia is not attested, but can be assumed. From the second century CE onwards, Christian communities were also established. Parthian rule did not constrain the expansion of Jewish and Christian communities. The complex internal history of the Jews under Parthian rule lies beyond the scope of this paper, nor can we describe the history of the development and expansion of Christianity. To illustrate the living conditions of Jews and Christians during the Parthian period, we will look at the caravan city of Dura Europos that was founded around 300 BCE. Around 114 BCE it was conquered by the Parthians, who ruled over Dura Europos until the city was conquered by the Sasanians in 256/57 CE (Fig. 17).

The map shows both the impressive number of temple complexes and the geographic proximity of the different religions. This is illustrated, for instance, by the relatively small distance between the synagogue and the house church.

The mural paintings of the synagogue and Christian house church are particularly relevant here. The paintings are in the characteristic Parthian style: they offer a frontal view of the people, with no three- dimensional perspective, and the figures are generally shown in Iranian clothing. Great emphasis was laid on the careful representation of details, such as jewels, weapons and hairstyle. The adoption of the Parthian style of painting in the synagogue as well as in the church shows an adaptation to Persian culture (Fig. 18).

SASANIAN PERIOD (224–651 CE)

By the beginning of the Sasanian era, Judaism was already well established in the Near East. In the Babylonian area in particular, there was a strong Jewish presence. Jewish communities existed as far east as India; the first Jewish communities in China were probably established after the fall of the Sasanian dynasty.[21]

As for Christianity, diocesan towns and their dioceses developed early on. As was shown by Ph. Gignoux[22] and others, metropolitan towns, and towns with an episcopal see, with the territories belonging to them, corresponded to the administrative units of the Sasanian Empire. At the Council of Mar Isaak in Seleucia-Ctesiphon in 410 CE, these Christian administrative districts were legally established. The six regular provinces – i.e., the hyparchies and their episcopal and archiepiscopal towns – had already

been formed at the end of the third century or during the fourth. The geographical extent of these six provinces of the western Sasanian Empire does not cover the whole area in which Christian communities lived at the time of the 410 CE council. In Canon XXI of the council's files – recorded in the *Synodicon Orientale* – bishops from the so-called 'remoter dioceses' are mentioned. This refers to the bishops of Persia, of the islands, namely, Bahrain, of the province Beth Madaye, southern Media, with the

FIG. 17

Map of the city of Dura Europos

from Kraeling, Carl H., 'The Christian Building, the Excavations at Dura-Europos', *Final Report VII, part II* (New Haven, 1967), frontispiece

FIG. 18

The Consecration of the Tabernacle and its Priests
with scenes from the Book of Esther

from Kraeling, Carl H., 'The Synagogue, The Excavations at Dura-Europos', Final Report VIII, Part I, New Haven 1956, Plate LX.

diocesan towns of Hulwan, Hamadan and Dinawar, the province Beth Razikaye, northern Media, with the episcopal town Ragae (i.e. Ray) and the region of Abarshahr or Parthia. The bishops of these regions did not participate in the 410 council, but in the *Synodicon Orientale* the council expresses the expectation that they will eventually come and sign the council's resolutions. This means that around 410 CE Christian communities already lived as far as the eastern borders of the Sasanian Empire.[23] At the end of the Sasanian period, Christian groups fled to the east and formed the first Christian communities in China.[24]

The Christians' adaptation to the Sasanian Empire even went as far as to use the Persian language besides Syriac for liturgical purposes. According to the Chronicle of Se'ert Ma'na II, a Persian-born metropolitan of Rev-Ardashir, who was present at the Synod of Acace in 486, he made a translation from Syriac into Persian of religious elegies, poems and hymns to be sung in church, which he sent to the Christians of Beth Qatraye. From Sachau's edition of Syrian law codes,[25] we know that an important collection of canon law compiled around 775 by Simeon of Rev-Ardashir was translated from the original Persian into Syriac by an anonymous monk from Beth Qatraye. Furthermore, Middle Persian translations of the Psalms have been found in Central Asia.[26]

Very much in contrast to these findings are reports on the repeated persecutions of Christians in the Sasanian Empire in the fourth and fifth centuries. It should be pointed out, however, that such persecutions always had a local rather than a systematic character, and invariably resulted from infringements of the law and were not arbitrary acts of despotism.[27] If one studies the Persian Martyr Acts in the edition of Assemani[28] and Bedjan,[29] two aspects immediately stand out. Given the large number of Christians settled in the Babylonian area up to Persis, the relatively small number of victims is striking – particularly in comparison to the number of Christian martyrs under Diocletian and others in the Roman Empire before the Constantinian shift. Moreover, the persecutions took place in certain limited areas, especially in Adiabene, Khuzistan and in the Ctesiphon region. No systematic persecutions of Christians throughout the Sasanian Empire ever took place in reality.[30] The question to what extent the persecutions of the fourth century were linked to the Constantinian shift and to the fact that Christianity was given the status of a state religion cannot be answered here. Although the Eastern Church had seceded from the Western Church and become independent from Byzantium in 410 CE and was becoming an independent Persian Church with its own Church leader, there were still persecutions of Christians in the fifth century. Particularly noteworthy are those that happened in the years 446 and 450 CE.

Interestingly enough, the Martyr Acts generally give another reason for persecutions besides the refusal to worship the Sasanian gods. For instance, in the Martyr Acts charges are brought against Bishop Simon of Seleucia-Ctesiphon. One is the systematically repeated accusation of rejecting Zoroastrianism, while the other is an indictment for treason, since he refused to pay a tax increase. Defending his decision not to pay the tax, the bishop argued as follows: 'Through the act of Jesus, the Christian people are freed from any worldly bondage.' From the point of view of the Sasanian Empire, this was treason in the legal sense, since the bishop had not only refused to pay the taxes himself but he had also instructed the Christians of his diocese to refuse to pay them.

Several facts suggest a certain proximity of Jewish, Christian and Zoroastrian believers, but these are generally individual cases that cannot be discussed in detail here. Around 400 CE it had already become common practice in the Eastern or Persian Church (and perhaps in the Near East generally) to hang up an eternal light from the ceiling close to the tabernacle. The eternal light served as a symbol of the constant presence of God. This custom was eventually adopted in the West in the thirteenth century. It is tempting to compare this everlasting light to the Zoroastrian symbolism of fire and light. If this is so, the question remains as to whether or not the custom was adopted consciously in order to show a closeness between Christianity and Zoroastrianism. In any case, if this custom was indeed adopted by Christians under Zoroastrian influence, this suggests that the two religious communities were in close contact and that the various peoples under the Sasanian crown could associate and interact freely with each other.

LIFE AND AFTERLIFE
Zoroastrian funerary practices and eschatological ideas

Sarah Stewart
SOAS, University of London

The Zoroastrian approach to the last rite of passage is guided by the eschatological teachings of the religion and the overarching theme of the cosmological battle between good and evil. Although the world is brought into being by Ahura Mazda first in a spiritual, or *menog*, state, it is to the *getig* or material state that it will return once evil has been rendered powerless for all time. Man's eschatological future is determined by two judgements, individual and universal. At death, the soul, *urvan*, leaves the body and is subjected to the first of these, which relates to the person's life on earth, and is rewarded or punished accordingly. At the final judgement, the soul will be reunited with its corporeal self. Purged of sin, it will return to a world that has been restored to its original perfect state.[1]

Zoroastrian eschatology as we know it is likely to represent an accretion of ideas that were consolidated during the Sasanian period and achieved their final form in the ninth-century Pahlavi books. Since Zoroastrian religious teachings were orally transmitted before that time, it is difficult to ascertain how they were understood by the Zoroastrian population until they were written down some time during the sixth century CE. Even then it is unlikely that written texts were widely disseminated. Adherence to eschatological teaching can be reconstructed to some extent through the remains of ossuaries dating from as early as the fifth to fourth centuries BCE and, according to Greek sources, from the rock-cut tombs that date from the Achaemenid period in the west of Iran.[2]

After the Arab conquest of Iran, Zoroastrian funerary rituals and methods of disposal of the dead were distinguished by the widespread use of the *dakhma* system. At the same time, certain salient features of Zoroastrian eschatology were likely to have been made more accessible to a wider public. Ideas about Heaven and Hell, for example, were detailed in the *Arda Viraz Namag*, a text that became popular in both Iran and India and which later found resonance

in the Islamic *Mi'raj Nameh* and Dante Alighieri's *Divina Commedia*. The importance attached to the soul, both in the *menog* and *getig* worlds, is unique to Zoroastrianism, as are the elaborate purity rites that surround death and funerary rites. This chapter will explore these ideas and their historical development.

ESCHATOLOGY

To what extent Zoroastrian ideas about the 'last things' – death, final judgement and existence thereafter – can be traced to the early Zoroastrian oral tradition is a matter for debate, though there are references in the Gathas to some concepts clearly recognizable in the later tradition.

The 'day of reckoning' is mentioned in Y.31:14, and there are references to the places of 'best' and 'worst' existence (Y.44:2, 30:4), though these do not have the developed characteristics of Heaven and Hell as described in the Pahlavi texts. In Y.44.10 there is a clear correlation between a person's good deeds on earth and the benefit they will bring to the soul at death:

> O Mazda Ahura, whosoever, man or woman, gives me those things which you know are the best of existence: reward for truth and power through good thought, and whom I stimulate to glorify those such as you, with all those I will cross of the Account-keeper's Bridge.[3]

The 'house of Song' (Y.50:4, 51:15) and 'house of the Good Mind' (Y.32:15) are portrayed in sharp contrast to the 'house of the Lie', described as 'a long period of darkness, foul food, and the word "woe" ...' (Y.31:20),[4] and leave no doubt as to the destination of the souls of the righteous and the wicked respectively.

Although there is no distinction drawn in the Gathas between individual and universal judgement, there is reference to the Saoshyant, Saviour (Y.48.9), who, according to later literature, will be present at the Last Day, Frashegird, when the world will be made perfect again. There is also reference to the 'red fire and molten metal' of Ahura Mazda (Y.51:9), which has been taken as an allusion to the river of molten metal that will have to be crossed at the final judgement.[5] Again, the fettering of the Daevas in iron (Y.30:7) is thought to refer to the final annihilation of Ahriman in Hell, into which the fiery stream will flow, thus bringing an end to evil in the universe for all time.

Zoroastrian doctrine teaches that, upon death, the souls of both men and women are led to the Chinvat Bridge, or Bridge of the Separator, which is guarded by two dogs. There it is judged by the *yazads* Mihr and Srosh, together with Rashn, who holds the scales on which to weigh the good and bad deeds. If the bad deeds outweigh the good, the bridge – itself part of the trial – becomes as narrow as a razor blade; the soul is met by the sum of its deeds in the form of a dreadful hag, naked and ugly, who plunges with it into Hell. The soul of the righteous, on the other hand, will be met by its own conscience, *daena*, in the form of a beautiful woman who will lead it across the bridge and up to Paradise.

A recurring motif in Zoroastrian literature is the insight into the next world, which serves to remind people that they can determine the nature of their existence there. Although the soul passes from the material to the spiritual world following death, its experiences continue to be markedly sensory in nature. The environs of Heaven and Hell are described as places that affect physical and emotional sensibilities, such as those of taste and smell and feelings of pain and sadness. The ninth-century Pahlavi books give substance to these ideas. A typical account is given in the Pahlavi *Rivayat* accompanying the *Dadestan i denig*, where the souls of the righteous and the wicked await judgement and are shown what the future holds for them. Here, as in other Pahlavi texts,

what is described for the righteous soul is contrasted with that for the wicked. In opposition to the world of mixture, *gumezishn*, from which the souls have recently departed and in which good and evil coexist, the dualism of Heaven and Hell is depicted as absolute. Whereas Paradise is altogether free from evil and, therefore, a much better experience than any that could be had on earth, the unmitigated misery of Hell is far worse than any suffering encountered in this world.[6]

[23.5] '… it seems as if all the most fragrant plants in the world were brought to this place, and he sits amid that fragrance of flowers, and he says: "This smell is so fragrant and pleasant which the breeze brings to my nose, never in the material world did I experience a fragrance such as this."'	[23.22] '… it seems as if (he is) in snow, and as if (all) the stench which is in the world around were brought to this place, and he lies down in it; when that stench assails his nose, he says: "Whence has the wind brought this stench which is so strong, that never in the material world did a stench such as this assail my nose?"'
[23.7] 'When the soul looks into that breeze, he sees a maiden whose whole body is bright and comely, and whose form is so lovely that he has never seen lovelier than her among the creatures of Ohrmazd.'	[23.23] '… When he looks into that wind, then he also sees his own Action (whose form is so ugly) that he has never seen uglier and filthier than her among the noxious creatures of Ahriman's miscreation.'
[23.8] 'And he asks: "Maiden, to whom do you belong?"'	[23.24] 'And he asks: "To whom do you belong?"'
[23.9] '… "Young man of good thought, good speech and good action, I am your Action, I belong to you."'	[23.24] '… "Young man of evil thought, of evil speech, of evil action, I am your Action."'

[23.15] 'Ohrmazd says: "Do not ask questions of him! For on account of love and affection for (his) body when he came out of the body, then it was difficult for him. And give him food!"'

[23.34] 'And he [Ahriman] says to the souls of the wicked: "Do not ask questions of him! And give him food of which he (is) worthy!"'

[23.16] 'The souls say: "Which food shall we give him first?"'

[23.25] 'And the wicked say: "Shall we give him the stench of freshly voided (filth)? Is it best if we give him that stench, or that which has not been freshly voided?"'

[23.17] 'Ohrmazd says: "Give (him) mare's milk, and cream and butter and sweet wine, or butter which is made in spring … because for the souls of the righteous when they depart from the material world, then this is the food for them until the Future Body."'

[23.36] 'Ahriman says: "Give him the fresh stench, because for the souls of the wicked, then this is the food for them until the Future Body."'

Perhaps because the ultimate state of existence is a material rather than a spiritual one, the sense of corporeality described above is present even at the end of time when souls are reunited with their bodies to undergo the final judgement. Also, Zoroastrianism abhors withdrawal from life in the form of abstinence or celibacy. Thus at Frashegird the world will become a place where physical pleasures exist, such as the taste for meat, and where, '… man and woman will have desire for one another, and they will enjoy it and consummate it but there will be no birth from them.' It will resemble a garden in spring in which there are all kinds of plants and flowers.[7]

In Zoroastrian literature eschatological ideas are also conveyed through accounts of journeys to the menog world, undertaken during times when the religion appears under threat, by the souls of worthy individuals whose purpose is to prove the authenticity of the religious tradition and its doctrine and rituals. The first of these appears in the inscription of Kirder, high priest under Shapur I (c. 240–70 CE), who seeks confirmation of the existence of Heaven and Hell and to ensure that those who read his inscription should benefit in both body and soul (see Kreyenbroek in this volume). A detailed account of Heaven and Hell is given in the Pahlavi book of Arda Viraz, in which the soul of the righteous Viraz journeys to the other world to determine the nature of its existence and whether or not Zoroastrian rituals are being correctly performed.[8] (Cat. 102)

According to the narrative, Viraz first prays for the departed souls and, after food, is given three bowls representing good thought, good word and good action and containing wine and a narcotic. He then falls asleep for seven days and nights, during which time he is watched over by his seven sisters – who are also his wives. The journey of his soul follows the familiar pattern of crossing the Chinvat Bridge and being led by Sraosha and Arda Yazad to witness the conditions first of Heaven and then Hell, where he sees the souls of the wicked enduring diverse and dreadful punishments (Cats 101 and 103). There seems to be no logic to the sins they have committed in terms of severity of punishment, but it is interesting to note that some relate to customs still observed today. For example, the soul of a man who is being beaten continuously is paying for the misdemeanour of washing his hair, face and dirty hands in stretches of standing water. According to Zoroastrian purity laws, hair and nails constitute dead matter, and contact between them and the seven good creations should be avoided at all costs. Thus Zoroastrians will only introduce impurity into running rather than standing water. When Viraz sees the soul of a woman being gnawed by reptiles, he is told: 'This is the soul of that wicked woman who in the world combed her locks of hair over the fire and threw hairs and lice and nits into the fire, and she placed fire under her body and held her body over the fire' (Fig. 19).[9] Weeping is a negative sentiment and as such belongs to Ahriman – hence Zoroastrians do not indulge in prolonged mourning. In Hell, Viraz witnesses the souls of women 'whose heads were cut off and separated from their bodies, and their tongues were ever crying', who 'in the world wept and lamented excessively'.[10]

The punishments described in the *Arda Viraz Namag* are vividly depicted in the illustrated manuscripts that began to appear in the seventeenth century in which the souls of the wicked are portrayed in the grip of Ahrimanic creatures.

FUNERARY PRACTICES

In keeping with texts that remained in oral transmission for many centuries, there are varying accounts and different terminologies that refer to methods of disposal of the dead in the Avesta and Pahlavi books.[11] The *Videvdad*, a text in Young Avestan, deals with this subject in detail. Here the term *dakhma*, which today refers to the Towers of Silence, refers to a structure (AV. *dakhma-uzdaeza*), possibly a tomb, which it is considered meritorious to destroy. The term also refers to a high summit in the open air where bodies should be left for carrion birds to devour, and where the rays of the sun will draw the soul towards its final destination. After the bones have been bleached by sun and rain, they are to be gathered and placed in an *uzdana*, or ossuary. If this is not possible – for example, for the poor – then the bones may be laid upon the earth, since they are by then free from pollution.[12] The custom of enclosing the summit of a hilltop as a place to expose the dead and the use of the more substantive stone towers are not attested before the Islamic period in Iran.[13] Whereas the type of exposure described in

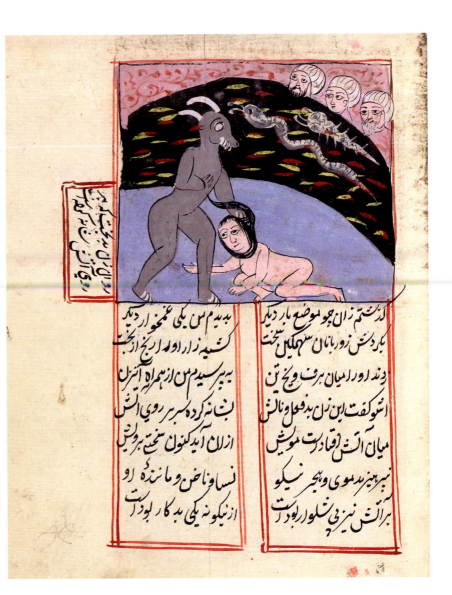

FIG. 19

The soul of the wretched woman who combed her hair over the fire

From Ms John Rylands Persian 41, f. 55r. © The John Rylands Library, The University of Manchester

FIG. 20

**Dakhma in the
village of Cham**
The central pit into
which the bones of
those laid out would
have been deposited
is clearly visible but
filled with rubble

photograph:
John Bugge

the *Videvdad* allows for the preservation of the bones in an ossuary, in the modern *dakhma* these are periodically swept into a central pit where they disintegrate (Fig. 20).

The survival of stamped ossuaries and fragments of the same from the seventh century in Central Asia points to the Zoroastrian beliefs of those who practised excarnation and is described in detail by Frantz Grenet in this volume. It is notable that the imagery depicted on these ossuaries is lacking in epigraphic information and appears to focus on the afterlife, for example, religious rites for the soul or, in some cases, the journey of the soul to the Chinvat

Bridge. The soul is depicted in human form, as described in the religious literature, and there are instances where the divinity Rashn is portrayed holding the scales of justice.

The adoption of a communal place of exposure in the form of the modern *dakhma* accentuated the notion of anonymity; those who enter become nameless – there is no means of marking their last resting places as individuals, no place for epigraphs and no distinction between rich and poor. Moreover, the *dakhma* system, though continuing an ancient tradition of exposure, was adopted after Zoroastrians became a religious minority in their homeland, as well as in the diaspora. As such it became a signifier of identity for the community, both in Iran and India. The historian Monier-Williams gives a detailed account of his visit to the Towers of Silence in Bombay in 1870. His guide was the then secretary of the Parsi Panchayat, Mr Nasarwanjee Byramjee, who explained: 'Here in these five Towers rest the bones of all the Parsis that have lived in Bombay for the last two hundred years. We form a united body in life, and we are united in death. Even our leader, Sir Jamsetjee, likes to feel that when he dies he will be reduced to perfect equality with the poorest and humblest of the Parsi community.'[14] In her account of death ceremonies in Iran in the 1960s, Mary Boyce cites the words of comfort for the soul spoken by the *salar*s when they set the body down on the stones inside the *dakhma*: 'Fear not and tremble not … It is the place of your ancestors, and or [our] fathers and mothers and of the pure and good, for a thousand years.'[15]

Despite the long separation between Parsi and Irani Zoroastrian communities, funerary ceremonies and prayer sequences have remained essentially the same. Prayers and offerings provide support for the soul when it is at its most vulnerable; apotropaic rituals are performed to protect it from evil. When *dakhma*s were still in use in Iran, funerary rituals were simple and adapted to the long journey between village and *dakhma* that had to be undertaken on foot. When a person was nearing death, a *patet* or confession would be recited on their behalf by a priest and a spoonful of *nirang* would be administered. Thereafter a dog would be brought to perform the first *sagdid* or ritual sighting of the corpse. As it is a dog that guards the Chinvat Bridge, so a dog was present to protect the soul from the *druj i nasush* or corpse-demon who settles on the body immediately after death, causing it to become full of pollution. A fire was kept burning near the head of the deceased and the corpse was washed first with *nirang* and then water, after which it was clothed in white cotton garments. While undertaking their work, the *salars* maintained *paiwand*, that is, they were joined by a *kusti* tied to their right wrist; this was also kept by the pairs of *salars* who carried the funeral bier to the *dakhma*. A furrow was drawn around the body with a nail, metal being the creation of Shahrevar and thus giving added protection. The dog performed the second *sagdid* before leaving the house, and the third and last at the *dakhma* itself prior to the body being committed. An account in *dari* recorded at the beginning of the twentieth century describes the meal that was eaten by those in the funeral procession. The *salars*, sitting apart, were offered 'eggs, potatoes, cheese, vegetables, wine, [and] vodka for the sake of the soul of the deceased. The relatives and others who come, they bring each a table cloth (containing food), spread it and sit around each other. They eat each one mouthful and ask for forgiveness (for the soul).'[16]

Just before dawn on the fourth day, when the soul is thought to be approaching the Chinvat Bridge and place of judgement, prayers were recited and roasted meat from the blood sacrifice was shared among the family, friends and the village community. At dawn on the fourth day, the priest would offer oblation of fat from the sacrificial animal to the fire on behalf of the soul.[17] It used to be customary at this time for mourners to declare how many prayers they would recite for the soul of the deceased over the following

ten days. If a man had no heir, one was appointed – a *pol-gozar*, or 'bringer over the bridge' – in order to ensure that the ceremonies critical to the soul's safe passage to Heaven were performed, as well as those in years to come.[18]

In India today, the procedure is adapted to fit urban dwelling, as well as contemporary life. A hearse is called immediately after a death, and the washing of the body usually takes place in one of the *bunglis* or buildings in the precinct of the Towers of Silence. In other respects, the rituals are the same as those described above. In both India and Iran, a fire is lit in the room where the deceased lies and the *Srosh baj* is recited as part of the funeral prayers. Prayers for the deceased are recited throughout five *gahs* or watches of the 24-hour period. From midnight to dawn, the priest recites the *Videvdad* to aid the soul and drive away the forces of evil. On the third day, the *uthamna* (Iranian *sevvom*) ceremony is performed. This is intended to prepare the soul for its departure from the *getig* world. Prayers are recited twice, both for the mourners and for the soul of the deceased, and include the *Khorshed*, *Mihr* and *Atash Niyayesh* and the *Srosh Yasht Hadhokht*.

The commemorative rituals for the soul are as important to Zoroastrians as those performed when a person dies, for the soul is considered to be in need of comfort and protection during the first year after death. Continued performances of the *Videvdad* are considered meritorious and should be done on the tenth and the thirtieth days in memory of the deceased. Family members and friends should attend the rituals and prayers performed on these occasions. In both rural Iran and Gujarat, it is customary to invite people to communal meals in honour of the departed soul. The endowment of *gahambars* ensures the continuation of such ceremonies, as well as bringing merit to the person making the financial commitment. Religious charity is one of the foremost ways for a Zoroastrian to address his or her spiritual needs

FIG. 21 (above)

Jadid cemetery, near Yazd
The older *jadid* graves are visible in the background. In the foreground are those of recent *jadid* burials

photograph: Sarah Stewart

FIG. 22

Jadid graves
Above right: the niche for the *divo*, or light, is visible at the head of the grave

Right: the stone convex inside the grave is clearly visible

photograph: Sarah Stewart

in the sense of accruing good deeds, as well as addressing the practical needs of society. Since Sasanian times, the system of *vaqf*, or charitable endowment, was a well-established institution. In both Iran and India, civic facilities such as schools and hospitals, as well as religious institutions, have been the result of such charity.[19]

The funerary ceremonies described above were adapted to accommodate burial in a cemetery once the *dakhma* system was abandoned in Iran. This development took place partly because of the difficulties of maintaining the *dakhma*s and of preventing their violation by Muslim vandals, and partly because the practice of exposure was considered at odds with modern living among the predominantly urban population of Tehran, where the first cemetery was established in 1933. However, the idea that contagious diseases, such as bubonic plague, remain in the earth and can resurface at any time lingers on among many Zoroastrians in rural Iran even today.[20] A Zoroastrian grave is distinctive in that it is lined either with concrete or stones to ensure that the body does not come into contact with and pollute the earth – the good creation of Spenta Armaiti.

In Iran, Zoroastrians have had to adapt their funerary rituals within a predominantly Muslim environment. In other parts of the world, they have, as part of a diasporic religious minority, had to negotiate compromises. An interesting example of the former situation concerns a group of Zoroastrians who for some time lived as a minority within a minority – the *jadid ul-Islam*. These are the descendants of people who converted to Islam unwillingly, perhaps because of the need for a job or other pressures, and who continued to practise Zoroastrianism. The children of such people (*jadid*s, as they are commonly referred to) might be brought up as Zoroastrians but were officially Muslims with Muslim names. Often they married other *jadid*s and continued to practise Zoroastrianism. When they died, they were not accepted into the *dakhma*, or subsequently into the Zoroastrian cemetery, and evidently escaped burial in a Muslim cemetery, though they were obliged to have the Muslim last rites performed by a mullah. If possible, a person would have the entire death ceremony performed by a *mobed* before his or her demise. Otherwise, immediately after death a stone would be taken to the *mobed*, who would perform the death ceremony over it. The grave would be dug in a special cemetery reserved for *jadid*s the day before the burial. The bottom would be lined with pebbles and the stone, and a *sudreh* and *kusti* placed inside. Over the grave would be placed a convex structure of solid stone that hid the contents. The next day, the body would be brought on an iron bier and a mullah would recite the prayers. An interesting aspect of these graves is that the structure includes a special niche for a light or *divo* such as would have shone in the old days from the tower facing the *dakhma* (Figs 21 and 22).[21]

With respect to Zoroastrians who settled in the diaspora, cemeteries are repositories of information concerning the history of the various communities. In Britain, for example, the Zoroastrian burial ground in Brookwood Cemetery, Surrey, marks the achievements of individuals and their prominent place in society with epigraphic commemoration and, in some cases, elaborate tomb architecture. Identity is expressed in the opposite way to that outlined above with respect to the *dakhma*. But in the diaspora, the record is important not so much for individual members but for the community as a whole within the host establishment (Fig. 23).

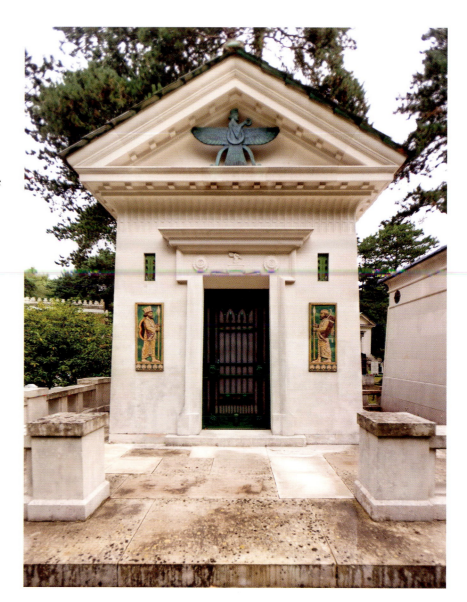

FIG. 23
Parsi burial ground in Brookwood cemetery
photograph: Bruce Benedict

THE ZOROASTRIANS OF IRAN
from the Arab conquests to the late nineteenth century

Albert de Jong

University of Leiden

In the final decades of the ninth century CE, two Zoroastrian priests who were brothers came into conflict with each other over the correct performance of the great purification ritual. The younger brother, Zadspram, had proposed that the ten-day ritual could be substituted by a much simpler procedure, for which he had found support in a passage from the Avesta. While there must have been members of his community who welcomed this decision, others decided to bring the case to his older brother, Manushchihr, who is known as a more traditional thinker and who outranked Zadspram in the priestly hierarchy. Manushchihr responded by writing three letters: one to the members of Zadspram's community who had brought the case to his attention, one to his younger brother himself and one in the shape of a general declaration, denouncing Zadspram's decision in very strong terms.[1] These letters have survived, as has one composition from each of the two quarrelling brothers: the *Religious Decisions* of Manushchihr[2] and the *Compilation* of Zadspram.[3] These two works do not address the supposed changes to the purification ritual, but they do reflect the differences in outlook of two leading priests and Zoroastrian intellectuals in the late ninth century. Of the two, Manushchihr is without doubt the more conservative, and probably also better versed in the vast Zoroastrian religious literature. Although he shows a keen awareness of the very real difficulties the Zoroastrians of his time faced on an almost daily basis, the dominant drive in his writings is that of upholding the tradition and using it to tackle these problems. Zadspram, by contrast, comes across as a more lucid writer and a more exciting thinker, with an open mind to ideas and developments that had taken place beyond the necessarily narrow confines of the Zoroastrian priestly tradition.

These brothers – the leading intellectuals of their generation – represent well the two different narratives that must be told about the Zoroastrians of Iran after the Arab conquests. One of these narratives is well known, having often been told and remembered by Zoroastrians themselves and by Western scholars who sympathized with them enough faithfully to reproduce it.[4] It is a story of loyalty, threat, attrition and marginalization. This is history by hindsight: since we *know* the state of Zoroastrianism in nineteenth-century Iran (and its later developments), the narration of this particular slice of Iranian history must necessarily work towards elucidating that particular situation. One cannot deny that the Iranian Zoroastrians suffered periodically, episodically perhaps, as a result of frequent organized acts of humiliation and violence, and were eventually reduced to a tiny portion of the population of Iran and located in marginal areas of the country. But this is evidently only half the story, and we will see that there is another narrative to be told that illuminates periods of flourishing, consolidation, resistance and especially *participation* in Iranian society.[5]

The history of the Arab conquests of Iran and Central Asia has most often been written by specialists in Islamic history.[6] For them, this is a crucial subject and the number of sources in Arabic is truly staggering. Most of these sources have a very particular focus, on the achievements of the Arab military forces, the weakness of Iranian resistance and the inevitability of the arrival and spread of Islam, and the inclusion of the Iranian world in a new world order. Zoroastrian sources add little to this history, for most of them studiously avoid the very subject of the Arab conquests. The only exception is a small cluster of apocalyptic-historical texts, in which the Arab conquests are seen as part of a world history that demands that towards the end of time the suffering of the faithful will become almost unbearable.[7] These texts add little topical information that historians of early Islamic Iran could put to use, and they have therefore generally been ignored. Sources in Arabic thus show little interest in the Zoroastrians of the newly conquered territories, and Zoroastrian sources only dimly reflect the new reality they faced.[8]

There is very little information on actual numbers of Zoroastrians (or Muslims, Christians or Jews) or on the spread of the religious communities over the Iranian world. Most importantly, however, the focus of much work on the first few centuries after the Arab conquests consistently contrasts the 'victors' ('Arabs' or 'Muslims') with the 'vanquished', those who were already there. This contrast is often translated in terms of a confrontation or 'meeting' between two segments of the new polity. This is a fatally flawed perspective, which should be replaced by one that takes into account the fact that the Zoroastrians did not *meet* the new polity, but *were part of it* and contributed to it in many different ways: economically, by paying taxes, growing crops and by producing and trading goods; administratively, by providing the new rulers with clerks and administrators; culturally, by keeping alive a well-established literary tradition and by enriching Islamic culture with an almost inexhaustible fund of stories, proverbs, genres and music, as well as through art, architecture and crafts; and even religiously, by provoking Muslim thinkers to sharpen their concept of the oneness of God in the light of an enduring Zoroastrian critique of the difficulty this creates in explaining the existence of evil. It has often been noted that the first five centuries of Islam witnessed what can only be called an Iranian takeover of the Islamic religion (and culture).[9] But few scholars have paused to consider possible ways of explaining it. Almost all of them, moreover, have strictly separated this 'Iranian' (in an ethnic, linguistic or 'national' interpretation) contribution from its Zoroastrian roots. The end result of this separation is the idea that only those texts in Middle Persian that have been preserved by the Zoroastrians illuminate 'Zoroastrianism', and the rest can only be used for general interpretations of 'Iranian' culture (Fig. 24).

In the Sasanian and early Islamic periods, the words 'Iranian' and 'Zoroastrian' were almost used as synonyms. This was part of a strong ideology that was developed to unite the Iranians under a single king as a people defined by its Zoroastrian religion. That notion is omnipresent in the Zoroastrian sources in Middle Persian from the early Islamic period.[10] It is only natural, however, that those Iranians who converted to Islam but remained geographically, linguistically and 'ethnically' Iranian enforced a split between the religious and 'cultural' aspects of Iranian civilization – they participated, that is, in Iranian culture in all meaningful contexts except the religious. While this has often been recognized, the attendant fact that the Zoroastrians equally participated in Iranian society has most often been glossed over in a process of restricting scholarly interest to their religious activities. Their presence, for example, in Baghdad – the intellectual, political, economic and artistic centre of the Abbasid caliphate – has barely been noticed,[11] even though scholars have always been aware of the fact that the most majestic of all Middle Persian writings, the *Denkard*, was composed there and shows, in the extensive debates between Zoroastrian priests and Islamic *'ulama* in the third book,[12] that it could *only* have been written in a society where representatives of a high intellectual culture of both religions actually encountered each other. The colophon of the manuscript of the *Denkard*,

FIG. 24

Taq-e Kesra, Great Iwan and the façade of the southern wing of the Sasanian palatial complex at Ctesiphon (Iraq)
A visual reminder of the greatness of the Sasanian Empire right in the centre of the new Muslim world

photograph: Ernst Herzfeld, 1907 (The Ernst Herzfeld papers), Freer Gallery of Art and Arthur M. Sackler Gallery Archives, Smithsonian Institution, Washington, D.C.

moreover, explicitly states that the manuscript was written in Baghdad in the *divan* of the Zoroastrians, an establishment whose existence has equally often been overlooked.[13]

ZOROASTRIANISM ON THE EVE OF THE ARAB CONQUESTS

Late Sasanian history is a tough subject, especially because historians have generally studied it in search of signs of weakness that could explain two facts: the crushing defeat of the empire by the Arabs and the (eventual) marginalization of Zoroastrianism as the chief religion of the Iranian world. For the former subject, there are rich materials that indicate that the late Sasanian Empire had indeed been beset by serious problems: strenuous (and often pointless) wars with the Byzantines, extremely rapid dynastic change, fluctuating support from the noble families in the regions, whose task was to ensure stability in the empire,[14] and unfortunate diplomatic choices, especially in the relations with client kings among the Arabs.[15] On the specific subject of religion, the sources are less abundant,[16] but the problems are equally obvious: in the West, Christianity, by successfully converting Iranians, had begun to pose a serious threat to the notion that being Iranian implied being Zoroastrian.[17] Something similar had long been going on in the East, with the persistence of strongly localized versions of Zoroastrianism and the growing popularity of Buddhism, Manichaeism and Christianity among the Iranian peoples of Central Asia.[18] And there was a considerable rift between the version of Zoroastrianism that was current at the Sasanian court – intellectually rigorous, combative, suitable for statecraft and tightly supervised – and the religion of ordinary Iranians and the priests who served them. Some of these difficulties had culminated in the trauma of the Mazdakites, an ascetic movement whose ambitious programme of religious and social change exposed the fragility of the social and religious establishment of Sasanian Iran.[19] The movement itself was ruthlessly suppressed, but its consequences were long lasting, since, in an attempt to prevent anything similar from ever happening again, certain measures were taken that, once again, transformed the religion. The most important of these was the writing down of the Avesta, with its commentary (the *Zand*), and thereby the establishment of a closed canon of texts. Access to that text was severely restricted: lay Zoroastrians were to learn the Avestan texts insofar as they were necessary for the performance of Zoroastrian rituals, but were to be banned from accessing (at least in writing) its *Zand*, the chief source of Zoroastrian theology.[20] This led to a system whereby every Zoroastrian had to select a priest who would be 'in authority' over him (*dastwar*).[21] That priest was supposed to have knowledge of (and access to) the *Zand* and thus to be able to answer questions from members of his community. His decisions were thought to be binding. The system was held in place through the attendant notion that having a *dastwar* was necessary for any ritual to be validly performed. In later texts in New Persian, the system can easily be recognized in the explicit injunction to priests to teach members of their community the Avestan script and in the equally explicit ban on teaching the Pahlavi writing system – which would be necessary for reading the *Zand*.[22]

Such developments exerted a huge influence on the lives of Zoroastrians after the Arab conquests, but their limits must be made equally clear. Zoroastrians had the freedom to seek another priest as their *dastwar* and considerable discretion in deciding which questions to bring to priests and which not. Where we see the system in operation, the cases decided by priests chiefly concerned matters of ritual, especially of the purity laws, and of family law. It is no coincidence that these are the two domains where Zoroastrians, under Islamic law, had the freedom to apply the requirements of their religion to their personal lives.

THE CONQUESTS AND
THEIR CONSEQUENCES

After the Arabs had crushed the Sasanian armies in a series of brilliant military victories, they obviously had to go through a much slower and more complicated process of holding and administering their newly conquered territories. Numerically the Arabs were submerged in an ocean of Zoroastrian (and Christian, Jewish, etc.) inhabitants, and since the shaping and sharpening of the former's religious identity and tradition virtually coincided with their military expansion, matters must have been very sensitive on different levels. Not only was there the problem of how to deal with the mass of what most people think of as 'religious minorities' (actually the vast majority of the population), but much effort also had to be invested in preventing the Muslims from allowing their religion and culture to be influenced too conspicuously by the evidently more robust and time-tested religions of the peoples they had defeated (Fig. 25). There was uncertainty among the Arabs, too, about the 'ethnic' versus 'religious' aspects of Muslim identity, and one can see different compromises and strategies in various parts of the new Arab polity. This period is, for Iran at least, very poorly documented, and many historical narratives give the false impression that institutions were imposed the day after the conquests, rather than as the end result of a long period of gestation.[23]

While many things thus remain unknown, there is one professional body of late Sasanian society that must indeed have suffered immediately from the change in rulers. These were the court priests, a powerful body by all indications, and one that literally became expendable overnight. Clerks and administrators could be (and indeed were) employed by the new rulers to continue their administrative work; interpreters, builders, artists and performers could equally hope to serve the new masters. But this hope seemed futile to those whose primary duties lay

in the sphere of religion. It is reasonable to assume that it was the communities that had to absorb the ecclesiastical organization that had grown at the Sasanian court. The only indications that this was so come from the time of Manushchihr, in whose works it becomes apparent that the communities were not witnessing a shortage of priests (which would have given his brother a reasonable argument for compressing the purification ritual). On the contrary, not only were there too many priests, but they had managed to continue a structure of the priesthood that presupposed the munificent state support that had, in reality, ceased generations earlier – with a division between priests who actually performed the rituals and priests who took care of the learned tradition, but were less qualified to perform rituals (and thus, in Manushchihr's time, of earning their livelihood), and a top layer of priests who 'arranged' the rituals and lent them prestige, but were not otherwise involved in their performance.[24]

Although in Manushchihr's time the signs of communal despair become increasingly alarming, this is also thought to be precisely the time of the composition and writing down of the bulk of Zoroastrian Middle Persian literature. The shorthand usage of 'ninth-century books'[25] for this literature has greatly delayed careful investigation of their context in time and place, but it has become clear by now that some of these Middle Persian texts are to be dated earlier, and many of them later than the ninth century. Yet there is an exciting cluster of original compositions that seem to belong chiefly to the ninth century: the *Denkard*, the works of Manushchihr and Zadspram and the final redaction of the greater part of the *Bundahishn*, a very important cosmological text. Although these texts all betray the influence of a type of Zoroastrian learning that goes back to Sasanian times, they can by no means be described as attempts at codifying existing knowledge. On the contrary, they are often strikingly original, carefully considered and obviously part of a much wider context of Zoroastrian intellectual life. The fact that they almost exclusively consist of religious texts has only rarely been raised as a problem, and has therefore never been interpreted. At most, scholars have expressed their (often implicit) amazement at the fact that we can glimpse the incomparable riches of Sasanian literature through the many translations of Middle Persian texts that have been preserved in Arabic and partly even in Persian, but none of this is reflected in Zoroastrian Middle Persian. That amazement only works if we continue to believe that Zoroastrians somehow did not participate in the wider culture that made so much use of these Sasanian texts, but this they obviously did. Zoroastrians had access, therefore, to part of their heritage through the mediums of Arabic and Persian literature, and invested (wisely) in preserving those parts of their tradition that were of little interest to a Muslim audience, that is, those that pertained exclusively to the practice of their religion. One can easily see that with the gradual erosion of Zoroastrian communities and the eventual shortage of priests (or of funds to maintain priests), the decision of which manuscripts

to copy – as earlier with the decision of which texts to write down in Middle Persian – came to be dominated by questions of direct and urgent practical use. But even in this later period, it is clear that other texts were produced, in Persian, both to instruct the communities and for purely literary aesthetic reasons.

THE MIGRATION OF THE ANCESTORS OF THE PARSIS

Recent investigations have stressed two facts about the early history of the Parsi Zoroastrian community: that it did not originate in a single wave of migration, but was the result of long-established trading and cultural ties between Iran and the western coast of India;[26] and that the traditional date of 'the' migration of the Parsis in 936 CE, which scholars had deduced from the most important narrative concerning this migration, the *Qesseh-ye Sanjan*, is historically worthless.[27] While this has been very important for a new appreciation of the *Qesseh-ye Sanjan* as a piece of literature, it has not yet been accompanied by an alternative history other than that of a steady stream of cultural interactions between Iran and India. The tenth century still is a reasonable time frame for a numerically significant migration from Iran to Gujarat. The communities in Gujarat must have taken a few generations to settle and acquire land to farm and places to live. In the eleventh and twelfth centuries, there are small traces of their presence in India, in particular a few inscriptions in the Kanheri caves near Mumbai, and the translation of major portions of Zoroastrian texts into Sanskrit. These translations (associated with the name of the famous priest Neryosangh Dhaval) show the first signs of what was to become a marked characteristic of the Parsis: their participation in the high learned culture of their surroundings, whether this happened to be conducted in Sanskrit, Persian or English (Fig. 26). In the fourteenth century, their presence was recorded by travelling European monks, one of whom described a community wealthy enough to have built its own *dakhma*.

As tiny as these traces may be, they derive some of their importance from the fact that a sizeable proportion of the Zoroastrians of the world had left Iran before it was ravaged and many communities made extinct by a succession of Turkish and Mongolian invasions that swept the country in the eleventh and again in the thirteenth centuries. It is particularly the latter invasion of the Mongols that seems to have put an end to whole regional communities of Iran's religious minorities.[28] It is not difficult to see how this could have happened. Although Muslims formed a clear majority of the population of Iran when the Mongols came, the country was still home to large non-Muslim communities, spread all over Iran. These communities were not targeted by the Mongol invaders, who simply killed at random, but it was evidently much more difficult for the religious minorities to replenish their numbers than for the rest of the population. So whole regions that once knew thriving Jewish and Zoroastrian communities, especially in the north, provide no evidence of the return to life of these communities once a stable situation had arisen. From this moment on, Jews and Zoroastrians seem to have followed different tracks of development: Jews remained strongly affiliated to the Iranian cities (Shiraz, Esfahan, Yazd, Kashan) and continued to participate in the cultural life of the Iranian world, which went through one of its most glorious periods of artistic endeavour, whereas the Zoroastrians increasingly withdrew into marginal areas of the country and entered a period of quietism, surviving by remaining as little noticed as possible.

PARSIS AND IRANIAN ZOROASTRIANS IN CONTACT

We possess important sources for this period, which was to last until the early nineteenth century and during which terrible episodes of violence overtook the chosen quiet of the Zoroastrians' lives with depressing regularity. Many of these sources are a reflection of the re-establishment of contacts between the Iranian and Indian Zoroastrian communities. Evidence suggests that both communities had been in contact earlier, but a lively correspondence began in the late fifteenth century and continued until the late eighteenth century. These letters, known as the Persian *Revayats*, deal mainly with the practical matters of leading a Zoroastrian life as a minority – something that was true of both communities.[29] Together with the colophons of manuscripts produced in India and Iran, they are the most important evidence we have for the period. Interestingly, they consistently show the Iranian Zoroastrians in the role of teachers and the Indian Zoroastrians as those in need of education. The colophons also show that certain texts were unknown and certain rituals neglected among the Parsis until they were re-introduced from Iran.

There was in this period a steady flow of manuscripts, scribes and advice from Iran to India, but this again is only half the story. It seems that the Indian Zoroastrians knew very well on which matters to consult their Iranian brethren, and on which not. On the markedly different division and workings of the Parsi priesthood, for example, advice was never sought, and some of the counsels given by the Iranian priests are unlikely to have been put into practice in India. In the miscellanies that were extracted from this correspondence, the letters were accompanied by poetry, and indeed poetry was produced by members of both communities.[30]

The meteoric social and economic rise of the Parsi community in eighteenth-century India coincided with a series of disasters in the Iranian communities, of which the massacre of the Zoroastrians of Kerman by the Afghans in 1719 was probably the most damaging. Developments in India and Iran followed

FIG. 26

The Sad Dar
A Zoroastrian book of rules based on earlier models but composed in the 15th century in a popular Persian verse format. This 17th-century copy is written in standard Persian and archaic Avestan scripts

Reg.16.B.1, ff. 174v–175r © The British Library Board

almost opposite paths: Zoroastrianism in India developed into an urban religion, with a strong, increasingly wealthy and increasingly educated lay elite, and (especially in the nineteenth century) intense participation in wider society in India and, following the British colonial empire, all over the world.[31] The Iranian Zoroastrians, by contrast, were socially marginal, living in rural isolated parts of Iran without access to education or to most other ways of participating in society.

Certain notions that are special to Shi'i Islam, especially the concept of the impurity of the unbelievers, have given Iranian Islam a greater potential for cruelty towards religious minorities.[32] It is certain that this potential did not necessarily have to be realized, and there are countless examples of pragmatic, friendly and harmonious relations in various parts of Iran and in various periods of Iranian history since the adoption of Shi'i Islam by the majority of Iranians in the sixteenth century. The nineteenth century was not such a period, however, nor was the city of Yazd – the centre of the dwindling Zoroastrian communities of Iran – such a place (Fig. 27). On the contrary, the religious minorities of Iran in the nineteenth century were taxed beyond their (very modest) means, and came to be bound by strings of humiliating and debilitating restrictions. Jews and Zoroastrians were saved, literally, by interventions from foreign co-religionists: the Alliance Israélite Universelle and prominent Jewish families of Europe came to the rescue of the Jewish communities of Iran, and the Parsis came to the rescue of the Iranian Zoroastrians. In both cases, they tried to improve two things: first, the abolition of the *jizya*, the poll tax for religious minorities, which had crippled the communities economically, and the organization of education.[33] They were strikingly successful in both areas, and within a generation, towards the late nineteenth century, the Zoroastrians of Iran began to emerge from their (partially self-sought) obscurity and to reclaim the possibility of once again becoming fellow-citizens of the Iranian state and participants in Iranian culture.

FIG. 27

The family of Dastur Tirandaz of Yazd
19th century

courtesy of
A Zoroastrian Tapestry: Art, Religion and Culture, 557, fig. 5

LOOKING BACK TO SEE THE PRESENT
the Persian *Qesseh-ye Sanjan* as living memory

Alan Williams

University of Manchester

The exhibition 'The Everlasting Flame' tells a story. Similarly, a story, such as the one that is the subject of this short essay, is an exhibition around which the reader may walk in the imagination, witnessing memories and artefacts from the past that live on in the present. This essay will therefore take the reader into *Qesseh-ye Sanjan* as an imaginative narrative not as an academic study. The narrative is an exhibition itself, and this essay is not intended merely as a study of a manuscript or physical relic of the past, or indeed of the historical context in which that story exists. Rather it seeks to display a living tradition, or myth, that is current today among the Parsi Zoroastrians of India and its diaspora, that celebrates and commemorates the past for the present and future.

The Zoroastrian textual tradition comprises of literature in several languages, including Older and Younger Avestan, Pazand, Pahlavi, Persian and Gujarati. One text alone in that tradition gives an account of the departure of Zoroastrians from their ancestral homeland of Iran and their migration to India, in the course of which they were forced to forsake Iran. Parsi Zoroastrians to this day believe that they came to India as migrant refugees from Iran, forced to leave by the oppressive conditions they suffered there at the hands of the Muslims. They believe that their forefathers travelled in one boat, arriving eventually, after many hardships, on the shores of India, to be granted permission to settle by a Hindu ruler who allocated to them a piece of land on which to build their own fire temple and consecrate a sacred fire. This single text is the extant source of lore about Parsi origins. A tale is told of an epic journey, occasioned by the tragic circumstances of the ruin of Zoroastrian Iran, of a journey of over 100 years, of centuries of settlement and wandering, of bravery, victory and defeat in battles, and eventually of the establishment of a community of Zoroastrians who became known to India and the world as the Parsis. As is well known,

Parsis have conserved traditions that are traceable to the Zoroastrianism of antiquity and the early Middle Ages. They became one of the wealthiest and most influential communities of India during the British colonial period. To this day, they hold in their collective memory a single text, the *Qesseh-ye Sanjan* (*QS*), 'Story of Sanjan', that tells of how they came to India and became what they are. It is a poem of some 430 Persian verse couplets (Fig. 28), which exists in several forms, in Gujarati and English translations of a Persian original text, and also in various versions in oral tradition. The written Persian text purports to have been completed in 1599, composed on the basis of oral traditions handed down from living memory to the writer who records his name as Bahman Key Qobad, a high priest (*dastur*) of the Sanjana priestly lineage of the town of Navsari, in Gujarat, India, at the end of the sixteenth century.

Though it is a *qesseh*, 'story', it is no *tarikh*, 'history'. It is more than history: it is a multi-faceted religious myth that looks back to Zoroastrian greatness in the Iranian homeland many centuries before, lamenting its loss and celebrating its rekindling on the shores of India, lasting down to the day of its composition. The text holds up this memory of the past as a beacon for the future. The term 'myth' is used of the *QS* to denote a story of great value that conveys a transcendence of historical time and interweaves strands of meaning to convey something of collective significance. In my recently published edition and translation of the text it was argued that the *QS* is a unique document, not as a primary source of events of the early Islamic period, but rather for what it reveals about religious memory that reflects sixteenth-century Zoroastrian self-understanding as a minority in India. This essay suggests that the *QS* is a text that stimulates the cycles of memory in the Zoroastrian imagination: it is not set on a linear trajectory of history, in which the past is the object of scrutiny for modern outsiders of the tradition. It is a religious poem, and is, among other things, a justification of the Zoroastrians' status as migrants, and a commemoration of how they came to be there, so far from their homeland of Iran.[1] One of the main indicators of this 'mythological', poetic nature of the text is the author's fluid use of temporality and his transporting of the reader into other times in a circular motion from past to present and future and back again. It is as if the reader walks – as does the mango tree – through the story, able to look ahead, behind and around about, guided by the view of the author, who draws attention here and there along the way (Fig. 29).

To judge by the number of copies that were made during the centuries after its composition at the end of the sixteenth century and which are still in existence, the *QS* seems to have been deemed to be an important text until the late nineteenth century, when a number of Parsi scholars debated its historical veracity. They variously took traditionalist, revisionist and literalist positions in regard to the narrative of the *QS*.[2] Without rehearsing the arguments of this discussion in any detail, it may be said that it is now generally agreed that for any chronological history of actual Zoroastrian Iranian settlement on the Indian subcontinent, this text is an altogether unstable foundation. Its concerns are, in fact, other than chronology; its memory is religious not historical, focused largely on the concerns of its author, Bahman Key Qobad, as indeed it refers to one date only, i.e. that of its composition. In short, events alluded to in the story stand in only vague relation to events known from historical sources. Scholars such as the Indian historian S. H. Hodivala and the priestly scholar Jivanji J. Modi argued with passion, in debates that lasted well into the twentieth century, about its historical significance for establishing a chronology. Hodivala's dating of the Zoroastrian arrival in India in the tenth century (936 CE) was based upon special pleading and what may now be seen as rather spurious evidence.[3] Various eighth century dates were computed from an arithmetical

calculation of the time periods mentioned in the text, principally by J. J. Modi (785 CE) and S. K. Hodiwala (716 CE), whereas the archaeologists H. Dhalla and R. Nanji, who have recently worked on the site at Sanjan, have favoured a date of early to mid-eighth century for the migration to Sanjan to have taken place. Such arguments and conclusions may be said, however, to be in pursuit of something that was never the concern of the author of the *QS*. Bahman wrote his poem for a more subtle purpose than the establishment of a chronological history: he wrote it with the past in mind for the present and the future, cast into the form of poetry in imitation, in miniature, of a literary model he himself knew from his reading of the Iranian national epic, the *Shahnameh* of Ferdowsi.[4]

A threefold development of the unfolding of events may be a virtually universal feature of narrative plot – the logical and historical ordering of things. Certainly, as we know from the Zoroastrian scriptures recorded in the Pahlavi books, Zoroastrian salvation history is underpinned by a scheme of eschatological time that is subdivided into three periods: Creation, Mixture and Resolution (Pahlavi: *bundahishn*, *gumezishn* and *wizarishn*). Such a structure is dramatically and mythologically significant in the unfolding of the *QS*. The time span of the *QS* is projected back to the very beginning of time, and reaches forward to eschatological future. These extremes take place in the introductory and concluding doxologies which enclose the text, as it is a convention of classical Persian literature, as in pre-Islamic Iranian literature, that the author will address God at the beginning and end of his work. So Bahman addresses God as if at the beginning of the world, availing himself of his authorial ability to jump time zones, to project himself back to the remote past, even pre-cosmic time – ranging from divine *present* to the divine *past* tense, as in the verses:

> You fashion with Your power man's form from clay,
>   [v. 11a]

and

> You gave a form and body to the seed:
>   within it You have made the world established. [v. 13]

Bahman continues in the perfect tense, celebrating the work of God in creating:

> Two eyes You've given him to use for seeing …
>   You've given him a tongue to use for speech [vv. 15a, 16a]

until he reverts to the intimate present tense of praise:

> 'Completest lordship is adorning You …' [v. 22]

Bahman is able to move between times, adopting a quasi-divine point of view, and thus may interject a timeless aphorism such as:

> All this existence was revealed by You,
>   You fixed the image in the world through wisdom. [v. 27]

Bahman establishes a personal present-tense relationship with God,

> I have no comforter except for You [v. 35a]

that leads him into the realms of his own personal eschatology, as he declares, in empathy with his mortal readership,

> At last shall fortune turn me into dust. [v. 44a]

and into imprecations for his future salvation, declaring the formal purpose of this doxological introduction, for example,

> I plead in lamentation at Your court
>   You would not put my name among the sinners. [v. 60]

This kind of reflection is suggestive of a religious scenario borrowed from the Qur'anic discourse of

Islam, which is amplified in many respects in the introductory doxology of the *QS*. I have argued that this is attributable to stylistic rather than theological imitation.[5] But as the *QS* is ostensibly a story about the past, it is to the past that Bahman turns, in his

> tales of wondrous things
> told from the lore of priests and ancient sages. [v. 64]

He says that he speaks through the words of a learned priest to 'tell the secret deeds of Zoroastrians' (v. 76). Again, demonstrating his ability to move through time with ease, he plunges back into sacred history to the days of Vishtaspa, Zarathustra's patron. The 'millennium' (i.e. the basic unit of Zoroastrian religious time) is not *recalled* from Bahman's future point of view, but rather is *predicted* in Zarathustra's own words as moving through alternating periods of oppression and recovery.

> In King Vishtaspa's days, religion's path
> was brought to light by Holy Zoroaster.
> He'd told of things to come in the *Avesta*,
> 'Oppressive kings will show themselves to you,
> Three times the Good Religion will be broken,
> each time the faithful will be crushed and wounded.
> The name of those same "kings" will be "Oppressor",
> and hence the noble faith become despairing.'
> [vv. 76–80]

The author has the prophet Zarathustra himself declare the eventual downfall of the faith. The passage then continues in the first person of the author, predicting how time will unfold, that thrice the good religion will be broken and the faithful will be crushed and wounded by oppressive tyrants (vv. 78–93). The author is now speaking retrospectively about the past from a future vantage point, for example,

> I speak now of Religion's work, so listen
> how once again the noble faith was weakened. [v. 81]

Alexander the Great and other tyrants will have come to destroy Iran, which will then be rescued by virtuous sovereigns, first Ardashir and his priest Arda Viraf, then Shapur and his priest Adurbad-e Mahrasfand. However, by the defeat and death of Yazdegird (i.e. Yazdegird III, d. 651), the millennium of Zarathustra will end and a new enemy, the infidels (*joddin*), i.e. the Muslim Arabs, will seize his throne and smash Iran. At this point, future prediction of the past meets historical reality as the text declares a *terminus post quem*:

> From that time forth Iran was smashed to pieces
> Alas! That land of faith now gone to ruin! [v. 97][6]

Having survived two previous periods of oppression, the Zoroastrians are now said to have lost Iran to the infidels, and they can survive this disaster only by fleeing for the sake of their religion. History is repeating itself, as was predicted by Zarathustra. The remainder of the narrative of the *QS* is the recovery from this lowest point.

The text announces the dispersal of the Zoroastrians into hiding, the abandonment of all their property, in fear of the infidel. The first leave-taking is therefore from their own homes. After this, they become dispossessed wanderers, embarked on what becomes a long journey to freedom in India, spread out over time and distance. The first of a series of halts is their seclusion in the mountains for 100 years (v. 101) until, 'on one occasion', 'a wise and virtuous man' (*i.e.* a priest) urges his companions that it is impossible for them to remain there and that they must leave for the city of Hormuz on the southern coast of Iran (Fig. 30). There, the text relates, they remained for 15 years until a wise man, this time named as a *dastur* or high priest, deduces from his astronomical tables that they must abandon Hormuz and set sail for India. They do so and land on an island called Dib, where they stay for 19 years (Fig. 31). History repeats itself a third time as an old *dastur* consults his star tables and

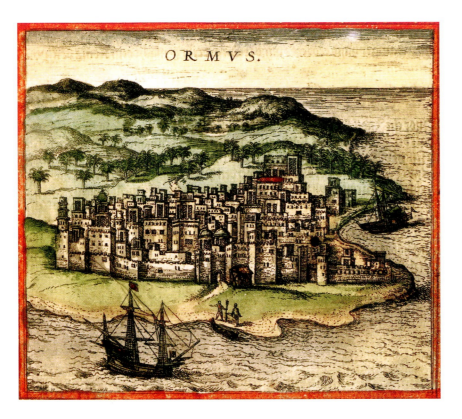

ORMVS.

FIG. 30

The medieval town of Hormuz, southern coast of Iran

Not the island of Hormuz in the Strait of Hormuz, but the town on the mainland. The town was moved, along with its name, to the island *c.*1300, after repeated attacks

S. H. Hodivala, *Studies in Parsi History*, Bombay, 1920, 100, n. 19

declares that they must leave Dib. This time there is rejoicing in the company, and they speed towards the Indian mainland of Gujarat. However, having set sail, they are thwarted by a new peril: a ferocious storm engulfs them in a whirlpool. The priests all cry out to God for help, calling especially on 'Victorious Bahram' (*bahram-e firuz*), a divine figure who has an eschatological role as the embodiment of victory over oppressors at the end of time.[7] The storm abates when they promise to light a fire of Bahram if they reach India, as the text announces:

> They were all blessed in their adversity,
>   by fortune of victorious Bahram's Fire.
> The very moment when their cry was heard,
>   God gave them succour in their difficulties.
> A fair wind blew, there was a glorious light,
>   the hostile wind then disappeared from there.

The captain uttered, 'By the Holy Name
    of God', and straightaway he steered the vessel.
All *dasturs* and all laymen tied the *kusti*,
    the boat was then propelled upon the sea.
And after that it was the law of Fate
    that every one of them arrived at Sanjan. [vv. 131–6]

The travellers appear to have crossed not only a sea but also a threshold presented by the natural elements, and in the process they have been blessed in their adversity – the only time blessing is mentioned apart from those blessings called down upon the author in his doxology. It is another critical point in the text, which is predictive of what will (and must) be done in fulfilment of their promise. The Zoroastrians are said to arrive safely at Sanjan on the Indian mainland.

In the encounter between the Zoroastrian *dastur* and the Hindu ruler, called Jadi Rana in the text, the first reaction of the latter is to fear for the safety of his throne. He sets a number of conditions they must satisfy to gain entry and a place in his territory, the first of which is to be informed of the customs of their faith. The Zoroastrian *dastur* obliges him with such an account, prefaced by assurances of Zoroastrian friendliness towards the land of India and a par-ticularly bold assertion:

> '… We are all friendly to the land of India,
>   we'll slash your enemies in all directions.' [v. 163]

This claim sits ill with another promise they have been told to make by Jadi Rana:

> '… they shall lay down these swords and weapons,
>   and never more shall gird them on again.' [v. 157]

However, the contradiction is resolved just over 100 verses later in the text, when many centuries have passed. A future Hindu rajah of Sanjan receives news of the imminent arrival of 30,000 cavalry of a hostile Muslim sultan who plans to sack his city. The rajah's

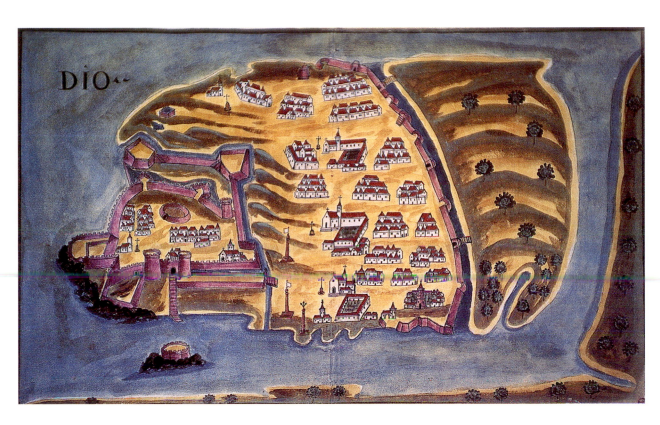

FIG. 31

**The Island
of Diu (Dib)**
off the southern
tip of the Kathiawar
peninsular in the
Indian state of Gujarat

photograph courtesy
of *A Zoroastrian
Tapestry: Art, Religion
and Culture*

first reaction, after recovering from shock, is to call all the Zoroastrians to him to ask their counsel and remind them of their ancient debt of gratitude, as he says:

> 'My forefathers have shown you preference,
>   in your affairs they showed you every favour.
> Now gird your loins in this my hour of need,
>   you will be in the vanguard of the battle.
> If you'll count up the kindness of my forebears,
>   you'll not withdraw yourselves from gratitude.'
>   [vv. 258–60]

The response of the Zoroastrian priest is reminiscent of the words of his 'forebears':

> '… My prince, do not be daunted by this army.
> So long as one of us remains alive,

we shall behead a hundred thousand foes …'
[vv. 261b–62]

In response, the rajah bestows honours on the Zoroastrians and, contrary to the condition of their original settlement in India made at v. 157, they take up arms to fight in battle – albeit on the side of the Hindu rajah. The battle against the Muslim sultan's forces rages for 40 couplets. The Hindus are routed, and the Zoroastrian leader takes the situation in hand:

> The faithful Zoroastrian told his comrades,
>   'I see no Hindu comrades anywhere.
> Now all the Hindu camp has been deserted,
>   Zoroastrians alone remain in battle.
> Now is the time for battle, o dear friends!
>   We must advance like lions to the front!

If we assault them in a mass together,
  we'll spill the enemy's blood with sharpened swords!'
  [vv. 284–7]

The Zoroastrians, outnumbered more than twenty to one, are led by a hero, Ardashir. In a series of encounters described in language that is strikingly reminiscent of Ferdowsi's *Shahnameh*, Ardashir leads the Zoroastrians in a battle that lasts three days and nights until the Muslim general is routed. The *QS* is triumphant in its celebration, which the author Bahman expresses as being a Zoroastrian victory over Islam, not merely an army:

Islam had fallen on that battlefield,
  slain in the battle with the noble prince. [v. 307]

This is clearly another instance of the author *looking back* to the downfall of Iran centuries before.

Yet the sweetness of revenge is tragically short lived: on the next day, Ardashir charges forth into the Muslim battle lines drawn up before him, and in the manner of an Achilles or a Rostam, challenges the Muslim forces to send out their warrior leader to fight him in mortal combat. In language that directly quotes a famous passage of the *Shahnameh* that describes the combat between Rostam and Sohrab, the *QS* tells how Ardashir slays his foe. However, the Muslim general, Ulugh Khan, demands total vengeance and orders Ardashir's death and the slaying of all on the Hindu side, including the rajah himself. The passage ends with a reflection on the hardness of fate, and a lament for the destruction of a kingdom:

Alas for that good Hindu prince who died!
On every side his kingdom was laid waste. [v. 352]

By this point the author of the *QS*, Bahman the priest, has mourned the downfall of the Iranian and now the Hindu kingdom, and he draws the parallel very

deliberately in the text. His point is surely that both disastrous losses have resulted in the scattering of the faith, but on both occasions the religious tradition of Zoroastrianism will have survived. In Iran the Zoroastrians had lost their royal patron, Yazdegird III, but now in India they will have had their own invincible monarch with them, the Iran Shah fire, which they had enthroned and consecrated as a result of their promise to God, made in the middle of the storm at sea. The remainder of the text of the *QS* will tell of how the Zoroastrians faithfully minister to their Iran Shah: the kingly and priestly role had previously been separate, in the figures of Vishtaspa and Zarathustra, Ardashir and Arda Viraf, Shapur and Adarbad-e Mahrasfand. Now, however, with the Iran Shah fire safe in the care of the Sanjana priesthood, as Bahman's story makes clear, the future of the faith will be secure. This, in short, is the inspirational message of the *QS*, which has necessitated its mythological expression: the myth transcends the vicissitudes of time that have brought secular decline. The *QS* is thus the story of the triumph of the King of Iran, who is a sacred fire, not a mere mortal.

In the *QS*, there is also the growing presence of another figure in Zoroastrian society, that of the faithful layman who takes up a civic duty (as distinct from a sovereign or sacerdotal one). He is embodied in the figure of Changa bin Asa, who is announced thus:

At that time there appeared a faithful layman,
  there had not been one like him for so long.
By Fate he came to succour the Religion,
  and several signs were manifested from him.
The Mayor he was, his name Changa bin Asa,
  who treated the Good Faith with soothing heart.
That man of goodly nature would not let
  the good religion come to nought in future. [vv. 367–70]

The next 33 verses are virtually a eulogy to the memory of this 'pure-born' layman, 'pious Governor, so full of light', 'of philanthropic heart', who brought the

Iran Shah fire safely to Navsari to be at the centre of the Parsi community of the day. Bahman implicitly includes himself at the end of the eulogy to emphasize his point:

> Peace in the world to him from me the servant!
>> Amongst the spirits may he have his place! [v. 403]

The remainder of the *QS* (vv. 404–32) is a concluding doxology, all expressed in the present tense, much of it directed at the future reader. Ever resourceful, Bahman even presumes to provide the reader with the words to be offered up in prayer for his soul:

> Be sure that when a pious man might read it
>> he will send up a prayer for me in future.
> 'A thousand times and more we bless that man
>> of noble heart and people of those times.
> May the Immortal Soul return his spirit
>> and ask God for forgiveness for his soul!
> May there be always praise upon his soul
>> and riches in his heart and soul for ever.' [vv. 416–19]

Bahman calls down blessings from the reader upon himself twice more in the text (vv. 423–5, 430). Yet the text is more than a showcase for himself and his priestly lineage.

The *QS* purposefully resolves a number of tensions and anxieties that must have troubled, and perhaps still do trouble, the Zoroastrian community of India and its diaspora:[8]

1. The shame of the defeat of the last Zoroastrian monarch by an invading *joddin* army.
2. The distress of having forsaken Iran and lost the motherland.
3. The fact of being non-Indian, disarmed on arrival.
4. Dispossessed of their own Persian language.

These tensions are resolved by:

1. Vengeance taken over the Muslim armies on the Indian battlefield.
2. The symbolic enthronement of the Iran Shah fire as the monarch at the centre of the community.
3. The sacrifice of Persian blood by bearing arms again on Indian soil for their Hindu compatriots against Islam.
4. Expressing all of this in Persian.

If the *QS* seems to be a heroic and romanticized poem, it is because it is just that. The author begins the journey with a nostalgic tale of loss: this sense of loss is gradually purged in overcoming a series of setbacks, down to the bloody struggle against 'Islam' on the Indian battlefield. With the defeat of the Muslim forces in the first encounter, and Ardashir's slaying of the Muslim warrior in the second, a brief but glorious vengeance is exacted: a 'poetic justice'. Fate again rears its head when Ardashir is immediately slain. The implication of the text, however, which continues with the story of the Parsis ultimately surviving this latter-day Islamic victory (vv. 353–403), is that, having lost Iran, they have earned their permanent home in India, at the cost of their warriors' blood. Loss and leaving of Iran are atoned for. Heroic virtue in action purges any residual shame felt for once having retreated from Iran. There is also, ultimately, the consolation that in place of a mortal monarch, they have the everlasting flame of their new king, the Iran Shah.[9]

THE LURE OF CHINA AND THE ART OF PARSI PORTRAITURE
in the eighteenth and nineteenth centuries

Firoza Punthakey Mistree

Zoroastrian Studies, Mumbai

with **Pheroza Godrej** (art historian)

The emergence of a collection of portraits in the eighteenth and nineteenth centuries and their later popularity is attributed in this essay to the rise of a wealthy merchant class and pervasive colonial influence. Until this time there is no evidence of the use of portraits as an art form among the Parsi community in India. The wealth garnered in the China trade prompted a natural assertion and jostling for power within the Parsi community. Portraits were used to signify the growing dominance of this new merchant class, who as co-partners in the flourishing China trade had made their name by building Bombay.

A repository of Parsi portraits that were painted in China, and the almost parallel appearance of portraits that were painted in Bombay by a few European and Parsi artists, form an interesting historiography of the leading merchants of the time. The earliest extant portraits of Parsi Zoroastrians are two sixteenth-century Mughal miniatures from the collection of A. C. Ardeshir,[1] which resulted from an ephemeral meeting in 1573 between the Mughal Emperor Akbar (r. 1556–1605) and a Parsi priest, Meherji, son of Rana (1514–91), on the outskirts of Surat city.[2] The emperor's fascination with different religions and his ambitious project of *towhid e-ilahi* (Islamic monotheism), designed to promote a universal monotheism, led him to invite the Zoroastrian priest to his court in Delhi.[3]

The Orientalist Father Henry Heras S. J. identified the priest in the miniature as the First Dastur of Navsari, Meherjirana.[4] The painting depicts him in the august company of holy sages and court dignitaries, in audience with the Mughal Emperor Akbar and his son Jahangir.[5] The second miniature, a 'Group of Sufi Mystics Engaged in Religious Discourses', is also said to depict a Zoroastrian.[6] In the miniature, the figure wearing a red felt *pheta*, trimmed with a yellow woollen embroidered band resembling the headgear of the Kadimi Zoroastrian sect, was also identified as

Meherjirana. This identification may not be accurate; the figure is wearing a long coat, trimmed with red collar and cuffs, and it is unlikely that a Parsi priest in the sixteenth century would have worn non-priestly attire. Thus this portrait is more likely to be that of Ardashir Nushirvan of Kerman, a Zoroastrian scholar and Kadimi priest from Iran, who met Emperor Akbar a few years after Meherjirana journeyed to Delhi.[7] These two paintings by the miniaturist Daswanth (d. 1584), mentioned in *A'in-e Akbari* as an artist of considerable repute, are the earliest paintings portraying Zoroastrians in India.

Remnants of this miniature style of painting continued to be seen in some Parsi portraits until the early nineteenth century, when European art styles began to overshadow Mughal miniature art.[8] The Mughal miniature style is still evident in the pose and use of traditional elements in the late-eighteenth-century portraits of Parsis, such as that of Manekjee Lowjee Wadia, a master builder of ships at the Port of Bombay, and Ardeshir Dhanjishaw Kotwal, the warden-general of Surat city. Evidence that Mughal miniatures were beginning to absorb new European styles can be seen in the miniature-style portrait of Dadabhoy Cowasji Jantliman (Leelauvala) (1744–1811), the first Parsi opium auctioneer. The essential European elements of a heavy drape, overhanging in the top left corner, juxtaposed by a Corinthian pillar, and the use of an umbrella with his hand resting on the ferrule end make it representative of this transitional period. The new elements introduced into miniature art gradually created space for the shadowy presence of European artistic intrusion. The complete absorption of European influence is conspicuous in the life-size portrait of Rustom Maneck Sett (1635–1721), broker to the East India Company. His portrait, painted after 1889, was probably executed from an earlier mezzotint engraving made during his visit to Delhi in 1660.[9] From the mid-19th century onwards, a number of Parsi portraits commissioned by merchants appeared in private and public places, prompted by

FIG. 32
**Nineteenth-
century
map of Asia**

courtesy Phillips
Antiques, Mumbai

the wealth accumulated from the China trade and the desire for recognition within the community.

THE LURE OF CHINA

In the early seventeenth century, Parsis who migrated from their rural farming environment to Surat began working as brokers, financiers, commission agents and traders with the Dutch, Portuguese and East India Company, who had set up factories there. By the eighteenth century, the East India Company gained economic and maritime importance, and its trading links with China emerged as the new main source of revenue. Lured by China, two Parsi brothers from Surat, Hirji and Mancherji Jivanji (later known as Readymoney) sailed there in 1756 and were among the first to settle in Canton[10] (Fig. 32).

In India, the increasing presence of the East India Company brought in its wake struggling European artists who came to paint the exotic Orient, the grandeur of the nawabs and the architectural splendours of India. Their main ports of entry were Bombay, Madras and Calcutta, where the writ of the Company was effective and its influence extensive. Artists such as Tilly Kettle, Zoffany, Winterhalter, Val Princep and later Chinnery introduced the art of European portraiture and landscape painting with a vanishing perspective. This eventually influenced the 'painted image'. Indian artists followed suit, with many working as copyists, studying under and learning from European artists.[11] A factory line of artists began reproducing paintings that simply 'sold' because of the subject at hand. Copies of the ruling nawab's portraits were given by the ruler as gifts, *nazr,* and some commissioned by loyalists were displayed in their homes as a sign of being close to the ruling house. Portraits became devices for the delivery of messages about power, loyalty, kinship and protection.

Until 1857, the East India Company's official policy of employing European artists defined the artistic landscape of India, but with the handing over of India to the Crown, patronage shifted to the nawabs, maharajas and wealthy merchants, especially the Parsis, for whom the 'academic realism' introduced by the influx of European artists had a certain appeal.

August Theodor Schoefft (1809–88), a Hungarian artist, came to Bombay in 1838 and lived there for a year.[12] He was credited with the remarkable ability to capture 'historical subjects' with astonishing speed.[13] Among his lesser-known works is the portrait of Pherozebai Shapurjee Batliwalla (1834–1906), the daughter of the China merchant, Jamsetjee Jejeebhoy. By the time Schoefft reached Bombay, Jejeebhoy was a man of extraordinary wealth, and it is possible that

Schoefft came to Bombay thanks to Jejeebhoy. Whether her portrait was painted from an etching or the child sat for Schoefft during his short stay is unknown. Schoefft was known to make quick sketches of the sitter, accompanied by elaborate notes.

Pherozebai's father Jamsetjee was partial to portraits and was known to have ordered several portraits of family, friends and business partners. In a letter written on 3 February 1849, Jejeebhoy wrote to his agent, Thomas Fox, in London,

> I have received from Mr. Hogg the likeness of our much respected and lamentable friend Mr. John Forbes which Sir Charles was kind enough to send me. I shall have this print framed and placed among the other pictures of the family already in my possession.

In another letter dated 3 December 1852, Cursetjee Jejeebhoy (1811–77), his son, wrote to T. W. Ramsay at the Oriental Club in London, requesting

> a Portrait of your goodself to place in our large room along with the likeness of the esteemed and valued friends and acquaintances. My Good Father is particularly desirous … to possess a portrait of your goodself to place in one of our large rooms along with the likeness of other esteemed and valuable friends and acquaintances.

For Jejeebhoy, portraits were used as *aides-mémoire* to honour old friends. In his letters, he demonstrated neither an appreciation of the art of portraiture nor did he express a desire to be painted by a notable artist. Yet he gave precise instructions for the size and frame to be used, a concern of little artistic value. He wrote:

> We should wish it uniform in size to other portraits in our possession and the canvas therefore on which it is painted ought not to be less than about 3 feet 2 inches in length and 2 feet 5 inches in breadth and as framing can be done much better in England than here I hope you will add to the obligation by sending us the portrait framed.[14]

This art form, used as an instrument to display the sitter's extraordinary wealth, power and position, appeared in fire temples and other institutions in the mid-nineteenth century. Portraits of merchants like Jamsetjee Jeejeebhoy, the first baronet, displayed in public institutions such as the University of Bombay (established in 1857) library, also attest to Jeejeebhoy's philanthropic activities. The leading China merchants, flush with Sycee silver, were able to recharge their aspirations to follow the lifestyle and culture of the English ruling class whom they admired.[15] Extant photographs of the drawing room of the Petits, Tatas and Readymoney families show large portraits by Royal Academy artists such as Edwin Ward, J. J. Shannon and others such as Boris Georgiev. This small but significant cache of paintings eventually formed a genre loosely referred to as Parsi portraiture.[16]

In the midst of this visual exploration of European art, Parsi merchants who traded with and on behalf of the East India Company and who lived during the season in Canton were influenced by the European penchant for owning a 'likeness' of oneself. They indulged in this with great enthusiasm, soon ordering portraits and shipping them to Bombay.

By the early 1800s, trade with China – notably of cotton, opium and tea – considerably boosted capital accumulation within the community. Parsi merchants were among the largest traders in opium and cotton. Many who had by the 1850s been in this trade for over 50 years – such as the Readymoneys, Jeejeebhoys, Banajis, Camas and Dadyseth families – controlled the ports and maritime trade, being both shippers and ship owners. Jamsetjee Jeejeebhoy, who dealt with Jardine Matheson and Forbes and Co., had an annual turnover of over £1 million in the mid-nineteenth century. His diaries detail deliveries of opium from Malwa and Bengal. His requests for remittances of more than £150,000 from trading partners in London were recorded for a single ship-

ment in May 1849.[17] Among the many gifts these wealthy merchants sent home were parcels of yellow damask silk, lengths of embroidered cloth, pearl necklaces, packets of the finest tea in China, jewels and portraits commissioned by them[18] (Fig. 33).

Upon arrival in China, the merchants' main port of call was Canton, situated on the lip of the Pearl River. By the 1850s this strip of land known as the 'foreign concession' was a bustling cosmopolitan centre where the dynamics of trade demanded a different approach. In Canton, concessions by the Celestial Imperial Court allowed foreigners to live in this

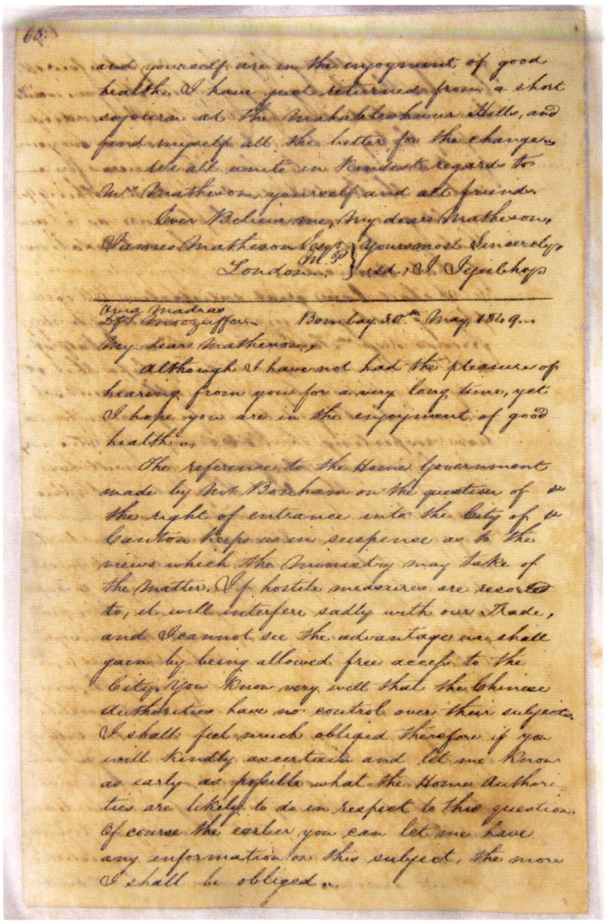

FIG. 33
Letter from Sir Jamsetjee Jeejeebhoy to Mr Cowie concerning the sale of opium
8 February 1849

Collection: University of Mumbai Library. photograph: Noshir Gobhai

Canton, where artists abounded, was as good a place as any to commission portraits. Well known among the artists living there was George Chinnery, who gained both notoriety and popularity and was perhaps the most sought-after painter of his time. His sense of colour, technique and style influenced Chinese artists, who were quick to learn, adapt, reproduce and copy his techniques, much to his annoyance and exasperation. Chinnery's portrait of Jamsetjee Jejeebhoy and his Chinese secretary captures the spirit of this remarkable China trader.

Lamqua, also known as Guan Qiaochang (1801–60), came from a family of professional painters. Although he claimed to have learned new European techniques from Chinnery, the latter dismissed him as an upstart and a usurper. In Canton, the ever-increasing demand for souvenir paintings from merchants, sea-captains, itinerant travellers and sailors kept the artists in business. The demand in India and England for expensive and cheap copies kept the factory-like ateliers busy in Canton. Charles Toogood Downing counted as many as eight to ten artists diligently working in Lamqua's studio in the rice paper department.[21]

The Parsi merchants were not far behind in wanting to indulge their family members with a portrait of a 'handsome likeness'. They approached the ordering of portraits with a determination to master the cultural tastes of their colonial rulers, which they learned in the factories they inhabited in Canton and at the social events they attended. With European merchants, scholars, Company officials and adventurers of all kinds, Canton was for Parsis a vast learning ground. The distance maintained in Bombay between official-dom and the ruled was blurred in the combustive trading forces of Canton. The Chinese view of foreigners as aliens to be tolerated created an us-versus-them syndrome, which forced foreign merchants – whether English, French, Indian or Parsi – to band together against the Chinese, as evidenced by the First Opium War.

exclusive gated area. The 13 Hongs who dealt with them ensured that they were kept at a safe distance, unable to pollute the Imperial Court with their *fan-qui*, foreign devil, ways.[19] The foreign concession strip comprised Armenians, Baghdadi Jews, Danes, French, Americans, Austrians, Indian and Parsi traders. It is somewhat of an anomaly that in the official records the Parsis, whom the Chinese called 'baitouyi' (white-heads), referring to their white turbans, were singled out as a separate group from the Indians, perhaps because of their numerically large number in Canton.[20]

Most of the ship owners, traders and commission agents from India were Parsis, so the Europeans were effectively forced to rub shoulders with them in the 13 factories. It is from this close exposure that wealthy Parsi merchants began to take a greater interest in things European. Back home, the opium wealth was spent on building lavish homes, filled with chandeliers, carpets, European-style furniture and Chinoiserie chic of every kind (Fig. 34). Merchants on long-haul stays in China brought photographs or miniatures of their family members, from which portraits were created.

By the mid-19th century, the art of portraiture had completely captivated the imagination of the Parsis, and initiation ceremonies and other family occasions were marked by celebratory portraits. The splendidly bejewelled portrait of Dhunbai Jamsetjee Tata who died in 1871 at the age of 10, is representative of portraits commissioned to commemorate special events (Cat. 148).

In his book *The Fan-qui in China in 1836–7*, Downing described in detail Lamqua's workshop, which he visited on a number of occasions. Downing mentions that Lamqua was instructed by Chinnery 'to paint in a tolerable manner after the European fashion'.[22] Downing rated Lamqua as the chief Chinese artist of Canton, since he often had more commissions than Chinnery. 'His chief occupation is in taking likeness of a small size in oil colours, of the transient visitors to the city.'[23] The Jamsetjee Bomanjee Wadia (1754–1821) portrait signed by Lamqua and housed in the Wadia fire temple is a magisterial portrayal of the master ship builder (Fig. 35).[24]

Downing's description of Lamqua painting while holding two paint brushes at the same time provides an insight into the prolific artist's organisational skills. Downing describes the paint boxes fitted with saucers of colours, brushes of every kind, bundles of Nanking rice paper and pieces of black India ink.[25] He records nature drawings, seascapes, landscapes, village scenes and even an unfinished portrait of a Parsi on the walls of Lamqua's studio. He mentions the atelier having the greatest appearance of order and neatness, born of Chinese precision and training and probably taught to him by Spoilum.

Spoilum (Guan Zuolin), who lived on Painter's Street, was Lamqua's grandfather and had learned the European method of reverse glass painting. By 1770 he was the largest producer of paintings on glass. His skill lay in his ability to execute precise mirror images of engravings brought over from

FIG. 35

Jamsetjee Bomanjee Wadia (1754–1821)

Artist: Lamqua Collection: H.B. Wadia Atash Behram photograph courtesy of *A Zoroastrian Tapestry: Art, Religion and Culture*

Europe. His portraits were said to sell for 10 dollars each. Such reverse glass paintings can be seen in many fire temples, with themes from the *Shahnameh* showing kings holding court or in equestrian pose.

Sunqua, another artist, lived on China Street and produced a series of paintings on the effects of opium smoking. The portrait he painted bears his name in yellow paint on the edge of the folded canvas (Cat. 142).

Until the eighteenth century, the Parsi Zoroastrians were largely iconoclastic, maintaining fire temples bare of adornments, with their attention focused on worship of the sacred fire. However, a trickle of miniature-style portraits and paintings on glass graced the walls of some fire temples, peaking with life-size portraits displayed in the outer halls during the China trade.

The portrait painted in Canton of Framjee Patuck and his son Kaikhushroo Patuck posing before a sacred fire burning in a silver fire vase suggests that the artist may have done sketches in the factory where the Patucks lived and where these religious artifacts were available. The background has European props of swathes of heavy ruby drapes and a pillar. Portraits such as that of the Patuck father and son were keepsakes of their time spent in China.

AT HOME IN BOMBAY

Back in Bombay, the Parsi merchants, with their immense wealth, sought to dominate community affairs according to their changing values. They schemed to tip the balance away from the traditional fulcrum of power – the Zoroastrian priesthood – by building and funding fire temples and employing subservient priests. Commanding portraits, philanthropic activity and power worked in tandem to deliver an image of powerful merchant princes who could not be ignored.

By the end of the nineteenth century, Bombay was a thriving metropolis where merchants of all types and from various parts of the world converged. They represented an ever-widening world where money was the main concern and profits tempered by charity were used to renegotiate an identity that had received a battering in the aftermath of the opium trade in China.[26] In India, the British rulers established art schools in Madras and Calcutta to introduce Indians to new artistic sensibilities. The *Great Exhibition of the Works of Industry of all Nations* in 1851 in London is said to have inspired Jejeebhoy to establish in 1853 a school of art in Bombay. John Lockwood Kipling, Rudyard's father, was employed to teach sculpture, and young Indians honed their artistic skills under the watchful eye of principal John Griffiths.

The Sir JJ School of Art and Architecture functioned as a training ground where young artists were introduced to the world of European art while tempering their own 'native' artistic styles.

With the East India Company relegated to the sidelines after 1857, the establishment of an art school was seminal in continuing the inclination for European aesthetics and with it a natural progression to the European way of life. Such adaptations were seen as being important for completing the assimilation process and control over the populace, facilitating the administration of India. The artistic strides of the Bombay Presidency were catered for by schools such as Lord Reay's Art Workshop and the Sir George Clark Technical Laboratories and Studios, where pottery making, the firing of porcelain and metal and woodwork were taught.[27]

Amidst all this emerged India's most talented painter, Raja Ravi Varma (b. 1848), who learned oil painting under the Danish artist Theodore Jensen, deputed to the Travancore Court. Jensen immersed the young painter in the techniques of mixing oil colours and showed him the effects and counter effects of the use of light and shade.[28] He painted several ethnographic portraits of Parsis.

By 1909 the Sir JJ School had 383 students.[29] Among the Parsi artists who made their mark was the diminutive figure of Pestonjee Bomanjee (1851–1938), who stands out for the sheer range of subjects he painted. He rose to fame when he worked as Griffiths' assistant to reproduce the frescos of Ajanta caves. In 1876 he worked under Val Princep, the celebrated painter who immortalized the Delhi Darbar. Bomanjee was trained in the style of Western realism and excelled at works depicting Parsi daily life and faith[30] (Fig. 36).

Today, the best-known Parsi artist is M. F. Pithavalla (1872–1937), a student of Griffths.[31] Pithavalla's portraits were exhibited at Simla, Darjeeling, Poona, Madras and Bombay.[32] Having mastered portraiture in oil, he travelled to Italy and London, where he painted 26 pictures using different mediums, some of which were reproductions of Old Masters. His exhibition at the Dore Gallery was followed by a reception given by Conservative MP Sir M. M. Bhownagree to introduce him to the art world in London. His series of 14 watercolours depicting Indian women was presented in 1911 to Mary, the Queen Consort.

Not so well known was Erach A. Bhiwandiwala (b. 1898), who worked in the Calcutta Studio of the Bengalee master J. P. Ganguli. He studied at the Chelsea Studios, London University (Slade School of Art), under Sir John Lavery RA, who painted the famous court portrait of Lady Dorab Tata, and the Academic de la Cluse in Paris.[33] His portraits of Prince and Princess Kaya of Japan, the socialite Countess of Howe and Bhownagree (presently in the collection of ZTFE) were widely acclaimed.

FIG. 36

Pestonjee Bomanjee (1851–1938)

Artist: Ardeshir Pestonji, 1911 Collection: Homi Ranina. photograph: Noshir Gobhai

Another portraitist, Jehangir A. Lalkaka (1884–1967), studied at the Sir JJ School of Art and in London at the St John's Wood and Westminster Art Schools. On his return, he painted the portrait of Viceroy Lord Willingdon and was invited in 1929 to participate in an exhibition held by the architect Edwin Lutyens. In 1931 he became the first Indian Vice-President of the Sir JJ School of Art. He created a series of family portraits and several of the Iranian prophet Zarathustra.

There are several artists who painted members of the Parsi community who have not been mentioned and could be the subject of another essay. However, it remains to be said that the art of portraiture, which derived inspiration from the officially sponsored Company artists who travelled to Bombay and Canton, influenced a new generation of Indian and Chinese artists who laid the canvas for a magnificent record of ethnographic portraits.

NOTES TO ESSAYS

WORDS WITHOUT CONTEXT

1. For a general survey, see Hintze (2009a). On the oral character of the Zoroastrian religious tradition, see Skjærvø (2007).
2. Hintze (2013a).
3. N. Sims-Williams (1998): 136; Kellens (1989): 35ff.
4. Gnoli (1989).
5. Schwartz (1990).
6. de Jong (1997).
7. Macuch (2008).
8. Mallory and Adams (2006): 102ff, 449 – and, for a discussion of the most viable theories, 460–3.
9. Varfolomeev and Evdokimov (2013): 301. For a summary of the cultural traits of the Indo-Iranians, see Mallory (2002): 21; Witzel (2003): 9.
10. For these dates, see the references in Witzel (2003): 3 (n. 13).
11. Hiebert (1998).
12. Lubotsky (2001): 307–8, 311, 313; Witzel (2003): 3 (n. 13), 25, 29–30.
13. Boroffka and Hansen (2010): 18.
14. Boroffka and Swerçkow (2007): 94; Lhuillier (2013); Kuz'mina (2007).
15. Lyonnet (1993): 431; Lhuillier (2013): 104.
16. Hale (1986).
17. On the relationship between the trisyllabic masculine agent noun *mazda-*, 'wise one', and the morphologically different feminine abstract noun *mazda-* = disyllabic Vedic *medh* – 'wisdom, insight', see Hintze (2007): 284–5.
18. For a discussion of details and references, see Hintze (2013b).
19. Note that this word lives on in Latin *deus* ('god') and *divinus* ('divine').
20. The texts are conveniently accessible in Boyce (1984): 45–53. See also Kreyenbroek (1993): 303–7.
21. For further details on the creation of the spiritual and material worlds, see Hintze (2013c).
22. For details, see Hintze (2009b).
23. For details and a full quotation of this and the following text passages, see Hintze (2013d): 32–35.
24. On blame poetry, see Skjærvø (2002): 29–67.
25. Hintze (2000).
26. Boyce (1984): 80–2.

ZOROASTRIANISM AS AN IMPERIAL RELIGION

1. Kreyenbroek (1996): 221–37.
2. See latterly Kreyenbroek (2010): 103–9.
3. Hinz (1987), 127, states that the Persians began to take possession of the land around 700 BCE; for an earlier date (850 BCE), see en.wikipedia.org/wiki/Persian_people#Ancient_history_and _origin.
4. See www.iranchamber.com/history/elamite/elamite.php.
5. See Henkelman (2008).
6. See Kreyenbroek (2010).
7. The core texts of the Zoroastrian liturgy, the Gathas and the *Yasna Haptanghaiti*, had probably been memorized word-for-word from the time of Zarathustra.
8. Texts and translations can be found in Kent (1953).

9. Kreyenbroek (2008): 48–50.
10. See Kreyenbroek (2010).
11. See Shaked (1984): 31–40.
12. www.sasanika.org/sasanika-library/agathias.
13. On Mazdak, see latterly Rezania (2012): 479–94.
14. See the articles collected in Kashani and Stoellner (2011).
15. See Kreyenbroek (2011).

ZOROASTRIAN FUNERARY PRACTICES

1. See in general Grenet (1984).
2. Chavannes (1903): 132–3, n. 5.
3. Bendezu-Sarmiento and Lhuillier (2013).
4. Unpublished, exhibited at the Afrasiab Museum in Samarkand.
5. See Grenet (2012), esp. 37–8, figs 10 and 11.
6. Livshits (2008): 49–58.
7. N. Sims-Williams (2012): 120–1, 130–1 (documents v and w).
8. This chronology was upheld in particular in Rapoport (1971). It appears that, too often, funerary remains have been dated by the structures in which they had been deposited and which can pre-date them considerably.
9. See Grenet (1984): 187–93, 327; Rtveladze (1997).
10. Sachau (2005): 222, 226.
11. Grenet and Marshak (1998): 5–18, esp. 11–12, with fig. 6.
12. See Grenet (1984): 149–53, 252–3, 260–1, pl. XLIV.
13. Grenet (1986): 97–131, figs 35–48. The late Boris Marshak accepted most identifications but proposed other Zoroastrian deities for some characters (Marshak 1995/96). The captions in the present catalogue are descriptive only.
14. Marshak (2001): 227–64; Lerner (2005); Grenet (2007).
15. Sheng (2005), esp. p. 168.
16. Riboud (2003); Grenet (2007): 470–1, with fig. 7.
17. Riboud (2012): 1–23.
18. See Grenet (2012): 39–43.
19. Summarized in Grenet (2007): 471–4.
20. Between the encounter with the *Den* and the advent in Paradise comes a scene that cannot be accounted for in Zoroastrian texts: a female figure falls backwards into space, threatened by a heavenly creature brandishing a small human statue. It is probably an insertion from the Manichaean myth of the end of time (other specifically Manichaean themes have been recognized in other panels).

JEWISH AND CHRISTIAN RELATIONS WITH ZOROASTRIANISM

1. See Oelsner (1986, 2002).
2. Ibid.
3. For further information on the various city layouts, see Joisten-Pruschke (forthcoming [a]).
4. For a detailed discussion on this topic, see Joisten-Pruschke (forthcoming [b]).
5. See Donner (1986).
6. On the edict to build the temple, the returning of the temple's treasure and the permission to return to Judaea/Israel, see Ezra 1, Ezra 6:1–18 and 2. Chron. 36:22–3.
7. On the history of the discovery of the Aramaic papyri, see Joisten-Pruschke (2008): 17ff.

8. Pilgrim (1999).
9. Ibid.: 141.
10. Pilgrim (1998).
11. See Dandamayev (1999): 271.
12. Papyrus Strassburg l.1ff.
13. Papyrus Sachau 1.8ff.
14. Papyrus Sachau 3.9.10.
15. See, for instance, Kottsieper (2002).
16. Razmjou (2004).
17. Especially *Nerangestan* 46. See Kotwal and Kreyenbroek (2003), vol. I: 196ff.
18. Papyrus Sachau 10.6.
19. See Kotwal and Kreyenbroek (2003).
20. See Oppenheimer (1983), and Neusner (1969).
21. Guandan (1984).
22. Gignoux (1983).
23. Sachau (1919): 17.
24. See Saeki (1916, 1951).
25. Sachau (1907–14).
26. Andreas and Barr (1933).
27. See Joisten-Pruschke (forthcoming [b]).
28. Assemani (1748).
29. Bedjan (1890–97).
30. Systematic persecutions of the Christians over the whole territory of the Roman Empire started with Decius (249–51), and were intensified by Valerian (255–60) and Diocletian (284–305). See Liesering (1933) and Stade (1926).

LIFE AND AFTERLIFE

1. Two terms exist for the soul that are at times indistinguishable from one another: *urvan* (an Indo-Iranian term), thought to inhabit the underworld after death, visiting its former home at the festival of Hamaspathmaedaya (All Souls), and *fravashi*, an Iranian word for guardian spirits who have the power to protect and aid those who worship them.
2. Grenet (1990): 560.
3. Humbach and Ichaporia (1994): 79.
4. Ibid.: 37.
5. See also Y.32.7.
6. See Stausberg (2009): 229, where he describes the focus on Paradise as a conscious effort to extract only that which is good from the present state of mixture.
7. Williams (1990): 88.
8. Though probably dating from the disruption caused by the conquest of Iran by Alexander the Great, this account is thought to have achieved its final form in the ninth to tenth centuries CE. It became popular in India and was translated into Gujarati as demand grew for religious texts in the vernacular.
9. Vahman (1986): 205.
10. Ibid.: 209.
11. See Boyce (1975a): 325–6.
12. See VD. VI: V 44 (92) and 51 (105) in Muller (1980): 73–4. See also Boyce (1975a): 326–8.
13. For the remains of such structures in Central Asia see Grenet in this volume.

14. Monier-Williams (1891): 82.
15. Boyce (1977): 152.
16. Vahman and Asatrian (2002): 45.
17. The blood sacrifice continued among Parsis in India until the beginning of the nineteenth century. It is no longer practised in Tehran and increasingly less in Yazd and surrounding villages.
18. In India, evidently there was a custom whereby the will of the deceased was read out, including the charities endowed by him. See Munshi (unpublished): 91.
19. See Stewart (2012): 61–4.
20. The perceived scientific basis for this idea was conflated with the teachings of the religious texts – for example, the *Videvdad*, which stipulates a period of 50 years during which a burial place remains contagious. See Modi (1995): 151–2.
21. From an interview conducted with a villager in Zeinabad in 2009 by this author. It seems that this custom began during the reign of Nasir al-Din Shah (r. 1848–96), but it has not been possible to verify this.

THE ZOROASTRIANS OF IRAN

1. These letters are known as the *Epistles of Manushchihr* and are fiendishly difficult. They were edited by B. N. Dhabhar (Dhabhar 1912), without a translation. The full translation of the text by E.W. West (West 1882: 277–366), although demonstrating an almost miraculous intuitive grasp of Middle Persian, is seriously out of date, and this is also true of the many chapters edited by M. F. Kanga, but the translation by this great Parsi scholar of the third epistle – the general declaration, which is the least convoluted of the three – aptly conveys its key message (Kanga 1975: 445–56).
2. This text, the *Dadestan i denig*, has been edited in two parts, but only the first part of this edition was ever published (Anklesaria 1976). Strangely – again with the exception of the full and equally intuitive translation of E.W. West (West 1982: 3–276) – this is also true of another translation of the text (Jaafari-Dehaghi 1998).
3. The new edition, translated by Ph. Gignoux and A. Tafazzolil (Gignoux and Tafazzolil 1993), has replaced the earlier edition of B.T. Anklesaria (Anklesaria 1964), at least for those who read French. Anklesaria's introduction, however (i–xliv), remains indispensable.
4. The classical statement is Boyce (1979): 145–95, which remains a very good example of this narrative. Although this author takes a slightly different approach, it must be stressed that Boyce was the *only* specialist of her generation to have even an interest in Zoroastrian history after the Arab conquests; the majority of her colleagues and contemporaries simply treated Zoroastrianism as a religion that was (or should have been) extinct.
5. Important recent studies are Choksy (1997), Stausberg (2002): 263–372, and Crone (2012).
6. An important exception is Howard-Johnston (2010), which takes a much broader perspective.
7. The classical statements are the text known as the *Zand i Vahman Yasn* (Cereti 1995), and the seventh book of the *Denkard* (Molé 1993). Josephson (2003) aptly stresses the fact that the chapters dealing with the 'present' difficulties derive much of their meaning from being part of a narrative of world history.
8. Note, for example, the memorable characterization of the economic

relations between Zoroastrians and Muslims in Khorasan in terms of a 'dual agricultural economy' (and the further social implications of this structure) in Bulliet (2009).

9. See especially Yarshater (1998).

10. The main sign of this is the use of the term *an-er* ('non-Iranian') as a synonym for 'non-Zoroastrian', and of *ag-den* ('of evil religion'). See, for example, *Dadestan i denig* question 40 (in Jaafari-Dehaghi 1998): 'Those whose judgment is this, that one should not believe in the Mazdean religion, in [whose] judgment it is said that [one] should leave the Mazdaean religion, and repudiate the religion and follow a non-Iranian faith; then how is it, and what is their sin? And what is the sin of him who goes over to a non-Iranian religion?'

11. Zoroastrians remain wholly unnoticed in Kennedy (2004).

12. These debates are highly significant, and can be found in de Menasce (1973), under the index entry 'docteurs'.

13. There is, remarkably, no modern study of this colophon, but the information in it is well known to specialists and parallels the information on the history of the *Denkard* in book 3, ch. 420, where the Zoroastrian *divan* is also mentioned.

14. Pourshariati (2008).

15. Howard-Johnston (2010): 436–41.

16. The best overview is Shaked (1994).

17. See especially Walker (2006).

18. See Rose (2011): 135–58.

19. See Crone (1991); de Blois (2012).

20. de Jong (2009).

21. Kreyenbroek (1994).

22. Thus, for example, the Persian text *Sad dar-e nasr*, 98–9, specifies that priests must teach members of their community the Avestan script, but are not allowed to teach the Pahlavi script to anyone who is not a priest.

23. An important exception is Levy-Rubin (2011).

24. Thus, brilliantly, Kreyenbroek (1987).

25. Although the expression was already traditional when it appeared, it has been given much (lasting) currency by Bailey (1971).

26. Wink (1990): 104–8.

27. Williams (2009). 'Historically worthless' should be taken to mean 'not reflecting an actual historical event'; the whole purpose of Alan Williams' book is to show how important the text of the *Qesseh-ye Sanjan* really is for the cultural, literary and intellectual history of the Parsis.

28. Boyce (1979): 161–5.

29. The texts (as found in topically arranged miscellanies, interspersed with poetry and other compositions) were edited in Unvala (1922), and translated (without the poetry etc.) in Dhabhar (1932). To this must be added the (excluded) last of the Persian *Revayats*, the *Ithoter*, which was edited and translated in exemplary fashion in Vitalone (1996).

30. The only recent study of (a small part of) that poetic heritage is Schmermbeck (2008).

31. See Palsetia (2001) for a survey.

32. The most extensive discussion, applied to the Jews of Iran, is Tsadik (2007): 15–32. For the specific situation of the Zoroastrians of Yazd, see the memorable testimony of the Christian missionary Napier Malcolm. Malcolm (1905): 44–52.

33. See Boyce (1969), for the Zoroastrians, and Cohen (1986).

LOOKING BACK TO SEE THE PRESENT

1. See Williams (2009).

2. See further my discussion of the nineteenth- and early twentieth-century debates in ibid.: 205–21.

3. Ibid.: 209–12.

4. As I have shown in ibid.: 195–8, 218–20.

5. Ibid.: 150–2, 158.

6. References are to the translated verses of my edition, cited above. In the references to verses, 'a' and 'b' refer to each of the half-lines of a particular verse.

7. See, for example, Boyce (1977): 71.

8. Williams (2012): 79–93.

9. On the history of the Iran Shah fire with bibliography, see Boyce and Kotwal (2006), also online at www.iranicaonline.org/articles/iransah

THE LURE OF CHINA AND THE ART OF PARSI PORTRAITURE

1. Mughal miniature, Shah Jehan School, from the collection of A. C. Ardeshir. See Darukhanawala (1939): 44.

2. Darukhanawala (1939): 55–6. Meherji was the first high priest appointed by the Parsi community after their arrival in India. He was acknowledged as their spiritual leader and given the title 'Meherjirana'. Successive descendants have taken this eponymous title.

3. Meherji visited Delhi in 1573 and 1578–79. See Modi (1903).

4. In 1926, Father Henry Heras founded the Indian Historical Research Institute, renamed the Heras Institute, at St Xavier's College, Mumbai. This museum houses an eclectic collection, which ranges from a Parthian rhyton to Christian statuary and Indian bronzes.

5. A later reconstruction of Meherjirana's image was painted by artist Jehangir A. Lalkaka in the twentieth century. The full-size portrait, which shows Meherjirana in priestly regalia on a moon-lit terrace, is displayed in the Anjuman Atash Bahram (fire temple) in Navsari.

6. Darukhanawala (1939): 46–54. This miniature was part of A. C. Ardeshir's collection and has been dated 1576–77.

7. Ardashir Nushirvan of Kerman is said to have contributed Avestan and Pahlavi words to the dictionary, *Farhang-e Jahangiri*. See also Shastri (1918): 9–14.

8. Darukhanawala (1939): 227, 308, 309, 492.

9. The etching of the Iranian Prophet Spitaman Zarathustra, inscribed in gold on the book held in Rustom Manek's hand, appeared in Zoroastrian prayer books after the publication Kiash (1889): plate LXI opposite p. 211. Its occurrence in the painting suggests that the portrait was created after 1889.

10. Patel and Barjorji (1891), vol. I: 41.

11. Llewellyn-Jones (2008): 13.

12. Aijazuddin (1979): 21–3.

13. Ibid.: 22.

14. The correspondence of Jamsetjee Jejeebhoy and his sons with their agents in China and business partners such as Jardine Matheson and Forbes is compiled in several volumes and housed in the library of the University of Mumbai, Fort branch. The volumes, written between 1826 and 1864, chronicle the historical China trade and record the economic trends, the merchants' political manoeuvrings, their attempts to influence the British parliament

during the ban on opium trade and the inner workings of the complex network of shippers in the maritime trade with China.

15. Sycee silver was the currency with which China merchants paid for commodities brought to China. Its weight was evaluated in taels.

16. A conservative estimate suggests that in the over 40 fire temples built by wealthy merchants in Mumbai, there are some 300 Parsi portraits, not counting those in other community institutions and private collections.

17. Jejeebhoy (1849).

18. Export of paintings from China began much earlier: 'On 27 December 1727 the commander of the British East Indiaman *Prince Augustus* added four cases of "pictures" to his usual cargo of tea, silks, and porcelain.' See Krauss (2005): 73.

19. The Hongs were representatives of the government. Low-ranking officials, they made vast sums of money facilitating foreign trade by working as commission agents. Their job involved ensuring that the many foreign firms and small traders operating from Canton's 13 factories obeyed the Imperial decrees.

20. Thampi (2005): 76.

21. Downing (1838). See vol. II: 94.

22. Ibid.: 90–1.

23. Ibid.: 91–2.

24. Oil on canvas, collection of H.B. Wadia Atash Bahram, Mumbai.

25. Downing (1838): 93–4. Rice paper was valued by an artist and sold according to size. The paper made from the pith of a malvaceous plant was flattened into thin leaves. Black India ink created by grinding lamp black with glue, was a valuable artist's tool as it contributed to the fineness of the brush work in traditional Chinese painting. The Chinese tested the quality by breaking a piece to check its internal shine, lustre and perfume.

26. Short ditties and rude songs about the merchants became popular and are an indication of the declining reputation of these merchants before they embarked on their strategic campaign of portraiture, institution building and philanthropy.

27. Edwardes (1910): 342–3.

28. Jaradi (2011): 17–18.

29. Edwardes (1910): 157.

30. Darukhanawala (1939): 188–9. Available at goaartgallery.com/bomanji_pestonji.htm (accessed 14 March 2013).

31. Ibid.: 190–2.

32. In all, he gathered a small cache of 24 gold and silver medals and won cash awards a staggering 45 times.

33. Now at Chhatrapati Shivaji Maharaj Vastu Sangrahalaya, formerly the Prince of Wales Museum in Mumbai.

THE CATALOGUE

1

THE ANCIENT WORLD

Jenny Rose

ELAM

Before the early first millennium BCE, there is no firm evidence for an Iranian presence on the plateau of modern-day Iran. It is thought that Iranian migration began some time in the late second millennium, preceded by a movement of Indo-Iranians or Indo-Aryans into upper Mesopotamia. Prior to that period, we have evidence of several substantial urbanized civilizations stretching from Egypt, through Mesopotamia, Iran and western Central Asia to the Indus Valley. By at least 4000 BCE there was a flourishing Elamite civilization centred around Susa in south-west Iran. From about 3000 BCE onwards Elam had its own cuneiform writing system, and by around 2500 BCE Susa was part of a vast trading network that extended to sites in south-east Iran such as Shahdad, Tepe Yahya and Jiroft. The high point of Elamite civilization came during the Middle Elamite period (c.1500–1100 BCE) with ambitious building programmes at Susa, Choga Zanbil and Haft Tepe, and the production of many splendid works of art. Amongst the more modest products of this period are numerous terracotta (baked clay) figurines, many of them apparently associated with fertility and childbirth. There is a long tradition of such figures in neighbouring Mesopotamia. From both the Middle Elamite period and the succeeding Neo-Elamite period there are baked clay bricks with inscriptions of rulers, some of which were incorporated into palaces and temples.

The Elamite civilization lasted until the Achaemenid period (c.559–330 BCE), although in a depleted form, when southwest Iran, together with most of the Middle East, became part of the Persian Empire. Some of the ancient iconography and religious symbolism of the conquered areas was adopted by Iranians living both on the plateau and in the lands of Transoxiana (north of the Amu Darya river).

1 • Painted pottery vessel
Iran, possibly from Susa • 4200–3700 BCE, Susa I period
Pottery • 7.3 x 9.2 cm
Alpaiwalla Museum: Susa 37

Pottery jar with ledge inside rim with brown painted decoration on a buff background. There is a decoration of chevrons within the widest brown band on the shoulder. This pottery vessel may belong to the first period of occupation at Susa (Susa I, 4200–3700 BCE). The Susa pottery of this date has close connections with the contemporary Ubaid period pottery of Mesopotamia.[1] JC

Right: Cuneiform tablet (see page 76)

2 · Amorous couple

Iran, probably from Susa
1500–1100 BCE, Middle Elamite period
Baked clay • 4.4 x 6.3 x 2.1 cm
Alpaiwalla Museum: Susa 12

Top part only of a plaque showing a couple lying
on a bed, making love. The frame of the bed is shown
with some kind of binding, but the mattress is plain.
On comparable plaques, the mattress sometimes
appears to be made of reeds. The man (on the left)
appears to be bearded, while the woman has long hair
falling over her shoulder. A number of comparable
baked clay plaques have been found in the French
excavations at Susa,[2] where they are dated to the
Middle Elamite period (1500–1100 BCE). At Ur in
Mesopotamia baked clay plaques showing beds are
dated to the earlier Old Babylonian period, c.1750
BCE.[3] The purpose of such plaques is uncertain. They
could show a religious ceremony, or they could be
votive, intended, for example, to induce pregnancy. JC

3 · Potsherd with bird

South-west Iran, possibly Susa • 2200–1600 BCE
Pottery • 6.4 x 6.4 x 1.6 cm
Alpaiwalla Museum: Susa 142

Potsherd with brown painted designs of birds and
linear decoration on a buff background. Such pottery
is known as 'kaftari' ware[4] (after the Persian word
kaftar, 'pigeon') and is known from Fars province
in Iran and from sites on the west side of the Persian
Gulf. Kaftari ware is best represented at the site of
Tall-e Malyan, and dates from c.2200–1600 BCE. JC

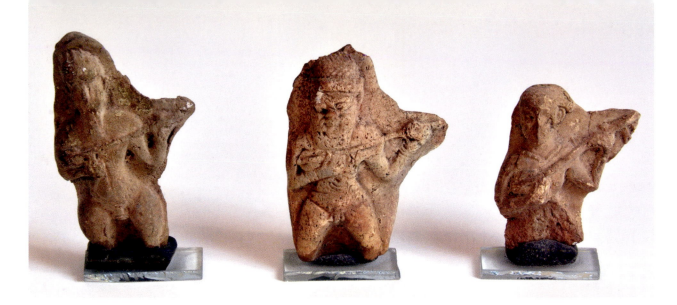

4 • Three lute players

Iran, probably from Susa
1500–1100 BCE, Middle Elamite period • Baked clay
l to r: 9.4 x 5.3 x 1.7 cm; 8.5 x 6.2 x 2.3 cm; 7 x 7.2 x 2 cm

Alpaiwalla Museum: Susa 9; Susa 11; Susa 10

Three baked clay plaques showing naked male figures playing lutes with either short necks (from the *oud* family) or with long necks (from the *tanbur* family).[5] From the French excavations at Susa there are a number of baked clay plaques showing figures, generally male and generally naked, playing lutes[6] which are dated to the Middle Elamite period (500–1100 BCE). From the excavations of W. K. Loftus at Susa are three baked clay figurines showing naked male figures playing lutes; two of the figures are bearded and one is beardless.[7] The purpose and significance of these figures is not clear. JC

5 • Naked woman figurine

Iran, probably from Susa
1500–1100 BCE, Middle Elamite period
Baked clay • 16 x 5.5 x 2.8 cm

Alpaiwalla Museum: Susa 1

Baked clay plaque showing a woman naked except for a pendant suspended around her neck. She has an elaborate hairstyle and has her hands cupped underneath her breasts. A collection of about 200 such figurines was found by W. K. Loftus in the south-west corner of the Ville Royale mound at Susa, of which about 40 are now in the British Museum.[8] Although superficially similar, they come from a number of different moulds.

There are also large numbers of these figurines from the French excavations at Susa, where they are dated to the Middle Elamite period.[9] These are clearly fertility figurines, and their association with childbirth is shown by the exaggerated breasts, hips and pubic triangles. Many of them even have stretch-marks on the belly. JC

6 • Part of naked woman figurine
Iran, probably from Susa
1500–1100 BCE, Middle Elamite period
Baked clay • 8.3 x 6 x 2.9 cm
Alpaiwalla Museum: Susa 3

Top part only of a clay plaque showing a woman naked except for a pendant suspended around her neck. She has an elaborate hairstyle with tiara, and has her hands cupped underneath her breasts. This figurine is similar to Cat. 5 above, except that in this case the woman appears to be wearing a tiara in the centre of her forehead. JC

7 • Cuneiform tablet (see page 73)
15.6 x 15.1 x 3.7 cm
British Museum K252

This cuneiform tablet comes from the royal library at Nineveh in northern Mesopotamia of the neo-Assyrian king Assurbanipal (668–c.630 BCE), but it is possibly the copy of a middle-Assyrian text from the second millennium BCE. The tablet is inscribed in cuneiform script and records the names of gods invited to a ritual meal. Among them is *as-sa-ra ma-za-ash*, which is widely assumed to represent an early form (with 's' between vowels preserved) of the name of the principal Zoroastrian deity Ahura Mazda. AH

MESOPOTAMIA

To the west and north-west of Elam, in Mesopotamia, a parallel urbanized and literate civilization had existed also from at least 3000 BCE. By the time of the Iranian migrations, there had been a shift in power from Sumer to Akkad, then to Babylonia and Assyria. The ancient cuneiform inscriptions that are known from Babylonia and Assyria provide many insights into the history of their people, particularly with regard to the rulers and their divinities. For instance, the Code of Hammurabi, inscribed on a black basalt stela, shows Hammurabi, the king of Babylon (c.1792–50 BCE), on his throne facing the god Shamash; the inscription tells us that Hammurabi was known as 'mighty King, King of Babylon' and 'King of the Four Quarters of the World'. Over 12 centuries later, the Ancient Persian king Cyrus the Great uses these same titles for himself on the clay cylinder recording his restoration works at Babylon (l. 20 Cyrus cylinder; Cat. 66). Inscriptions on smaller clay tablets, or foundation cones, give important historical, social, economic and religious information. A tablet from Assurbanipal's library at Nineveh may contain the earliest reference to Ahura Mazda. The practice of foundation inscriptions was continued by the Achaemenid kings.

8 • Clay tablet with list of workers
Ur III period • c.2100 BCE • 4.7 x 4 x 1.5 cm
Alpaiwalla Museum

The tablet records barley rations issued to female workers. The Ur III Empire has left us plentiful records documenting the detailed functioning of its large institutions. Many people worked in the fields, tended flocks and manned the workshops that were the powerhouse of the economy.

9 • Foundation document
Sin-kashid of Uruk
Old Babylonian period, c. 19th century/1850 BCE
6.2 x 3.9 cm (base diameter)
Alpaiwalla Museum

This type of document is found in large numbers, especially examples from the reign of Sin-kashid, king of Uruk. They were a type of time capsule placed in the walls of major buildings – temples or palaces. This particular one reads: 'Sin-kashid, mighty man, king of Uruk, king of the Amnanum …'

IRON AGE IRAN

The arrival of Iranian or Iranian-speaking people on the Iranian plateau is difficult to document in the archaeological record. Early Iron Age grey ware (c.1200–800 BCE), as attested at sites such as Hasanlu near Lake Urmia, Tepe Sialk near Kashan, and Marlik in Gilan province, is thought by some to indicate the migratory path of the Iranians, but such changes in material culture cannot be 'responsibly linked' with language or ethnicity.[10] Whether or not this grey ware can be associated with the Iranian migrations, from the ninth century BCE onwards the Persians and the Medes are mentioned in Assyrian inscriptions. At the same time, local cultures continued to flourish in areas such as Luristan, just to the east of the Zagros mountains, where horse-rearing cultures produced a prolific number of distinctive bronze artefacts, mostly related to horse training, riding and ornamentation.

10 • Spouted pot
Probably Tepe Sialk, Iran
Iron Age • 9th–8th century BCE
Pottery • 18 x 38 x 20 cm
British Museum 129072

Painted pottery vessel with a long bridge-spout and handle. The shape and decoration of this pot were inspired by several different media. The elongated shape of the spout copies contemporary metalwares, whereas the painted designs are typical of pottery made in the Sialk area of central Iran. It is decorated with reddish-brown painted designs showing a bull with arched neck reminiscent of a horse. Moreover, the square chequer pattern resembles contemporary painted clay tiles found at the contemporary site of Baba Jan in Luristan (western Iran) and both may have been inspired by woven floor coverings, although sadly no traces of such survive from these periods in Iran.[11] St JS

11 · **Humped bull**

Northwest Iran · Iron Age, 9th–8th century BCE
Pottery · 17 x 20 x 9 cm
British Museum 132973

facing page

12 · **Luristan bronze, 'Master of Animals'**

Luristan, Iran · Iron Age, 9th–8th century BCE
Bronze · 13 x 6.2 x 2.1 cm
British Museum 115514

The function of this object is uncertain but as it is hollow it was presumably used to hold and pour liquids from the top of the head. It may have been a ceremonial type of vessel which was later placed in a grave. Many others of this class are known, although few come from controlled excavations, the notable exceptions being from the cemetery of Marlik in north-west Iran. Scientific analysis of this example shows it was made by coiling the clay, followed by burnishing, and has since been carefully restored. These techniques are typical of Iron Age pottery traditions in northern Iran in the late second and early first millennia BCE.[12] St JS

Copper alloy 'master of animals' hollow standard-finial, cast using the lost wax technique. It represents an unarmed Janus figure (indicated by its facing in two directions) grappling a pair of rampant stylized lions who are biting his large ears. The body of each lion is fused into the central tube. The representation of the lions with elongated necks, prominent rears and curly tails is in typical Luristan style, yet the motif of a hero overcoming wild beasts was popular over much of the ancient Near East and lasted for several millennia. The parallel ridges around the tube imitate tightly wrapped cord. The fact that the central figure was intended to be seen from both sides supports the idea that such objects were mounted rather like the whorl on a spindle rather than being the head of a pin thrust through a cloak.[13]

St JS

above

13 • Luristan bronze, horse-bit

Luristan, Iran • Iron Age, 9th–8th century BCE • Bronze
cheek-pieces (one) 9.7 x 8.5 cm; (two) 9.6 x 9.2 cm;
cross-piece 18.1 cm (length)

British Museum 134746

Horse-bits with elaborate decorated cheek-pieces
are one of the most typical features of Luristan
metalwork. The bits are formed of a single bar
fitted into cheek-pieces on each side. These examples
are decorated in the form of winged animals with
human heads wearing horned headdresses. They have
spikes on the inner side which were designed to be
uncomfortable when the bit was pulled and therefore
helped the rider to control the horse. A large number
of such horse-bits are reported from Luristan and
some are said to have been found reused as head-rests
in ancient graves but none has yet been found
in controlled archaeological conditions.[14] St JS

WESTERN CENTRAL ASIA AND INDIA

Many bronze objects have also been discovered in western Central Asia, apparently in Bronze Age burials of the late third to mid-second millennium BCE. Since these artefacts are largely the result of clandestine archaeology, their provenance is uncertain, but their similarity to objects excavated from the Bactria Margiana Archaeological Complex (BMAC) site of Namazga-Tepe indicates that they belong to the same culture. BMAC sites stretch from Namazga, just to the west of the Pamirs, all the way to the northern foothills of the Kopet Dagh mountains along the border between Iran and Turkmenistan. Although Soviet-era archaeologists found evidence of a 'pre-Zoroastrian' cult in certain BMAC cities, particularly Gonur Tepe, Togalok and Anau, current thinking, driven by linguistics, is that the population was either Indo-Iranian or Indo-Aryan.[15]

Other BMAC materials have been discovered to the east of Iran, in sites identified as part of the Indus Valley civilization, and finds at BMAC locations inform us that there was trade between Central Asia and both Indus Valley and Elamite cities. The Indus Valley civilization, which seems to have emerged rapidly from advanced local village cultures in the mid to late third millennium BCE, extended from Shortugai on the Oxus river near the northern border of Afghanistan down to the south-western coast of Pakistan, near Iran, and across to Lothal in Gujarat, India. Steatite seals excavated from these urban centres display beautifully carved scenes of animals and deities alongside an as yet undeciphered script. Much of the iconography of these early deities was later incorporated into the forms now associated with Hindu gods and goddesses.

One of the most important original Hindu deities, Indra, who is lauded in the Ṛg Veda as chief of the gods, seems to have an entirely proto-Indo-European derivation, as a god of war and thunder/lightning. An early fourteenth-century BCE Mitanni treaty with the Hittites, found at Bogazkala in Turkey, invokes Indra as one of four Indo-Aryan or Indo-Iranian deities to witness the pact. Although Indra is demonized in Zoroastrian texts (*Videvdad* 10.9, 19.43, and *Greater Bundahishn*) his epithet *vritrahan* – 'smiter of the snake/dragon Vritra' who held back the life-giving waters – is cognate with the name of one of the Zoroastrian deities, Verethragna, who epitomizes 'victory'. Recollections of an ancient snake-smiting story, although not connected with Indra, are found in Iranian mythology preserved in the Avesta and some Middle Persian texts, as well as the *Shahnameh*, concerning several heroic figures who slew snakes or dragons.

14 · Indra

Nepal · 19th century · Bronze and turquoise
CSMVS Museum, Mumbai

Turquoise matrix ornament of a seated bronze figure of the Vedic deity Indra.

Indra is the most popular god of the people of Vedic India and praised in numerous hymns for his heroic feats, particularly for setting the waters free and slaying the serpent. He is incited to war-like deeds by drinking large amounts of Soma, the sacrificial drink prepared in the Vedic ritual. While his name is also mentioned as that of a god in the Mitanni treaties, in the Avesta Indra is the name of a demon. AH

2

SACRED TEXTS

Almut Hintze

AVESTAN LITERATURE

The sacred texts of the Zoroastrians are composed in an ancient Iranian language, Avestan, and assembled in a body of literature called the Avesta. The oldest parts (the Gathas, *Yasna Haptanghaiti* and two prayers) probably date from some time in the mid to late second millennium BCE. Their language is more archaic than that of the rest, the Younger Avesta, which is not only linguistically more recent, but also much greater in volume and is evidence of a more advanced stage of the religion's development. The Gathas are traditionally believed to be compositions of Zarathustra, the eponymous founder of the Zoroastrian religion.

left
15 • **16th-century copy of the Yasna ceremony**
Copyist: Herbad Ardashir, son of Mobed, son of Jiva
India • 20 Avan 925 Yazdegerdi (1556)
Provenance: Samuel Guise (1751–1811)[1]
Ink on paper
British Library MSS Avestan 17, ff. 127v–128r

The daily Yasna ceremony, which priests are still required to learn and recite by heart, is the most important of all Zoroastrian rituals and includes 17 hymns, the Gathas, which are attributed to Zarathustra. This opening (Y.43.3–7) contains Gathic verses about the reward and retribution for good and bad deeds and the encounter of Zarathustra with Good Thought, one of Ahura Mazda's spiritual creations. Later tradition, as preserved in the Zarathustra legend, regards this encounter as the first occasion on which Ahura Mazda revealed the Mazdayasnian religion to Zarathustra.

This highly decorated manuscript is the oldest-known dated copy of the *Yasna Sadeh* (the simple text of the ritual without any commentary), copied in India in 1556 by Herbad Ardashir Mobed Jiva who here traces his genealogy via Ardashir Ram Kamdin Shahriyar Neryosangh back to Hormazdyar Ramyar. Ritual directions are given in Gujarati (written upside down because Gujarati reads from left to right, whereas Avestan reads from right to left). AH, USW

Right: An illustrated *Videvdad Sadeh* (see page 85)

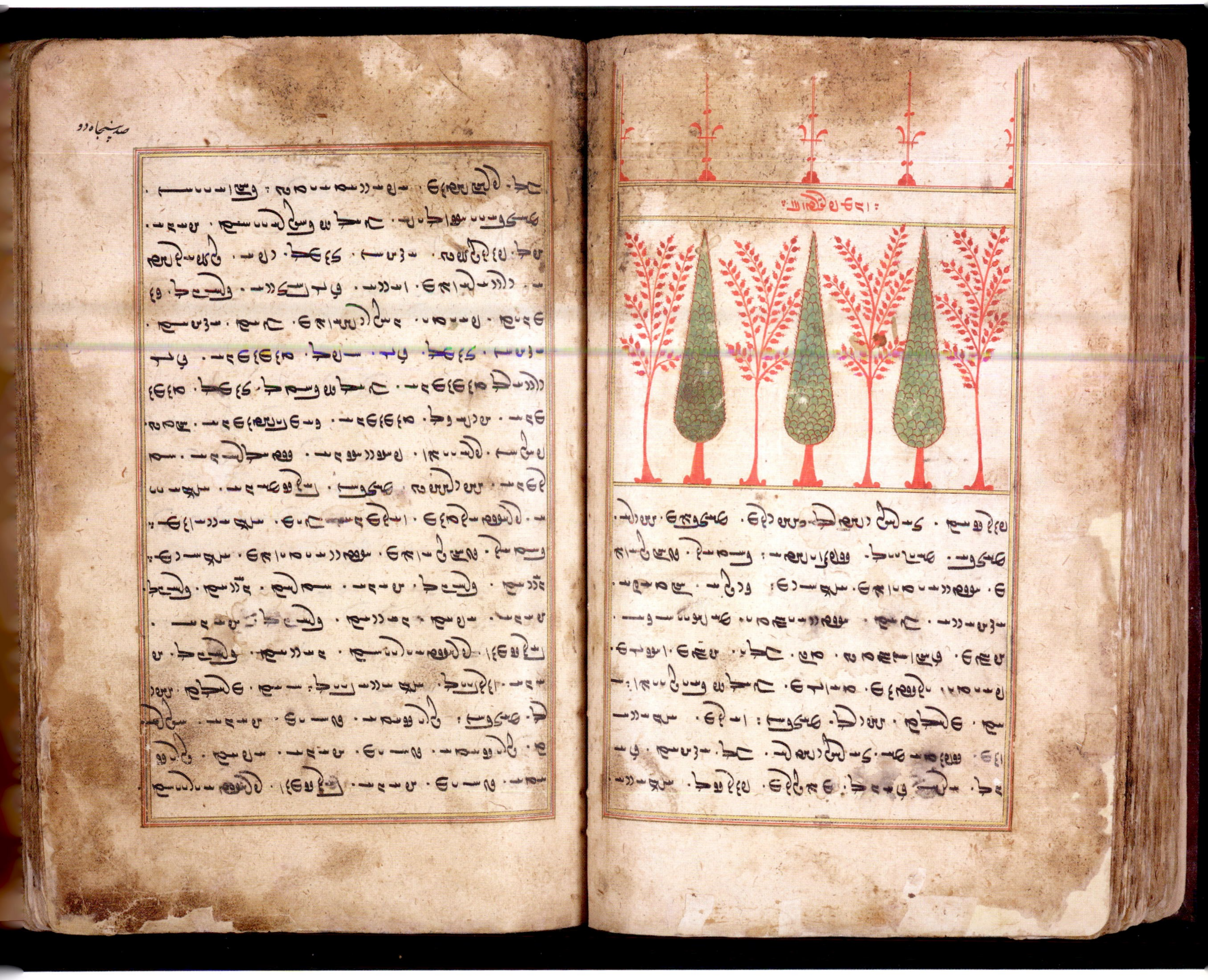

16 • On the creation of the universe

Iran • early 17th century • Ink on paper
Provenance: Thomas Howard, 2nd Earl of Arundel
(1586–1646)
British Library Arundel Or.54, ff. 96v–97r

17 • The creation of the good and the evil spirit

Copyist: Darab Hira Chanda
India • 7 Ardibihisht 1030 Yazdegerdi (1661)
Ink on paper • Provenance: Thomas Hyde (1636–1703)[2]
British Library Reg.16.B.5, ff. 74v–75r

Folios 96–7 of this copy of the *Yasna Sadeh* contain the end of *Yasna* 43 and the beginning of *Yasna* 44. Arguably one of the most poetic sections of the whole Avesta, *Yasna* 44 consists of rhetorical questions posed to Ahura Mazda about the creation of the universe, such as who established the path of the sun and the stars, who made the moon wax and wane, and who holds the earth down below and prevents the clouds from falling down. The implied answer, of course, is that Ahura Mazda has arranged all of this.

The Avestan text of this manuscript includes ritual instructions in Pahlavi written in red ink. This seventeenth-century copy was written in Iran and was probably the first Zoroastrian sacred text to be brought to Britain. It is tempting to think that it might have been presented to the Earl of Arundel by Sir Thomas Roe, ambassador to the Mughal court, 1615–19, who acquired many of his artefacts for him. In India, Roe had been a personal friend of the lexicographer Jamal al-Din Inju, whose assistant, the Zoroastrian Ardashir Nushirvan, was summoned from Kerman by the emperor Akbar to help explain Zoroastrian technical vocabulary. AH, USW

This opening contains verses one to six of *Yasna* 30 which includes a dialogue between the two primordial forces, one life-giving and the other destructive. The concept of two mutually exclusive opposites who have nothing in common is the foundation of the Zoroastrian dualism of good and evil. Only that which is good comes from God, Ahura Mazda, while evil has a separate origin. Human beings have the freedom to choose between the two, but only the choice of the good path is the right one.

This manuscript was copied by Darab Hira Chanda, who, like the scribe of Cat. 15, also traces his lineage back to Hormazdyar Ramyar. The unusual quality of the binding and the burnished paper indicate the relative importance of this manuscript, which was acquired in the seventeenth century on behalf of Thomas Hyde, professor of Hebrew and Arabic at Oxford University. AH, USW

While the Gathas are composed in a syllable-counting metre, the poetic form of the *Yasna Haptanghaiti* differs in that it is governed by the rhythm of its words rather than the number of its syllables. We cannot be sure about the original pragmatic function of the Gathas, but there is no doubt that the *Yasna Haptanghaiti* is a liturgy intended to be recited during a religious ceremony (see section 9). References in the text itself to the actual ceremony indicate that a group of people are in the presence of the ritual fire for the purpose of worshipping their god, Ahura Mazda, or 'Wise Lord', and his spiritual and material creations. Whereas the Gathas are chiefly spoken by one person ('I'), the *Yasna Haptanghaiti* is couched in the plural 'we'. Moreover, the Old Avestan form *yazamaide*, 'we worship', characteristic of the middle part of the *Yasna Haptanghaiti*, subsequently dominates many of the Younger Avestan texts, a fact that illustrates the extent to which large portions of the Younger Avesta were composed in the vein of the Older Avesta.

It is possible to distinguish different strata in the post-Old Avestan literature. While the language displays a number of non-Avestan dialectal features, certain texts of the Younger Avesta, for instance *Yasna* 58, belong to an earlier layer of ritual composition. The Younger Avestan parts of the *Yasna* are comprised of passages that further increase the volume of the Older Avestan core ritual by means of insertions of text at key points (such as the short sections before and after the *Yasna Haptanghaiti*, and between the fourth and fifth Gathas) and by substantial accretions before (Y.1–27.10) and after the Older Avesta (Y.55–72).

A further expanded ritual is the Visperad ceremony, in which additional sections in Younger Avestan have been inserted into the *Yasna*. The Visperad ritual in turn was further extended by means of insertions, after the *Visperad* ones, of sections of the *Videvdad*, 'the law against the demons', thus creating the longest of all Zoroastrian rituals, the Videvdad, or Vendidad, ceremony. The manuscripts of the Videvdad ceremony are called *Videvdad Sadeh*, for which the British Library manuscripts RSPA 230 (Cat. 18) and MSS Avestan 5 (Cat. 209) are examples.

page 83 and above
18 · An illustrated *Videvdad Sadeh*
Copyist: Mehrban Anushirvan Bahram Shah
Yazd • 15 Esfandarmoz 1016 Yazdegerdi (1647)
Provenance: Burjorji Sorabji Ashburner (fl. 1817–95)
Ink on paper
British Library RSPA 230, ff. 151v–152r

The *Videvdad* is chiefly concerned with reducing pollution in the material world and represents a vital source for our knowledge and understanding of Zoroastrian purity laws. The opening shows the beginning of Chapter 9 of the Zoroastrian law book, the *Videvdad*, which concerns the nine-night purification ritual (*barashnom noh shab*) for someone who has been defiled by contact with a dead body (see also Cat. 136).

This beautifully written and decorated copy of the *Videvdad Sadeh* (i.e. the Avestan text without any commentary) was copied in Yazd, Iran, for a Zoroastrian of Kerman in 1647. Most unusually, it contains seven coloured illustrations, all of trees. The heading here has been decorated very much in the style of an illuminated Islamic manuscript. Two other manuscripts similarly decorated, by the same scribe, have recently come to light in Iran. AH, USW

The Yasna, Visperad, Videvdad and other rituals based on them are recited and performed by priests inside the fire temple. In addition, the Younger Avesta comprises devotional texts recited by both priest and lay members of the community, male and female alike. There are 21 hymns, or *Yashts* (Yt), dedicated to a variety of divinities whose praise is not only legitimized but demanded by Ahura Mazda, who presides over them all. In the Zoroastrian calendar, each of the 30 days of the month is dedicated to one particular deity whose name it bears and whose hymn, or *Yasht*, is recited on that day. The individual deities are also invoked for particular tasks. Mithra, for instance, is the deity who watches over contracts, while Anahita is especially close to women and helps them conceive and give birth. In addition, there are short prayers, blessings and other texts collected in the Small, or *Khordeh*, Avesta (Cats 19 and 186). Priestly ritual literature survives in the texts called *Nerangestan* 'ritual precepts' and *Herbedestan* 'religious education'.

19 • The *Khordeh Avesta*, the Zoroastrian prayer book

Copyist: Hormazyar Faramorz Qiyamdin Sanjaneh
India • 30 Ordibehesht 1042 Yazdegerdi (1673)
Provenance: Thomas Hyde (1636–1703)
Ink on paper
British Library Reg.16.B.6, f. 1r

The *Khordeh Avesta* ('Small Avesta') contains prayers, hymns and invocations recited by priests and lay people in daily worship. This opening shows the first page of a manuscript which begins with the *Yatha ahu vairyo* ('Just as he should be chosen by life') and the *Ashem vohu* ('Good order'), two of the holiest Zoroastrian prayers. Zoroastrians should pray five times a day while standing before a source of light: the sun or the hearth fire (or a *divo*) by day, and the moon at night.

This copy was acquired in India for Thomas Hyde. It is beautifully written and was used by Hyde as a model for the special Avestan type he created for his *History of the Persian Religion* published in 1700 (Cat. 139). AH, USW

ZOROASTRIAN EXEGETICAL LITERATURE

As the Older Avestan language gradually became archaic and eventually obscure, priests of the Younger Avestan period continued to compose their own liturgical compositions in the oral tradition while at the same time being inspired by the Older Avesta. In addition, they carried out their own exegesis of the Older Avesta. That an exegetical literature in Younger Avestan, now largely lost, once existed is borne out by Younger Avestan commentaries on the three holy prayers (the *Ahuna Vairya*, the *Ashem Vohu* and the *Yenghe Hatam*, Cats 19 and 27), which survive as chapters 19–21 of the *Yasna*. From the late Achaemenid period onwards, as Old Iranian dialects evolved into their various Middle Iranian descendants, Younger Avestan also gradually ceased to be understood and increasingly required exegesis. Zoroastrian priests therefore translated the Avesta into Middle Iranian idioms. An example of a bilingual manuscript is the British Library Pahlavi *Videvdad* (Cat. 46). As the tradition of the Avesta was entirely oral, its translation and explanation would have been memorized together with the Avesta, although the exegesis, called the Zand, was more flexible and open to being revised and expanded. The Avesta was eventually written down, presumably in the late Sasanian period, in an alphabet designed especially for this purpose and developed on the basis of a cursive form of the Pahlavi script. The tradition of the Avesta and its exegesis that has come down to the present day is that from the province of Pars, the centre of imperial and priestly power during the Sasanian era.

PAHLAVI LITERATURE

Most of the Avestan texts that have survived have a liturgical function. However, a summary of the 21 *Nasks* of the Avesta in the Middle Persian *Denkard*, or 'Acts of the Religion', shows that at the time of its composition in the ninth–tenth centuries there still existed a much greater body of Avestan literature, which included systematic accounts of Zoroastrian teachings, cosmology and cosmography. This corpus, now largely lost, provided the basis for systematic re-workings and re-interpretations in the Middle Iranian period. For instance, a Pahlavi text on cosmology, the *Bundahishn*, explicitly bases itself on the Avesta, the *den*. Its source is likely to have been an Avestan composition on creation, the *Damdad Nask*, now lost, the contents of which are summarized in the *Denkard*. Moreover, some sections of the *Bundahishn* agree with parts of the Avesta. Chapter 9 of the Iranian *Bundahishn*, entitled 'On the nature of the mountains', for example, is based on an Avestan list of mountains which survives as the opening part of the *Zamyad Yasht* (Yt 19). Chapter 27 of the Indian *Bundahishn* (Cat. 20) describes a great variety of plants. It starts with that of the Gaokarena tree, the tree of immortality, also called the White Hom. The tradition is based on the Avesta, where the Gaokerena is a single tree around which hundreds of thousands of medicinal herbs grow.

These examples indicate that many of the theological parts of Pahlavi literature, although compiled as late as the early Islamic period (ninth–tenth century CE), are not original compositions but Middle Persian versions and re-workings of Avestan material.

20 • The *Bundahishn* ('Primal Creation')

India • 17th or 18th century • Ink on paper
Provenance: Samuel Guise (1751–1811)
British Library MSS Avestan 22, ff. 82v–83r

The *Bundahishn*, or 'Primal Creation', is a Pahlavi text on cosmogony and cosmography based on the Avesta. It includes a detailed account of Ohrmazd's perfect creation, which was attacked by evil, Ahriman, and afflicted with disease and death. The cosmic drama culminates in the resurrection of the dead and the defeat and removal of evil from Ohrmazd's world and its perfection at the end of time. The cosmographical parts of the text include descriptions of the world's lands, rivers, lakes, mountains, plants, animals and peoples.

The *Bundahishn* is preserved in two distinct recensions, an Indian and a better and more complete Iranian one. This manuscript has the text of the Indian *Bundahishn* in Avestan script, called Pazand. The opening shows the beginning of chapter 27 marked with three circles in line 10 of fol. 83r and followed by the title of the chapter: 'On the nature of the plants'. AH, USW

21 • The *Menog i Khrad* ('Spirit of Wisdom')

Copyist: Mehraban Mahyar Padam
Navsari • 18 Bahman 890 Yazdegerdi (1520)
Ink on paper • Provenance: Samuel Guise (1751–1811)
British Library MSS Avestan 19, ff. 132v–133r

The *Menog i Khrad* ('Spirit of Wisdom') discusses various philosophical questions, such as the nature of truth, wisdom and the creation of the world. This Pazend and Sanskrit copy was made at Navsari for Bahram Pahlan. The final page, on view here, shows the Sanskrit colophon (upside down). The floral and geometric decorations are a feature of this manuscript. AH, USW

22 • The Pahlavi *Rivayat* Accompanying the *Dadistan i denig*

Copyist: Gobedshah Rostam Bundar[3]
Iran • 16th century • Ink on paper
Provenance: Burjorji Sorabji Ashburner (fl. 1817–95)

British Library RSPA 228, ff. 36v–37r

This text, commonly referred to as the Pahlavi *Rivayat*,[4] usually positioned before or after another work, the *Dadestan i Denig* ('Judgements of the Religion'), is a Pahlavi treatise without title or author, dealing with the ritual, cosmology, eschatology and epic history of Iran. The pages illustrated here are from chapter 23.17–28 and describe the dialogue between the soul of the wicked and its *daena* ('religion' or 'conscience'), pictured as a hideous hag embodying the bad deeds of the deceased. As usual in Zoroastrian manuscripts, the name of Ahriman is written upside down (right folio, line 9, and left folio, lines 3 and 4). AH, USW

❋

According to Zoroastrian doctrine the most potent source of ritual impurity is dead matter. Death represents the triumph of Ahriman over the righteous person, and the rituals following a person's death are designed to prevent the demoness of death, the *Druj i Nasush,* from spreading pollution. In addition the funerary rituals – in particular the night-long recitation of the *Videvdad* – affords protection for the soul on its journey to the spiritual world. Exposure of the dead, in order to avoid the pollution of fire, water or earth, is detailed in the *Videvdad* and there is evidence from Central Asia that this was an ancient custom (see page 32). It is not until the Islamic period in Iran that the widespread use of the *dakhma*, or circular tower in which bodies were disposed of collectively, is attested. From the mid-eighteenth century *dakhma*s in Iran were built on the Indian model. While they are no longer in use today in Iran, the Towers of Silence are still used by Zoroastrians in India and Pakistan.

overleaf
23 • Tower of Silence model
2010 • 8 x 79.5 x 54 cm
Heatherwick Studio

After the funeral the deceased is carried on an iron bier to the *dakhma* where it is placed near the entrance by the *nasasalars*, or corpse-bearers, for the mourners to pay their last respects. The priests maintain ritual contact with each other, *paiwand*, by holding the ends of a strip of cloth. Once the body is placed inside the *dakhma* vultures and other carrion birds dispose of it quickly and efficiently. At periodic intervals the sun-bleached bones are swept into a central pit to further decompose.

The decimation of the vulture population in India as a result of the use of diclofenac on cattle has threatened the system of disposal of the dead. Some Parsis now prefer to adopt alternative methods of disposing of the dead, namely cremation and burial.

In 2010 Heatherwick Studio was commissioned by the Bombay Parsi Punchayet to design an aviary in Mumbai to enclose the *dakhma*s and nurture the vulture population. Its planted sides have the advantage of preventing nearby residential tower blocks from overlooking the site. SS, FPM

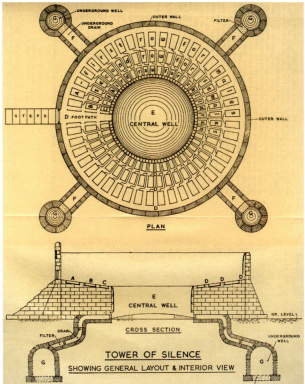

24 • Dakhma chart

from *History of the Bombay Parsi Punchayet 1860–1960*

Line drawing of a cross-section of a *dakhma*. Bodies are laid on the stone plinths that form three concentric circles: the outer one for men, the central one for women and the inner one for children. The central well, *bhandar*, leads into four underground drains at the end of which are charcoal filters. SS

25 • Rostam in the Dead of Winter
Artist: Fereydoun Ave
Mixed media and print on canvas • 100 x 150 cm
courtesy of Janet Rady Fine Art and Rossi & Rossi

Vulture painting by Fereydoun Ave in black,
white and gold.

3

THE SILK ROAD, CENTRAL ASIA AND CHINA

Frantz Grenet
with Nicholas Sims-Williams and Pavel Lurje

Textual sources providing information on Zoroastrianism in pre-Islamic Central Asia are scattered. Historians of Alexander's expedition mention next-of-kin marriage and exposure of the dead to flesh-eating animals, two characteristic Zoroastrian practices of the time. Both are again mentioned by later Chinese travellers, who also describe other features more specific to Central Asia, such as the lamentations associated with the cult of Nana (Fig. 11) and the presence of statues in temples. The travellers record the major importance of Buddhism in Tokharistan (formerly known as Bactria) and the reverse situation in Sogdiana, where Zoroastrianism remained predominant until the Arab conquest, side by side with small Christian and Manichean communities and some Buddhist monasteries.

Few writings on Central Asian Zoroastrianism can be qualified as primary, i.e. contemporary and written by Central Asians. Although the texts comprising the 'Young Avesta' originated in Central Asia, they took their final shape in Iran and only a few sections explicitly refer to those regions: the general list of 'Aryan', i.e. Zoroastrian countries, in *Videvdad* 1, the *Mihr Yasht* centred on the Bamiyan area, and the *Zamyad Yasht* centred on Sistan. Lands situated to the north of Sogdiana and the Pamirs (the latter probably the *Airyanem Vaejah*, the mythical homeland of the Aryans) are not included in this list, but cult practices circulated both ways.

Due to the predominantly oral transmission of Zoroastrian teaching in the pre-Islamic period, very few texts survive from Central Asia and then only in Sogdian. By far the oldest is a ninth-century fragment which includes the Avestan prayer the *Ashem Vohu*, transcribed in Sogdian script (Cat. 27). A painting from Panjikent dating from *c.*740 CE shows the bust of the god of prayer, Srosh, emerging from an object which looks like a codex, in this case most probably an Avestan prayer book.[1] Another early 'Zoroastrian' painting is the 'Ambassadors Painting' (Cat. 26) which celebrates the court festival of Nowruz (the Zoroastrian New Year).

26 • Ambassadors painting, Afrasiab (ancient Samarkand)

20th-century copy of original wall painting of 660–63 CE
Original from aristocratic or royal house ('sector 23') at Afrasiab (now exhibited in the Afrasiab Museum)
Watercolour copy • 11 x 1.90 metres
Institute of Archaeology, Samarkand

The 'Ambassadors Painting' was created for King Varkhuman who ruled Samarkand in the 650s and early 660s, and was recognized by the Chinese as King of Sogdiana. On the main, the western, wall Varkhuman receives envoys from various countries, including China. The northern wall shows scenes of the Chinese court, and the eastern wall has picturesque scenes from India. The southern wall, partly illustrated here, shows Varkhuman leading a procession to the mausoleum of his parents on the sixth day of Nowruz (the day reserved for royal celebrations). He is accompanied by his wives and by two dignitaries (shown here) riding camels and holding clubs in order to kill the animals, according to the Zoroastrian ritual, by stunning them beforehand. The sacrificial animals, a saddled horse and four geese, are led by characters who are probably priests, as indicated by the *padam*.[2] FG

27 • A Zoroastrian prayer
Dunhuang • *c.* 9th century CE
Stein, 2nd expedition: Dunhuang, Cave 17
Ink on paper • 24 x 27 cm
British Library, Stein collection Or. 8212/84 (Ch.00289)[3]

This short fragment contains one of the few Sogdian texts which are wholly Zoroastrian in content. The main part, written in normal Sogdian of about the ninth century, describes Zarathustra addressing an unnamed 'supreme god' (presumably Ahura Mazda). However, the true significance lies in the first two lines which are a transcription in Sogdian script of one of the holiest Zoroastrian prayers, the Avestan *Ashem Vohu*, copied 300 years or more earlier than any surviving Avestan manuscript. Most remarkably, the language of the prayer is neither Sogdian nor Avestan as we know it, but a much older Iranian language, perhaps an archaic form of Avestan. The prayer must have been preserved orally in this ancient form, which remained unaffected by the codification of the Avesta in the Sasanian period, when the sacred texts were first committed to writing. NSW

28 • Bactrian document addressed to the god Mihr
Afghanistan • *c.* 5th century CE
Ink on parchment • 13.6 x 25 cm
Private collection

During the last 25 years many letters and other documents in Bactrian have come to light. These documents are almost entirely secular in content, though the persons mentioned often bear characteristic Zoroastrian names. The letter shown here is highly unusual in being addressed to a god, named as 'Mihr Yazad, the king of the gods'; it is concerned with the collection of taxes payable by the god himself. Other Bactrian documents bear the seal of a god – presumably in fact that of his temple-priest – witnessing a legal contract.[4] NSW

❁

Bactria, the area to the north of the Hindukush mountains in northern Afghanistan with its capital at Balkh, is mentioned in the first chapter of the *Videvdad* as one of the central lands of Zoroastrianism. Traditionally it was the birthplace of Zarathustra. Bactria, which had formerly been a satrapy of the Achaemenid Empire, was conquered by Alexander the Great in the fourth century BCE. At this time the Greek language and script were adopted for administrative purposes; later this role was taken over by the local Iranian language, Bactrian, for which the use of Greek script was retained.

Particular forms of the Zoroastrian calendar were used in Bactria, Sogdiana and Chorasmia. In all such calendars, each day of the month is named after a Zoroastrian deity. The earliest documentary evidence for this is found in two Aramaic letters issued by the chancery of the satrap of Bactria at the very end of the Achaemenid Empire (Cats 29 and 30), in which Aramaic was the usual language of written communication.

The lists of month names attested from the fourth century CE onwards are less homogeneous and include Babylonian month names, as well as that of the 'festival of Demeter', a legacy from the period of the Greek kingdoms.

29 • The earliest use of Zoroastrian day names
Afghanistan • 4th century BCE
Ink on parchment • 41.5 x 9.6 cm
The Khalili Collection of Imperial Aramaic Documents, IA 22

This badly weathered Aramaic document is dated 20 of Shebat, year two of an unspecified king. It lists provisions for various officials and mentions 'the day *Dīn*' and offerings for the *farvardin* (the spirits of the dead). It is the earliest known use of Zoroastrian day names. FB

Another document from Bactria mentions a 'libation for the temple, to Bel' (Cat. 30), which probably refers to a temple of Ahura Mazda, the name of whom was regularly translated as 'Bel' in Aramaic. The name used for the temple, *bagina* or 'place of the god', is an Iranian loan word and reappears in Sogdian as *vaghn*, the usual designation of temples, whose priest, as in the case of the fourth-century document from Dunhuang (Cat. 31), is the *vaghnpat* (*bagina-pati*) or 'master of the *vaghn*'. *Moghpat*, corresponding to the Western Iranian *mowbed* 'chief Magus', is also attested in Sogdian, but more rarely. Similarly, Bactrian inscriptions from the Kushan period (first–third centuries CE) identify the royal temples as *bagolaggo* [*vaghlaang*] *baga-danaka*, 'containing the god'.

30 • Achaemenid document from Bactria
Afghanistan • 4th century BCE
Ink on parchment • 33.0 x 39.5 cm
The Khalili Collection of Imperial Aramaic Documents, IA 21⁵

This Aramaic document records provisions for a certain Bayasa (Bessos) 'when he passed from Baxtri [Balkh] to Varnu [possibly modern Kunduz]'. It is dated to Kislev of the '1st year of King Artaxerxes', but does not specify which of the several kings of this name is intended. The 50 lines of text contain a long list of live animals, different sorts of wine, flour etc. required for the journey. In addition to provisions, the text lists flour, wine and other goods to be used for offerings to the gods, who include both the Semitic god Bel and the Zoroastrian Wata (Wind). One of the persons named is Wakhshu-bandaka, 'servant of the Oxus', attesting the worship in Bactria of the deified River Oxus. FB

31 • A Sogdian community in China

Dunhuang • c. 313–14
Stein, 2nd expedition: Dunhuang limes
Ink on paper • 26 x 42.7 cm
British Library, Or.8212/98 (T.XII.a.ii.3)[6]

By the early fourth century CE the Sogdians were well established as traders travelling the length of the Silk Road as far east as the Chinese capital, Luoyang. Their commodities included gold, silver, camphor, pepper, musk, wheat, silk and other kinds of cloth. This Sogdian letter is one of two from Miwnay, a member of the Zoroastrian community in Dunhuang, who has been abandoned by her merchant husband Nanai-dhat. Here she addresses her husband, complaining that he has left her destitute without answering her letters. The letter opens with conventional pleasantries, but by the end Miwnay cannot conceal her anger: 'I obeyed your command and came to Dunhuang … Surely the gods were angry with me on the day when I did your bidding! I would rather be a dog's or a pig's wife than yours!' In a second letter, to her mother Chatis, Miwnay describes how she lives, destitute, dependent on charity from the local Zoroastrian priest. NSW

❋

About ten 'local' (i.e. non-Buddhist and non-Hindu) temples belonging to the Kushan and post-Kushan periods are known from archaeological excavations. Though quite varied in their scale, architecture and ornamentation, they do not conform to the type of the *chahar-taq*, the standard form of the fire temple in Iran. They have an axial plan inherited from Greek models, usually with a succession of courtyards and porticoes leading to a room (sometimes tetrastyle), which sheltered one or several cult statues, while other images of gods were displayed in other parts of the temple.

The cult is addressed to the statue, not to the fire – or if it is so it is confined to a subsidiary *chahar-taq* built next to the main temple structure (two examples are known: at Surkh-kotal and Panjikent, both from the fourth and fifth centuries, a period of strong Sasanian influence). The most interesting set of cult utensils was found in the temple at Dzhartepa (Cats 32 and 33). The former is of a type probably similar to that often shown in Sogdian paintings, included in private dwellings where libations to an image of the god or pair of gods regarded as protectors of the family were performed by the master of the house (Cat. 34).

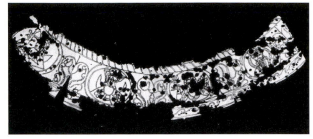

above

32 • Plaque from the Dzhartepa temple

Dzhartepa temple (near Samarkand)
Late 7th or early 8th century
Copper • 45 x 7 cm
Institute of Archaeology, Samarkand

Like Cat. 33, this plaque was found during excavations at Dzhartepa, between Samarkand and Panjikent. The temple's wall paintings suggest that it was dedicated to the goddess Nana, of Babylonian origin, who was the chief goddess of Sogdiana and was probably identified as Anahita, goddess of the waters. These objects were stored in a tower that served as sacristy. The plaque was probably used to decorate the base of a portable fire holder or incense burner. Four medallions show busts with crowns, which symbolized water, moon, fire and sun. Water is alluded to by the ephedra twig used for the preparation of the *hom*, which purifies it in the Yasna ritual.[7] FG

33 • **Human-headed mace from the Dzhartepa temple**
Dzhartepa temple (near Samarkand)
Late 7th or early 8th century
Iron with bronze head • 50 x 5 cm (head)
Institute of Archaeology, Samarkand

This mace was probably carried by the priest on solemn occasions, like those still used today in some Parsi fire temples in India. Here the mace is topped with a human head, instead of the ox head used by the Parsis (which represents the mace of the legendary King Faridun, who delivered Iran from the oppression of Zahhak). The display of weapons (maces, swords, daggers and shields) in the fire temples, occasionally worn in processions, symbolizes the role of the temple in the struggle against the forces of evil.[8] FG

above right
34 • **Sogdian in front of an altar**
*c.*740 • Panjikent (Tajikistan)
Wall painting on plaster • 67 x 45 cm
The State Hermitage Museum, St Petersburg, CA-16157[9]

Fragment of a wall painting from a deep-vaulted niche in the reception hall of a large rich villa. The walls were entirely covered with paintings on a red ground with scenes of feasting and included the statue of a four-armed deity seated on a throne in the form of a lion. This fragment depicts a middle-aged man, possibly the owner of the house who ordered the paintings. The paintings date from *c.*740, when there was a revival of life in Panjikent, which had been abandoned since the capture of the town by the Arabs in 722. LYK

In most cases, the gods depicted in Sogdian art (mainly wall paintings) of the fourth to eighth centuries look like Indian gods, seated on a specific animal and sometimes with four arms. However, these foreign models were sometimes altered in order to conform better to the Iranian god they were supposed to represent and in whose name they were worshipped. Twenty-three among the canonical list of 30 Zoroastrian deities have so far been identified among Sogdian images, with various degrees of plausibility. This appears to be consistent with an eighth-century Chinese description of the Sogdian temple at Dunhuang (perhaps the same one to which the *vaghnpat* of Cat. 31 ministered four centuries before), where 'twenty niches' with paintings of deities are mentioned.[10] In the Kushan Empire, which dominated Bactria and north-west India in the second and early third centuries CE, the Zoroastrian pantheon was almost as widely represented on coins, with the names of the gods inscribed in Bactrian. However, at this stage, the iconography was borrowed from Greece, although some gods were already modelled on Indian ones (notably Vayu, god of the atmosphere, depicted as Shiva, a type which was to continue in Sogdiana). Another trend, which appears mostly in Sogdian funerary art and is perhaps more 'conservative', was to create original types differentiated mainly by their crowns and by the attributes held in their hands. Examples are the Yumalaktepe ossuary with the scene of the weighing of the soul (Cat. 35), and the Biya-Nayman ossuaries (Cats 38–41) which possibly originally displayed the series of the six Amesha Spentas (see reconstruction, page 23).

Ossuaries are in many ways an essential source of information on Chorasmian (Cat. 37) and Sogdian Zoroastrianism (Cats 43 and 44).[11] Chorasmia, on the lower Oxus, has the longest history of ossuary burials. From the fourth century BCE we find 'burial vessels', large pots with anthropomorphic upper parts, which preserved bones. Somewhat later, statuary ossuaries as well as tower-shaped ones appear which were superseded by chest-shaped ossuaries like the one exhibited. From the seventh century, baked clay ossuaries were finally replaced by alabaster chests. The early chest-shaped ossuaries often contained zoomorphic elements. The ossuary was equipped with a lid, which was attached by two cords to two apertures on its body. Other ossuaries have apertures for a canopy (Cat. 37).

The ossuary tradition, which can be regarded as Zoroastrian, even though it is hardly attested in Iran itself, coexisted in Chorasmia with other burial practices. There were inhumations and possibly even cremations at the fringes of the oasis; the rulers of earlier periods erected mausoleums such as the monumental Koj-Krylgan-kala. The Zoroastrian tradition is also evident in a Tower of Silence in Chilpik erected in the first centuries CE – probably the earliest construction of this type known – and used until a much later period. Even the burial traditions of modern inhabitants of Chorasmia, although Islamic in essence, preserve a number of Zoroastrian relics, such as the prohibition of contact of the corpse with the earth.[12]

35 • Yumalaktepa ossuary

6th–7th century • Yumalaktepa (near Shahr-i Sabz)
Found during the excavation of a channel
Baked clay, stamped • 50 x 32 x 40 cm
Shahr-i Sabz Museum

The long sides carry a composition executed from a stamp, half of which is also applied on each short side. The context is the fourth morning after death, when the *chaharom* service is performed for the sake of the soul (lower register) at the time when it is judged in heaven (upper register). The priest wearing the *padam* is holding a long *barsom* (ritual twigs), or perhaps tongs. Alongside him are the four offerings prescribed for the dead: flour (in the shape of loaves of bread, *dron*, on the tray), sheep, wine (in a jar between them) and a saddled horse (probably a symbolic offering); the widow presents a flower.

On top, the soul is shown as a naked boy in a slanting position between two pans or bags containing his good and bad actions which are attached to a balance held by the god Rashn. To the left, the god enthroned in Paradise, symbolized by musicians, is probably Ardvahisht; to the right, the other seated god is either Vahman (who clothes the soul after the judgement) or Srosh (fighter against the demons whose threatening presence is indicated by the two swat bearers – for the demon of carrion takes the shape of a fly). A curious detail is the priest apparently lowering the right pan in order to make the balance decide in favour of the good deeds located in the upper half of the body.[13] FG

left
36 • Mullakurgan ossuary

*c.*7th century • Provenance: Mullakurgan (near Samarkand)
found by farmers • Baked clay • 52 x 28 x 69 cm

Afrasiab Museum (Samarkand)

Like the ossuary from Yumalaktepa (Cat. 35), this
shows a Zoroastrian ceremony on the lower register,
and on the upper one a heavenly scene. That the
scene depicts a major ceremony is suggested by
the presence of two officiating priests. The one to
the right using bellows is the *raspig*, assistant priest,
while the one to the left is the *zot*, main priest,
holding short *barsom* and kneeling on the ground
as required when reciting the Gathas. Paradise is
evoked on the lid, not by a judgement scene, but
by astral symbols, plants and two dancing girls in
transparent dresses. The Pahlavi text *Selections of
Zadspram*, 30.61, mentions *houris* (*ramenagan* or
'pleasure givers') in Paradise.[14] FG

above
38–41 • Biya-Naiman ossuary fragments

7th century • Biya-Naymen (Uzbekistan)
Baked clay • 28 x 11 cm (41); 27 x 27 cm (38);
13.5 x 13 cm (40); 19.5 x 22 cm (39)

The State Hermitage Museum, St Petersburg,
CA-2913 (222); CA-2918 (225); CA-2822 (226); CA-2765 (227)[15]

In 1908 about 700 fragments of terracotta ossuaries
and their covers were found at Biya-Naiman, near
Kata-Kurgan on the way from Bukhara to Samarkand.
They were discovered by N. B. Kastal'sky (1868–1943),
a military engineer resident in Samarkand, an
amateur and local historian and a well-known
collector of antiquities. Here we see four ossuary
fragments, possibly representing the six Amesha
Spentas, divine Zoroastrian beings, each holding a
ritual implement. Fragment 41 shows a female figure
holding a covered vessel and a crenellated object
resembling a key. Fragment 38 shows a crowned
female figure holding a pestle and mortar, and an
object with two rods sticking up from it. On her left
a partially preserved figure holds an incense burner.
Fragment 39 depicts a male figure holding an incense
burner with his left hand resting on a sword with an
animal-headed hilt. Fragment 40 shows a male with
his right hand resting on a sword with an animal-
headed hilt, and a short implement tucked into his
belt. Of the female figure beside him there remains
only part of the head and her fist grasping a covered
vessel (see page 38). LYK

37 • Chorasmian ossuary

*c.*2nd–3rd century CE • Chorasmia, Kalaly-ghyr 1
Baked clay • 60 x 39 x 28 cm

The State Hermitage Museum, St Petersburg, XP-725

Early chest-shaped ossuary with animal-like feet
(see page 98). PL

above
42 • Base of a funerary couch
*c.*550–77 • Northern China (Hebei or Shanxi)
White marble • 2.43 x 0.11 x 0.55 metres
Victoria and Albert Museum, Collection Eumorfopoulos, A. 54-1937

below
43 • Sogdian ossuary
7th–8th century • Samarkand region, possibly Biya-Nayman
Baked clay, incised and stamped • 78 x 33 x 30 cm
The State Hermitage Museum, St Petersburg, CA-3038

This base belonged to the funerary couch, not pre-served, of a rich Sogdian living in northern China during the second half of the sixth century, presumably in the territories of the northern Qi dynasty (550–77). It shares iconographic motifs with three other bases and three complete beds of the same period and later: two guardians, two male and two female dancers (the men dressed as Central Asians, the women as Chinese), a row of musicians playing Central Asiatic instruments (from left to right: mouth-organ, tri-angular harp, cymbals, defaced instrument, trans-verse flute, drum and panpipes), and two 'bird-priests' tending with long spoons a fire holder set on a pedestal of lotus flowers. The detail is damaged, as are the faces. The 'bird-priests', iconographically derived from traditional Chinese and Indian motifs, were re-interpreted in a Zoroastrian context as representing the god Srosh in the fire ritual (according to *Videvdad* 18.14, the cock is Srosh's assistant-priest).[16] FG

This house-shaped ossuary has only one decorated side, which is in the form of the façade of a dwelling. In the central part are two carved openings, separated by a modelled pilaster, with a base and a leaf above, similar to the entrances of fortresses and other works of Sogdian art. Along the top is a moulded border of scales with moulded leaves above it. The surface is decorated all over with a stamped W- motif. On the base at the corners are round openings cut before the ossuary was fired. LYK

44 • Sogdian ossuary

7th–8th century • Samarkand region, possibly Biya-Nayman
Baked clay, incised and stamped • 78 x 32 x 27 cm
The State Hermitage Museum, St Petersburg. CA-3043

House-shaped ossuary decorated on one side with arcs; above are stamped human heads in winged crowns and a crescent at the centre. The surface of the walls is decorated all over with plain stamps. Above is a relief band with pinched decoration. LYK

❋

Arab accounts of the Islamic conquest contain piecemeal but precious descriptions of the local practice of Zoroastrianism, notably the existence of 'idol temples' (evidently, as far as Sogdiana was concerned, the temples with cult images of Iranian gods), side by side with 'fire temples', which are the only temples mentioned in Iran. Most of the information we have on calendars and festivals was transmitted by al-Biruni (973–1050), notably in his *Chronology of Ancient Nations*. The local *Tarikh-e Bokhara* (Cat. 45), preserved in a Persian redaction, is a precious source on pre-Islamic survivals in the tenth century, especially the lamentations for Siyavush.[17] This legendary hero was probably an acceptable 'cover' (as a legendary king of the past) for the young god mourned by Nana, the high goddess of the Sogdians, identified as Anahita but preserving many features of her Babylonian origins.

45 • The history of Bukhara

AH 1246 (1830) • possibly Bukhara
Presented by Captain Sir Alexander 'Bokhara' Burnes (1805–41)
Royal Asiatic Society Persian 159 (1), ff. 51v–52r

The *Tarikh-e Bokhara* ('History of Bukhara') was originally written in Arabic by Narshakhi in AH 332 (943/4 CE). This abridgement of a Persian translation dates from 574 (1178/79). Bukhara, at the time of its annexation by the Arab general Qutayba ibn Muslim in AH 90 (709 CE), was a prosperous, semi-independent oasis in the valley of the Zarafshan River with Zoroastrian, Manichaean, Nestorian and Buddhist inhabitants. Despite having nominally converted, the people of Bukhara apostatized three times following their invaders' departure. Qutayba's fourth attempt is recounted here, wherein 'he made war [and] seized the city and established Islam there after much difficulty. He instilled Islam in their hearts, and made [their religion] difficult for them in every way.' Further, he ordered Bukharans to 'give one-half of their homes to the Arabs' to discourage backsliding and effectively eradicate 'the precepts of the fire-worshippers'.[18] BW

4

THE JUDAEO-CHRISTIAN WORLD

Ursula Sims-Williams

The close contact between Jews and Zoroastrians from the sixth century BCE onwards has left numerous traces in Jewish biblical literature and theology. One area where this is especially noticeable is in the field of Jewish law (civil, criminal and private), particularly in the Babylonian Talmud.

The Babylonian Jewish community began with the Exile, the deportation of the Jews to Babylon by Nebuchadnezzar II from 597 BCE, not long before Cyrus II became the first king of the Achaemenid Empire in 559 BCE and captured Babylon in 539 BCE. After Alexander's conquest of the Achaemenid Empire in 330 BCE, the Jews of both Babylonia and Palestine came first under Seleucid rule and then under that of the Arsacids/Parthians (second century BCE to third century CE). What little is known of Babylonian Jewry from this period comes primarily from traditions preserved by the Jewish historian Josephus Flavius (first century CE). From the beginning of the Sasanian Empire (224–650 CE), however, we can trace the history of the Babylonian Jews more systematically.

The Talmudic period in Babylonia, which began when the legendary teacher Abba Arikka (better known as Rav) moved from Palestine to Babylonia (approximately 220 CE), largely overlaps with the Sasanian Empire and lasted until the Arab conquest. It was during this period that the most important source of Jewish law, the Babylonian Talmud (the *Bavli*), was produced by the Babylonian rabbis. It shared numerous intellectual and cultural concerns with the Zoroastrian priests, their neighbours at Ctesiphon-Mehoza, capital of the Sasanian Empire, which affected matters of civil and criminal law, private law, theology and even ritual.

Like the Pahlavi *Videvdad*, the *Bavli* apparently reached its final, oral, form during the sixth or seventh century. We do not know when these texts were first written down, but probably by the ninth century at the latest. The earliest complete manuscript of the *Bavli* dates from the fourteenth century and is roughly contemporary with British Library MSS Avestan 4, dated 1323 (Cat. 46).

46 • A Zoroastrian law book, the *Videvdad*

Copyist: Mehrban Key Khosrow
Navsari • 1323 • Ink on paper
Provenance: Samuel Guise (1751–1811)
British Library MSS Avestan 4, ff. 46v–47r

This copy of the Zoroastrian law book, the *Videvdad*, dating from the early fourteenth century, is one of the oldest surviving Avestan manuscripts. It consists of short passages of the Avestan text, followed by a Pahlavi translation, often accompanied by brief comments and/or lengthy commentaries and discussions based on legal decisions made by the priests 'of old'. The text shown here features commentators from the Sasanian period: Soshans, Weh-shapur, Mahgushasp and Gogushasp.

These pages, containing part of chapter 3, exemplify discussions among Zoroastrian priests from the time of the Avesta to the Sasanians and beyond (early first millennium BCE to the tenth century CE) about how sins may be erased, and contain the statement that 'the Mazdayasnian (Zoroastrian) Tradition casts away the believer's sins just as the westerly(?) wind wipes the sky clean.' Also seen here is the importance of repentance and a firm intention to sin no more as a prerequisite for sins to be erased. POS, YK

above
47 • The Babylonian Talmud
12th or 13th century • Ink on parchment
Provenance: Edward Harley, 2nd Earl of Oxford (1689–1741)
British Library Harley 5508, ff. 69v–70r[1]

The Babylonian Talmud was composed and transmitted orally, and was probably first written down between the seventh and ninth centuries CE. The pages from the last chapter of *Tractate Yoma* (concerned with the laws of Yom Kippur, the day of atonement) contain a rabbinic discussion of repentance in many respects parallel to what we see in the Pahlavi *Videvdad* (Cat. 46). Here we read: 'Repentance is indeed great, as (by it) deliberate crimes are transformed into merits,' a sentiment matched throughout the Pahlavi literature. Related concepts such as repentance in thought only or also in words, contrition, penitence and payment for 'sins' are also discussed.

Both the Zoroastrian priests and the rabbis aimed at constructing a system of laws to create a coherent penitential system. In both traditions, the discussions are based on the sacred texts, the Avesta and the Bible. Both developed in a non-literate, oral context, were written down fairly late and were influenced by contemporary political and social contexts. POS; YK

By the mid-third century CE there were communities of Syriac-speaking Christians co-existing alongside their Zoroastrian neighbours. Relations, however, became very strained at the time of the Sasanian campaigns against the Roman Empire, resulting in periods of persecution under Shapur II (r. 309–79) and Yazdegerd I and his successors Bahram V and Yazdegerd II in the fifth century. Two examples of largely polemical Christian literature dating from these periods are the fifth- or sixth-century Syriac martyrdom of the Lady Tarbo (Cat. 79) and Bishop Eznik's Armenian work 'Refutation of the Sects' (Cat. 80).

Iranians and Greeks were in varying degrees of contact from the early Achaemenids up to the advent of Islam, but because the Zoroastrian scriptures were transmitted orally, the earliest accounts of Zoroastrianism are in fact those preserved in Greek and Roman sources. From Herodotus (fifth century BCE) up to Byzantine times, there was a steady flow of information, though it is not known what sources this information was itself derived from. We learn from the works of Plutarch (first to second century CE) and Diogenes Laertius (third century CE) that Zoroastrianism was of great interest to the philosophers associated with the Platonic Academy in Athens in the third and fourth centuries BCE (Cat. 51). Zoroastrians were almost always referred to as Magi (from which the term 'magic' is derived).

48 • Three Magi in Parthian Dress
Original mosaic in Basilica Sant' Apollinare Nuovo
Ravenna • 6th century CE
photograph: Almut Hintze

Detail of the sixth-century nave mosaic in the Basilica of Sant' Apollinare Nuovo, Ravenna, depicting the three Magi who are named above the figures as Balthassar, Melchior and Caspar. Guided by an eight-pointed star they approach and offer their gifts to Mary and the Child seated on a throne and surrounded by four angels. The Iranian provenance of the Magi is indicated by their Parthian attire of trouser suits with leopard-print leggings, breeches, fluttering cloaks and Phrygian caps. Shoes with upturned toes are typically worn by Zoroastrian priests to the present day (Cat. 207). The Basilica was built by the Ostrogoth King Theoderic the Great as his palace chapel. AH

49 • The Empress Theodora and her retinue
Original mosaic in Basilica San Vitale
Ravenna • 6th century CE
photograph: Almut Hintze

This mosaic, located on the right side wall at the foot of the apse showing Christ Pantocrator in the Basilica San Vitale, Ravenna, depicts Empress Theodora accompanied by two men and seven court ladies, standing in the anteroom of a church, possibly San Vitale. Theodora offers a large chalice with the wine of the Eucharist to the man next to her to be taken to the sanctuary. The theme of gift-giving recurs on the hem of her purple royal robe, which is decorated with the Adoration of the Magi in a composition that is similar to that of the mosaic of Sant' Apollinare Nuovo. The mosaic was completed in 547 CE, a year before Theodora's death. AH

50 · *School of Athens*
from the Stanza della Segnatura

Raphael (Raffaello Sanzio of Urbino) (1483–1520)
Vatican City • 1510–1511 • fresco

Vatican Museums and Galleries, Vatican City / Giraudon /
The Bridgeman Art Library

The *School of Athens* by the Italian Renaissance artist
Raphael (1483–1520) was painted between 1509 and
1511 as a part of a commission to decorate rooms
in the Apostolic Palace in the Vatican. The painting
is one of a group of four frescoes depicting different
branches of knowledge: philosophy, poetry (including
music), theology and law. Plato and Aristotle appear
as central figures, but the identification of many of
the other philosophers is uncertain. Twenty-three
are named in the key (Cat. 51) by Giovanni Volpato
(1740–1803). Zoroaster (as Zarathustra is known
in the Judaeo-Christian world), usually thought to
be represented by figure 16, on the far right holding
a globe, is here identified as figure 17. USW

51 · **Effigies cognitae in Scholae Atheniensis**

Etching on paper • 1750–1803 • 25.6 x 37.9 cm

British Museum 1869, 0410.2132

Key, by Giovanni Volpato (1740–1803), to the 23
philosophers depicted in Raphael's *School of Athens*.

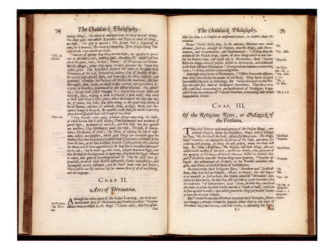

52 • *History of the Chaldaick Philosophy*
London: Thomas Dring • 1662 • Printed book
Wellcome Institute, CG [Stanley] fol, pp. 74–5

Thomas Stanley (1625–78), poet and translator, is
best known for his history of philosophy published
between 1655 and 1662, the first of its kind to be
written in English. The final book, *History of the
Chaldaick Philosophy*, is largely devoted to Zoroaster.

Stanley's *History* was very thoroughly researched
and was based, as can be seen here, on a wide range
of classical sources. Page 74 is an English translation
of Plutarch's famous account of the Zoroastrian
creation myth, unique in classical literature, given
in Chapters 46 and 47 of *De Iside et Osiride*, which
refers to the two rival gods: the better being the
creator of good, Oromazes (Ohrmazd), born from
purest light, and his rival, Arimanius (Ahriman),
born from darkness. Oromazes created six gods:
good will, truth, good order, wisdom, wealth, and
the sixth, the creator of pleasure in beautiful things.
Some of these correspond approximately to the six
Amesha Spentas ('Beneficent Immortals') mentioned
in the Avesta (Cat. 241). Plutarch also refers to the
dualistic categorization of plants and animals and
the merit derived from destroying the 'evil' reptiles
– here described as 'aquatile'! USW

53 • *Zoroaster's Egg*
Romæ: Ex Typographia V. Mascardi 1652–54 [1655]
Printed book • Provenance: Aby M. Warburg
Warburg Institute, NOH 1050 L.S.v. 3. p. 275

The Jesuit scholar Athanasius Kircher (1601/2–80)
was based in Rome from 1635, where he taught
mathematics at the Jesuit Collegio Romano. Famous
as an inventor of the most complex mechanical
devices, he also wrote prolifically on Coptic, ancient
Egypt, geology and medicine.

Kircher had a high regard for Zoroaster, whose
'oracles' (Cat. 56) were, he wrote, very ancient and
full of hieroglyphic explanations. In this context,
in his *Oedipus Ægyptiacus* he refers to the world as
'Ovum Zoroastræum', i.e. Zoroaster's egg, in which
Oromazes (Orhmazd/Ahura Mazda) had placed 24
gods and Arimanius the same number in opposition,
thus causing good and evil to become mixed
together. This idea was based on Plutarch's account
of the creation (see also Thomas Stanley's translation,
Cat. 52). USW

Medieval Christian traditions, based on classical literature, often focused on the figure Zoroaster who, especially after the Renaissance, with its increased awareness of Greek and Hellenistic literature, came to be regarded as a master of magic, a philosopher and an astrologer. In the eighteenth century, a more nuanced interpretation developed which took additional account of texts written in oriental languages and travellers' reports.

54 • Zoroaster, the founder of magic

Copyist: Bartolomeo di Lorenzo of Fighine
16 March 1425 • Ink on parchment
Provenance: Henry Yates Thompson (1838–1928)
British Library Yates Thompson 28, f. 51r

This Italian work, *Il Tesoro*, is one of several included in this manuscript of 1425. It is a translation by the thirteenth-century writer Bono Giamboni of the early French encyclopaedia *Li Livres dou Trésor* by Brunetto Latini (1230–94). Latini's work enjoyed considerable popularity, as is attested by the many surviving manuscript copies. His sources included Aristotle and Pliny. Latini placed Zoroaster in the era of Abraham, writing, 'And at that time a master called Canoaster [i.e. Zoroaster, presumably a misreading of the original French 'Çoroastres'] discovered the magic art of spells and other wicked words and wicked things. These and many other things happened during the first two ages of the era that finished in the time of Abraham.'

The lower painting on the right-hand page shows Canoaster bidding a pair of demons. The upper painting illustrates the building of the Tower of Babel. USW

55 • **Zoroaster, founder of the seven liberal arts**
*c.*1475–80 • Ink on parchment
Provenance: Sir Robert Cotton (1571–1631)
British Library Cotton Augustus V, f. 25v²

This outstanding copy of the *Trésor des histoires*, more commonly known as the *Chronicle of Baldwin of Avesnes*, was made in Bruges in the late fifteenth century. A secular text originally compiled between 1275 and 1282, it was repeatedly copied for and read by French-speaking nobles from then onwards and is one of several vernacular world chronicles covering the period from the creation up to the anonymous author's time. It consists of 763 chapters, of which the eighth is devoted to the philosophers Zoroaster and Hermes Trismegistos. Zoroaster, as in the *Tesoro* above (Cat. 54), belongs to the age of Abraham. Depicted here at his desk, surrounded by musical and mathematical instruments, he is described as the founder of necromancy and the seven liberal arts: grammar, logic, rhetoric, geometry, arithmetic, music and astronomy. We are also told that altogether he wrote 2,000 verses and that he laughed as soon as he was born, a tradition also found in Zoroastrian literature, for example the Pahlavi *Denkard* (DK. 7, 3:2), and in the Persian *Zaratosht Nameh* (Cat. 133).

This copy belonged formerly to King Henry VIII of England (r. 1509–47) and was probably collected for Edward IV (r. 1461–83) who acquired most of his manuscripts from Bruges, one of the most important centres of painting in the late Middle Ages. USW

56 • The Oracles of Zoroaster

Parisiis: Apud Ioannem Ludovicum Tiletanum • 1538
Provenance: Thomas Grenville (1755–1846)
Printed book
British Library G.7768(2)

57 • Rameau's opera *Zoroastre*

Original published: Paris: Chez la Veuve Boivin [1750]
photograph: British Library. British Library printed book E.110.a, p. 72

The Byzantine scholar Gemistos Plethon (*c*.1355–1452) was one of the most influential philosophers of the Renaissance. His *Magika logia ton apotou Zoroastrou magon* or 'Chaldaean Oracles', as they were known, consisted of 60 Greek verses which he believed were by Zoroaster, whom he regarded as the wisest and most ancient of all philosophers. In this volume, published in 1538, the poems are followed, as shown here, by Plethon's own commentary.

The poems are thought to have been originally composed by Julian the Theurgist in the second century CE and reflect a Hellenistic syncretism favoured by Neoplatonic philosophers. Although they have little to do with the Iranian Zoroaster, they were nevertheless largely responsible for transforming the popular medieval image of Zoroaster as a magician into that of a wise man from the East. USW

Zoroastre by Jean-Philippe Rameau (1683–1764), with words by Louis de Cahusac, was first performed in Paris in December 1749. In the preface to his libretto, published in Paris in 1750, Cahusac wrote that Zoroaster acknowledged a good and an evil principle in ceaseless combat until such time as the Author of Good, namely Oromase or Light, would be victorious over the Author of Evil, namely Ariman or Darkness. Amongst his sources, Cahusac mentioned the works of both Thomas Stanley (Cat. 52) and Thomas Hyde (Cat. 139).

This opening shows the beginning of Act 3: Zoroaster descends among the crowd in a chariot of fire. USW

5 IMPERIAL AND POST IMPERIAL IRAN

Jenny Rose and Sarah Stewart
with Ursula Sims-Williams and Burzine Waghmar

Some time between 1200 and 1000 BCE, Iranian peoples migrating from Central Asia began to settle in the region of the inner Zagros mountains. The Medes appear to have occupied the Mahi Dasht (modern Kermanshah) and the plain of Hamadan, while the Persians moved further south to the Elamite kingdom of Anshan, which later became known as Parsa. The fact that the language of the Zoroastrian texts, Avestan, is not a western Iranian dialect has given rise to a number of theories concerning the arrival of the religion in western Iran.[1]

The Persians were settled in Anshan for several generations before Cyrus II (r. 559–530 BCE) founded the first Persian Empire. According to Darius I (r. 522–486 BCE), the Persians traced their ancestry back to one Achaemenes, who gave his name to the dynasty. In this dynastic line, Cyrus II was the son of Cambyses I of Anshan and Mandana, his wife, the grand-daughter of Cyaxeres, who founded the Median Empire following the death of the last great Assyrian king Assurbanipal (r. 668–627 BCE). The Persians borrowed much from their Elamite subjects, including, it seems, aspects of their system of government, which they employed Elamite scribes to administer.

It is during the Achaemenid period that the 'Persian religion' enters recorded history through the accounts of Greek authors such as Herodotus and Xenophon. In addition, there are archaeological remains and inscriptions in Old Persian, Elamite and Aramaic.[2] Cyrus II founded his dynastic capital at Pasargadae, on the Dasht-e Morghab, a site that provides the earliest examples of Ancient Persian monumental architecture and iconography. The great palaces of Darius I at Persepolis and Susa reflect a variety of influences, no doubt derived in part from the workmanship of subject peoples, including Babylonians, Egyptians and Ionians.

ARCHITECTURE

58 • Fragment of carved limestone relief
Persepolis (Iran) • 6th–5th century BCE, Achaemenid period
Limestone • 58.5 x 42 x 12 cm
Presented by George Hamilton Gordon,
4th Earl of Aberdeen
British Museum 118845[3]

This fragment was found fallen from the north side of the Apadana at Persepolis in 1811. It shows a guardsman wearing so-called Persian dress with a pleated headdress, possibly made of felt, holding a spear in both hands and wearing a strung bow with tips ending in birds' heads over his left shoulder. There is a tasselled quiver on his back. Beneath is a cornice decorated with 12-petalled rosettes. Isolated microscopic specks of Egyptian Blue pigment survive on the face of the stone near the spear tip. Such figures are popularly identified with the 'Immortals' described by the Greek historian Herodotus and are shown at Persepolis along with figures of the king, courtiers, officials and tributaries. All were originally highly coloured but few traces of the original paints survive. St JS

59 • Fragment of a limestone relief
Persepolis (Iran) • 6th–5th century BCE, Achaemenid period
Limestone • 30 x 30 cm
Presented to the British Museum by George John James
Gordon, 5th Earl of Aberdeen
British Museum 118855[4]

Fragment of a limestone relief showing a bearded
figure wearing so-called Median dress, a form of
riding costume, a cap that covers his ears and chin
and holding a bowl with a rounded lid. This fragment
belongs with those series of reliefs that show figures
climbing staircases, bearing food, drink and live
animals. They have been interpreted in different
ways, either as priests bringing offerings for a
religious ceremony or as symbolic of servants
bringing provisions for a banquet. St JS

**60 • Fragment of limestone relief
showing a bearded male archer**
Persepolis (Iran) • 6th–5th century BCE, Achaemenid period
Limestone • 35 x 26 x 14 cm
Presented to the British Museum by George John James
Gordon, 5th Earl of Aberdeen
British Museum 118866[5]

This fragment was originally part of the decorative
façade on the north side of the Apadana and was
found at Persepolis in 1811. It shows a bearded male
archer wearing a pleated headdress and holding a
spear with both hands, his right hand placed above
his left. He wears a strung re-curved bow with birds'
head tips slung over his left shoulder and a quiver with
hanging cords with egg-shaped tassels on his back.
St JS

61 • Glazed brick with rosette designs

Susa (Iran) • 6th–5th century BCE, Achaemenid period
Glazed composition • 22.4 x 8.4 x 4.6 cm
Alpaiwalla Museum: IR 56.1

Part of a polychrome glazed brick, broken at the left-hand side. Bricks such as these possibly decorated the sides of staircases in the palace of Darius (522–486 BCE) at Susa. The rosettes would have been borders for elaborate lotus-flower decoration.[6] Whereas in the Assyrian and Babylonian periods glazed bricks were made of baked clay, and the surfaces painted, in the Achaemenid period they were made of 'sintered quartz' and the surface colours were dropped into compartments formed by low ridges. JC

62 • Fragment of glazed brick with chevron pattern

Susa (Iran) • 6th–5th century BCE, Achaemenid period
Glazed composition • 8.3 x 6.0 x 2.9 cm
Alpaiwalla Museum: IR 56.2

Fragment of polychrome glazed brick probably from a panel showing a royal guard who would have been dressed in a richly decorated Persian costume with a bow, a quiver and spear, perhaps one of the king's personal bodyguard. This fragment probably comes from the hem of a guard's tunic and shows a row of embossed circles between rows of triangular motifs.[7] It is likely to have come from the east courtyard of the palace of Darius (522–486 BCE) at Susa. Originally these panels would have lined the walls of the courtyard. JC

ACHAEMENID JEWELLERY AND OTHER ARTEFACTS

The lion motif was a popular adornment of the time: depictions of Darius I, Xerxes I and Artaxerxes I at Persepolis show each king in the same royal robe with striding lions 'embroidered' onto the blue-edged hems of skirt and sleeves. The notion of the king actively defending the realm is present on the doorjambs of the Tachara Palace and elsewhere at Persepolis, where a royal figure in Persian dress combats a bull, a lion or a fabulous beast.[8]

63 · Gold lion figures
Said to be from Iran · 6th–4th century BCE,
Achaemenid period · Gold · each 1.4 x 1.1 cm
British Museum (*left*) 132117 and (*right*) 132118[9]

Asiatic lions roamed the Middle East as late as the twentieth century but are now extinct. Ancient artists emphasized their ferocity and usually showed them roaring, making them a suitable subject for royal hunts. Using them as designs for personal adornment was perhaps intended to bestow some of their power on the wearer. St JS

64 · Gold fittings; lion in repoussé
6th–4th century BCE, Achaemenid period · Gold
L: 3.5 x 2.5 cm; R: 3.1 x 2.5 cm; roundel diameter: 4.3 cm
British Museum (*left*) 132109, (*right*) 132108) and (*roundel*) 132111[10]

These were clothing ornaments. The pair of lions has tiny rings on their backs to enable attachment, whereas the roundel must have been stitched onto a cloth backing. The use of gold sheet appliques sewn onto clothing was adopted in Achaemenid Iran during the fifth or sixth century BCE but was introduced from the north, where it was normally felted and popular among nomadic tribes. St JS

65 • Silver deep bowl with central omphalos

6th–4th century BCE, Achaemenid period
Silver • 5.8 x 13.7 cm
Bought in Beirut • acquired by the British Museum in 1925
British Museum 1925, 1019.1[1]

This bowl belongs to a classic type of drinking bowl used throughout the Achaemenid (Persian) Empire. They are represented on palace reliefs at Persepolis, and were widely imitated by local craftsmen in metal and even pottery. They were also placed in graves, underlining the notion that feasting was so important that it ought to be remembered or continued in the afterlife. This particular bowl was carefully designed to be filled as far as the rounded shoulder, and therefore held just under a third of a litre. The low boss in the centre allowed it to be securely held in one hand, with the fingertips underneath. St JS

66 • Cyrus cylinder

2013 • Made by the British Museum • L: 22.86 cm

commissioned for The Everlasting Flame exhibition, SOAS
courtesy of Farrokh K. Kavaranah

A replica of the Cyrus cylinder that was found
in 1879 at Amran, Babylon, and acquired by the
British Museum in 1880. The original was buried
as a foundation deposit marking the capture of the
city by the Persian king in 539 BCE. The inscription,
in Babylonian cuneiform, follows the tradition of
Babylonian and Assyrian kings of recording their
achievements. Cyrus II was seen as a deliverer from
the tyrant, Nabonidus, whose people had been forced
by him into sacrilegious acts, thus causing the local
gods to depart from the city.

Cyrus is presented in the inscription as the chosen
instrument of Marduk, the principal god of Babylon,
who 'had him take the road to Tintir (Babylon)
and, like a friend and companion, he walked at his
side'.[12] Following the bloodless defeat of the city, the
inscription goes on to describe how the king became
a provider for the local shrines and increased the
offerings to them of ducks, geese and pigeons. He
returned statues of gods to their sanctuaries, allowed
exiled peoples to return home and embarked on
restoration work in the city.[13]

The benevolence shown by Cyrus towards the
Babylonian gods and the gods of his other non-
Iranian subject peoples has been the cause of spec-
ulation about his own religious beliefs, of which we
know very little. The remains of what may have been
fire holders at Cyrus' palace at Pasargadae, combined
with the way in which his body was entombed without being in contact with the earth and the fact that
his successors were worshippers of Ahura Mazda,
have been cited as signs that he, too, was a Mazda
worshipper.[14] Elements of the Cyrus cylinder
proclamation are echoed in the biblical text of Isaiah,
where Yahweh 'takes Cyrus by his right hand to
subdue nations before him and strip the loins of
kings, to force gateways before that their gates
be closed no more' (45.1).[15] Moreover, it has been
noted that the rhetorical questions about creation
in *Yasna* 44 are similar in nature to those of Isaiah 40,
suggesting a relationship between the two traditions
that may have been introduced via the Persians:[16]
'Who was it measured the water of the sea in the
hollow of his hand and calculated the dimensions
of the heavens …' (40.12). '… Who made these stars
if not he who drills them like an army, calling each
one by name …' (40.26).[17] SS

67 Glass etching of decorative stone relief

2013 • Hamza Taher of Daudbhoy, M. Tayebally
and Khuzaima Badani workshop • Mumbai
(with David Barnett of Morris Associates • London)
Glass • 2.4 x 10.5 m
commissioned for The Everlasting Flame exhibition, SOAS

The etching is of the plaster cast in the British Museum
taken from the stone reliefs on the western façade of the
west staircase of the palace of Darius at Persepolis.
The reliefs were probably added during the rule of
Artaxerxes III (r. 359–338 BCE), as indicated by the
inscription on the central panel. Climbing the stairs
are gift-bearers from different parts of the empire.
The figures on the left are in Median-style trousers
and short tunics, while those on the right wear the
long Persian-style dress. Facing the central panels,
on both sides, is a powerful scene depicting a lion
clawing the hindquarters of a rearing bull and biting
into its back. This imagery is repeated numerous
times on the façades of Persepolis, indicating its
importance as a motif, although its exact significance
is unknown. One of the most popular interpretations
relates to astronomy, with either the bull, as the house
of Taurus, giving way to the lion, the house of Leo,
at the time of the spring equinox, or the bull as the
moon, being supplanted by the lion, as the sun.

The inscription

The Old Persian inscription in the central panel
of the relief is one of four copies of an identical
text replicated on the north wall of the terrace
of Artaxerxes I's palace at Persepolis. The lineage
outlined in the inscription identifies its author as
Artaxerxes III Ochus. The opening lines of this
sole text attributed to Artaxerxes III present Ahura
Mazda as foremost, using a formulaic expression
first used by Darius I in the inscription over his
tomb at Naqsh-e Rostam (DNa 1–8): 'A great god is
Ahuramazda who created this earth, who created
yonder heaven, who created man, who created
happiness for man, who made me, Artaxerxes,
king, one king of many, one lord of many.'[18]

The text also parallels similar appeals by Artaxerxes
III's predecessors for Ahura Mazda to protect the
king, the country and its institutions from any kind
of assault. Although Artaxerxes II had expanded
this appeal for protection to include both Anahita
(the female *yazata* of the waters) and Mithra (the
male *yazata* of the contract), the inscription of his
successor refers only to Mithra (*Mithra baga*).[19] JR

PARTHIAN AND SASANIAN

Following the relatively brief period of Seleucid rule, the second Iranian Empire – that of the Parthians – endured for nearly 500 years (248/7 BCE–224 CE). Until recently it was thought that the Parthians were 'Hellenized' and did not continue the practices and beliefs of their Achaemenid predecessors. The 'good religion' was understood to have been restored under the Sasanians after a long period of neglect. In the last few decades, however, much data has been collected or re-examined that challenges this view, including over 2,000 ostraca from Old Nisa in Turkmenistan. The Nisa ostraca demonstrate that the Parthians retained their traditional Zoroastrian calendar, using Avestan months and day names, rather than the Seleucid calendar and Greek script. Many names are theophoric, incorporating the *yazata* Mithra, such as Mihrbozan, Mihrdatak and Mihrfarn.[20]

From a Zoroastrian perspective, the Sasanian period (224–651 CE) is characterized by several significant developments, including the growth of the cult of fire. One of the ways in which Ardashir I (r. *c.*224–240 CE) and his successors sought to legitimize their sovereignty (since they were from a southwestern Iranian family, whereas the Parthians had come from the northeast) was through the establishment of regnal fires, which burned throughout their reign. Ardashir's personal fire was represented on the reverse of his coins, a practice that was continued by his successors. Shapur I (r. *c.*240–270 CE) established five sacred fires in the name of his immediate family members. The second great high priest of the Sasanian period, Kirder, refers to the founding of sacred fires in his inscriptions. He is the first among non-royalty to have his inscription carved, thus showing the power and pre-eminence accorded to the Zoroastrian priesthood.

The creation of a priestly hierarchy, together with the development of the temple cult of fire, gave the 'church' independent sources of income enabling priests to become wealthy in their own right. The writing down of religious texts was another important development during the Sasanian period. It meant that texts could be collected, translated and interpreted by priests, thus consolidating their authority and scholarly status. The later Sasanian period saw the establishment of the Christian Church of the East in Iran, with bishoprics being set up in the major towns. Conversion from Zoroastrianism, together with the rise of the Mazdakite movements, diminished the power and prestige of the Zoroastrian establishment and led to recriminations and at times severe reprisals.

PRE-SASANIAN ARTEFACTS

above
68 · Baked clay figurine in the form of a horse's head
Iran or Mesopotamia
1st-6th century CE, Parthian or Sasanian period
Terracotta baked clay • 4.5 x 2.5 x 5.7 cm
Alpaiwalla Museum

The horse wears a headstall of rope or twisted leather with decorative discs or *phalerae* mounted on the strap junctions. There is an additional disc in the centre of the browband, and suspended from it, lying on the horse's nose, is another short section of strap with a disc. This type of harness with the addition of decorative bosses is well attested in the Parthian and Sasanian periods on rock reliefs and silver bowls.[21] JC

69 • **Leaded bronze figure of a winged beast**

Helmand region (Afghanistan) • possibly 1st–2nd century
Bronze • 24.9 x 32 x 12.5 cm • Presented by the Art Fund
British Museum 123267

This object was found in a region loosely controlled by Parthian rulers and their eastern Kushan rivals. It has often been interpreted as a monster possibly symbolizing Angra Mainyu (Middle Persian, Ahriman), the 'destructive spirit' of Zoroastrian texts. The date of the object has attracted radically different views, ranging from the fourth century BCE to the eighth century CE. The stylized leaf decoration on the chest resembles that on Roman furniture legs, and the holes through the front paws indicate that it was originally fixed to another object and might have been part of a piece of furniture. One wing was crudely repaired at a much later period, when an inscription in *nasta'liq* script was added, possibly in AH 832 (1428/29). St JS

70 · **Parthian terracotta with the name of Mithra**
Uruk? (Iraq) • 1st–3rd century CE, Parthian
Fired clay • 12 x 9.8 x 1.4 cm
British Museum 120076[22]

A bearded man with bushy hair and radiate crown
wearing a long-sleeved belted tunic with a vertical
decorated strip along the front, baggy trousers
and shoes with long ribbon-ties. He reclines on a
decorated mattress or bolster with a cushion below
his elbow. Many similar fired clay plaques are known
from Iraq, especially Uruk, but this is unusual in its
detailed representation of dress and the absence of
a drinking bowl. Moreover, it is unique as it is also
inscribed in Parthian with a dedication to Mithra,
the 'Lord of the Contract' and one of the most
important Iranian deities.[23] St JS

SASANIAN ARTEFACTS

71 · **Sasanian seal with name of possible employee of the fire temple at Adur-Gushnasp**
Sasanian • possibly 4th century
Nicolo • 1 x 1 x 0.3 cm
Donated by the trustees of Henry Christy, 1867
British Museum 120252[24]

Circular nicolo ring bezel engraved with a crescent
at the top, with a Pahlavi inscription which
may be transliterated as *zy'twl gwshnsp*, i.e. 'of
Aturgushnasp', possibly indicating that the seal
belonged to an individual in the employ of this major
fire temple at Takht-e Suleyman. This seal has a
carefully bevelled edge proving that it was originally
mounted within the bezel of a finger ring but was
later detached and the ring is missing. St JS

72 • Sasanian seal with 'Rostam' brandishing a bull-headed mace

Afghanistan? possibly Kushano-Sasanian • *c.*4th century
Chalcedony • 2.7 x 2.7 cm
British Museum 1905, 0530.1[25]

Pale green chalcedony domed stamp-seal engraved with a contest between a 'hero' (Rostam) in Iranian dress, and a demon. The demon is characterized by dishevelled hair, ragged beard and pointed ears. From his mouth protrudes the upper part, head and arms of a human figure (a child), which he seems to be devouring. The 'hero' grasps the demon by the hair, threatening him with a bull-headed mace; the shape resembles a dome but the reverse is worked in the form of a portrait in relief.

In his discussion of this seal, D. Bivar suggested that the scene represents Faridun subduing Zahhak. The head on the reverse has been compared to representations of Kushans, Avars and Huns, which would support an eastern Iranian origin of this seal.
St JS

73 • Sasanian ox-headed mace

Iran? Sasanian • 3rd–7th century • Brass, iron • 8.4 x 7.6 cm
British Museum 129396[27]

Brass head of an iron mace; lost wax cast. Only the upper portion survives but the head is formed by the conjoined heads of three bulls, each facing outwards, with long dewlaps; at the base are the smaller heads of three calves turned sideways. Several other bimetallic maces are known in other collections. The earliest are first millennium BCE but the latest examples are attributed on stylistic grounds to the Parthian and Sasanian periods.

The *Shahnameh* refers to the Iranian mythical hero Faridun commissioning a mace of this shape; by 'taking compasses [he] showed to the smiths the pattern upon the ground. It had a buffalo's head.'[26] Another passage describes how Lohrasp was armed with an ox-headed mace when he defended Zoroaster and the fire temple against marauding Turks, and the same weapon is said to have been used by Giv, Esfandiyar, Goshnasp and Bahram V. In more recent times, ox-headed maces were considered prestigious symbols and attributes of Iranian kings and Zoroastrian priests, and are carried by the priest during his initiation, as well as in other ceremonies. St JS

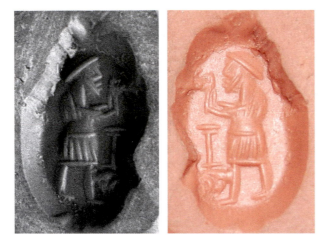

74 • Ellipsoid cornelian stamp-seal
Late Sasanian • 5th–7th century CE
Cornelian • 1.4 x 0.8 x 1.7 cm • Donated by Col. H.A. Dale
British Museum 114702[28]

Ellipsoid cornelian stamp-seal, pierced for suspension and engraved with a standing figure wearing a knee-length tunic facing right, his arms raised above a schematically represented fire holder.

The fire holder with a blazing fire is very close in style to that depicted on the tomb reliefs and seals of the ancient Persian kings, although it lacks the stepped base. A second-century CE relief on a large boulder at Bisutun shows a priest, or possibly a ruler, making an offering over a similar fire holder. Such ritual activity is also displayed in later Sogdian frescoes and on the Sogdian ossuary found at Mullakurgan (Cat. 36). It may reflect the ritual offering to fire, referred to in MP Zoroastrian texts as *atash zohr*. St JS, JR

75 • Stamp-seal with priest by fire holder
Late Sasanian • 5th–7th century CE
Cornelian • 1.9 x 1.7 cm
British Museum 119390[29]

Ellipsoid cornelian stamp-seal engraved with a male figure who appears to be wearing a short belted tunic in front of a fire holder. Originally catalogued as representing a priest, it might equally represent a private individual, especially in the absence of an inscription. St JS

76 • Bezel with mixed Zoroastrian and Christian imagery
Late Sasanian • 5th–7th century CE
Cornelian, silver • 1.3 x 0.9 *(bezel)* x 1.6 *(ring)* cm
British Museum 119616[30]

Cornelian bezel set in a crude modern silver engraved ring, with a robed figure standing before a fire holder. Above the fire holder is a lightly engraved symbol. This has been interpreted as a Greek cross and the seal has therefore been regarded as depicting mixed Zoroastrian and Christian imagery. However, it is not clearly cut and may have been intended to represent a flame. Initially catalogued as a priest, it is more likely to represent a private worshipper. St JS

77 • Silver bowl with figure by fire holder

Sasanian • *c.*5th century CE • Silver • 4 x 4 x 15.2 cm
British Museum 124088[31]

Semi-complete low hemispherical silver bowl with plain interior, and exterior decorated with four equally spaced medallion-like roundels, each containing a figural scene. The scene presumably illustrates one or more fables, the most important representing a female figure wearing a long, loose ankle-length gown with ribbons, standing in front of a fire altar on a stepped base, which is surmounted by a bird. The other roundels represent (1) a similar figure behind whom is a floral scroll apparently composed of palmette elements; (2) the head and bust of a similar figure (much destroyed) holding what appears to be a hemispherical bowl, with a tall plant in front; (3) a bearded man wearing a short belted tunic and close-fitting cap, with stooped back, holding a tall staff with curled top, a large crouching hare in front. St JS

left

78 • **Lead scroll probably inscribed in Mandaic**

Southern Mesopotamia or south-west Iran
3rd–7th century CE, Sasanian period
Lead • 29.5 x 4.8 cm
Alpaiwalla Museum

Thin strips of lead such as this were inscribed with magical texts and then tightly rolled up. There is an important group of Mandaic lead rolls found near Qurna in southern Mesopotamia and now in the British Museum. The Mandaeans, who wrote in a dialect of Aramaic, are sometimes erroneously called 'St John's Christians' because they claim descent from St John the Baptist, but their religion contains various elements including Gnosticism. Mandaic is a north-west Semitic language related to Aramaic and Syriac; inscriptions also appear on incantation bowls of the same date as the lead rolls. The texts usually contain incantations designed to ward off evil spirits. JC

TEXTS

By the mid-third century CE, there were established communities of Syriac-speaking Christians throughout the Sasanian Empire. Their numbers were swelled by prisoners captured during the campaigns of Shapur I against Rome, culminating in the capture of the Emperor Valerian in 260 CE. However, widespread persecution of the Christians did not occur until the early 340s under Shapur II (r. 309–379), a period which coincided with renewed conflict against the Roman Empire.

While one may question the historical significance of hagiographical accounts such as the martyrdom of the holy woman Tarbo (Cat. 79), they nevertheless represent a literary tradition of the early Christian communities based on the realities of persecution under the Sasanians. The story of Tarbo was evidently very popular, with translations existing in Greek and also in Sogdian, as far afield as the monastery of Bulayiq in northern Xinjiang (China).

facing page (above)
79 • **The martyrdom of the Lady Tarbo, her sister and her servant**

5th or 6th century CE • Ink on parchment • 23.5 x 18.5 cm
British Library Add.14654, ff. 13v–14r[32]

A very early Syriac manuscript dating from the fifth or sixth century CE that includes accounts of 11 martyrdoms. The story on display describes in gory detail what happened to the martyrs Tarbo, her married sister and her maid. Tarbo's brother Simeon, bishop of Seleucia-Ktesiphon, had been executed, probably in 341, and the three women were subsequently arrested on the pretext that they had cast a spell on the queen in revenge for their brother's death. Tarbo, whose 'beautiful looks and fine appearance excelled that of all other women', resisted the *mobed*'s offer of freedom in exchange for marriage. The king (Shapur II) intervened, offering to spare them if they were prepared to worship the sun. Protesting, 'we will not worship the created sun in place of our Creator', they willingly succumbed to martyrdom.[33] USW

Towards the end of the fourth century the Armenian Christians faced increasing pressures from different 'heretical' factions. Yazdegerd II's accession to the throne in 438 also heralded a period of enforced re-imposition of Zoroastrianism on his Armenian subjects. It was in this climate that Bishop Eznik wrote his *Refutation of the Sects* (Cat. 80).

80 • Bishop Eznik's *Refutation of the Sects*
Smyrna • 1762 • Printed book • 16 x 10.3 cm
British Library 17026.b.14

Bishop Eznik Kolbac'i wrote this polemical treatise around 440 CE.[34] In it he attacks the beliefs of four 'sects': the 'heathens', the Persians, the Greeks and the Marcionites, focusing on the importance of rationality, free will and evil as a consequence of human action. His views on the Persians were directed principally against the various forms of dualism. His work is valuable as a contemporary account of Zoroastrianism at a time when the scriptures were still transmitted orally, a fact which Eznik himself mentions as a reason for the existence of so many conflicting views.[35]

The frontispiece of this first edition of *Girk' end dimut'eanc'* shows Eznik instructing his pupils. USW

نگون بخت را زنده بر دار کرد
سر مرد بی‌دین بدو خوار کرد
وزان پس بکشتش بباران تیر
تو گر باهشی راه یزدان بگیر

بزرگان شدند ایمن از خواسته
...ن و زراده و باغ آراسته
همی بود با شرم و خندی...
ز نون زندگی بیکد... باد
بر رویش ببخشید بسیار چیز
بیاتشکده خلعت افکند نیز
ز کسری جهان شاد شد گیتی
شب و روز گردی ز فرزند یاد
وزان پس همه رای با داد دید
سخن هرچه گفتی بدو بستدی
ز شاهیش چون سال شد بر چهل
غم روز مرگ اندر آمد بدل
یکی نامه بنوشت پس بر حریر
بدان خط شایسته خود دبیر
تخت آفرین کرد بر داد کسری
که او داد دین و کمال و هنر
بباشد همه پیمان هرچه گفت
به در آشکارا چه اندر نهفت
سر پادشاهیش را کس ندید
نشد خوار هرکس که او برگزید
هر آنکس که پیوند خط قباد
بگنج بد کسری بگیرند یاد
بکسری سپردم سزاوار گفت
بسی از تاج با داد بود و گنج
که بر داد از آن بور خشنود باد
دل بدسگالانش پر دود باد
ز گفتار او هیچ برآکنید
بدو شاد باشید و گنج آگنید
بر آن نامه بر مهر زرین نهاد
بر موبد رام بر زین نهاد
بهشتاد شد سالیان قباد
بند روز پیری غم از مرگ شاد
بمرد و جهان مردی ماند از دنیا
شد از جهد و پیمانش زنگ و بو
تنش را بدیبا بیاراستند
گل و مشک و کافور دمی خواستند
یکی دخمه کردند شاهنشهی
یکی تاج شاهی درخت سهی
نهادند بر تخت زر شاد را
ببستند تا جاودان راه را
چو موبد بپرداخت از سوگ شاه
نهادند یکی نامه بر پیش گاه
بر آن انجمن نامه بر خواندند
ولی عهد را شاد بنشاندند
چو بنشست کسری بر گاه نو
همی خواندندی ورا شاه نو
بشاه بزرگ آفرین خواندند
بسر بر شش گوهر برافشاندند

Mazdak, a Zoroastrian heretic, is generally believed to have been executed along with his followers in 528/9 by Khosrow Anushirvan (r. 531–79) who convinced his father, King Qobad (r. 488–96, 498/9–531), an erstwhile supporter, to take action against him as a result of the chaos arising from popular revolt. Famous as an anti-elitist and ascetic revolutionary whose radical doctrines had socialist overtones, Mazdak is remembered for urging the egalitarian redistribution of wealth and women. In fact, almost nothing is known of his origins, birth or teachings. All our sources, chiefly Islamic, are unanimously hostile to him, as were his opponents among the Sasanian clergy and nobility.

left • 81

The execution of Mazdak from the *Shahnameh*

Iran • copy dated 6 Jumadi I [8]94 (7 May 1489)
Ink on paper • Purchased in 1885 from Zuhur al-Din Khan, relative of the Nawab of the Carnatic
John Rylands Per 910, f. 426r

In this scene from the *Shahnameh*, Mazdak, disgraced and defeated in debate with Khosrow Anushirvan and the Zoroastrian chief priest, is strung up on the gallows and shot with arrows. BW

SASANIAN SILVER

It was a custom for the Sasanian monarch to present a silver cup as a ritual gift to guests at banquets, along with a flowering branch. These state banquets were solemn events, celebrated in the presence of Haurvatat and Ameretat, the two 'Life-Giving Immortals' (Avestan *Amesha Spentas*) of Zoroastrian cosmology who are guardians of the elements of water and plant-life respectively, representing the respective qualities of 'wholeness' and 'immortality'.[36]

above

82 • **Lobed wine boat with footring**

Iran • Sasanian period • Silver, with partial gilding
Length 28.5 cm
Nasser D. Khalili Collection of Islamic Art, MIW 961

This lobed bowl is typical of the Sasanian period. Seventh-century Sogdian frescoes from Panjikant, Tajikistan, depict similar vessels in ceremonial banquets. The theme of feasting, including the drinking of wine, is prominent in Sasanian art and literature, as are illustrations of grapes and vines on Sasanian silverware. One late Sasanian Middle Persian Zoroastrian text, 'The Judgments of the Spirit of Wisdom' (*Dadestan i Menog i Khrad*) (see Cat. 21), discusses the benefits and ill effects of wine consumption, depending on the 'good' or 'bad' spirit of the drinker (*Dadestan i Menog i Khrad* 16.20–64). The text goes on to note that although the drinking of wine could be beneficial, moderation is necessary.[37] JR

83 · Dish with fish and birds
Iran · *c.*5th–6th century CE
Silver, partial gilding · Diameter 21 cm
Nasser D. Khalili Collection of Islamic Art, MIW 1666

84 · Dish with vertical sides and lion
Provincial or peripheral Iran · *c.*7th–8th century CE
Silver, partial gilding · Diameter 14.2 cm
Nasser D. Khalili Collection of Islamic Art, MIW 251

The motifs of the outer circle of ducks with ribbons around their necks and the stylized fish on this expertly worked dish indicate Sasanian influence. Yet the shape and 'star-burst' composition with its central Greek-style ornamentation are not typically Sasanian.

A bird wearing a ribbon around the neck or holding a necklace in its beak (or both) was a common element in later Sasanian metalwork, seals and textiles Both the ribbon and the necklace of pearls or other jewels are thought to symbolize the *khvarrah* (NP *farr*), the divine fortune or glory; the duck, although not mentioned in the Avesta, was one of the birds depicted in this manner in Sasanian times. On this dish, each duck holds a fish in its mouth, rather than a necklace, signifying, perhaps, the abundance of the waters. JR

Both the repoussé central lion and the surrounding symmetrical vegetal ornamentation of this dish are motifs common to Sasanian art, but the vertical sides indicate that the piece probably belongs to the early Islamic period.

The lion, although considered one of Ahriman's miscreations by Zoroastrians (see, for example, *Denkard* 7.8.45), had been incorporated into Iranian representations of royal power by the early Achaemenid period (see, for instance, Cats 63 and 64), and is found in variant forms on Sasanian seals, and as a protome for a crown worn by a prince on Bahram II's relief at Naqsh-e Rostam. The balanced plant scroll design on the dish is characteristic of the Sasanian (Zoroastrian) emphasis on order at both microcosmic and macrocosmic levels. Such ornamental motifs were popular on both the interior and exterior of Sasanian silver dishes, and continued to be copied well into the Umayyad period. JR

85 · Wine boat or oval dish
Iran · 7th–8th century CE
late Sasanian or early post-Sasanian period
Silver, partial gilding · Length 18.7 cm
Nasser D. Khalili Collection of Islamic Art, MIW 1401

86 · Dish with winged animal
Eastern Iran · 6th–7th century CE
Copper alloy · Diameter 23.9 cm
Nasser D. Khalili Collection of Islamic Art, MIW 543

This elliptical bowl with the central duck in a roundel and surrounding fish was probably used for wine. The single bird or animal in a roundel (often delineated with large pearls) was characteristic of later Sasanian art, and became a popular motif in countries outside Iran. The portrayal of a single duck is found on seals, and ducks were also popular motifs on textiles, reliefs or frescos depicting textiles (such as at Taq-e Bustan and Afrasiyab respectively) and on silver vessels.[38] When the duck is occasionally represented with fish, as here, a connection to water – and therefore to fertility and growth – may be assumed. Fish are mentioned in the *Bundahishn* as female, like the waters, and mythical *Kar* fish protect the Gaokerena tree, which grows in the middle of the ocean and is necessary for the final renovation (*Bundahishn* 13.10.26; 18.1–5). The watery imagery on this bowl could derive from an original association with the *Amesha Spenta*, Haurvatat ('wholeness'), the protector of the life-giving waters (Cat. 84). JR

The winged animal at the centre of this dish is reminiscent of the Parthian-era bronze winged beast from Afghanistan (Cat. 69), but here the beast should be considered as beneficent. The surrounding radiating petal design occurs in pre-Achaemenid Near Eastern art through to Sogdian metalwork and frescoes of the sixth and seventh centuries.

During the Sasanian period, as in the previous Ancient Persian and Parthian periods, lion-griffins and griffins were associated with royalty: they are depicted on Sasanian-era throne legs, stucco moulds and seals and on a Sogdian fresco from Panjikant in Tajikistan.[39] JR

87 • Ewer representing the *Simorgh*

Iran • 6th–7th century CE
Silver, traces of gilding • H: 31.5 cm
Found in 1823 as a part of a small hoard near Pavlovka
in the Kharkov region (Ukraine)

The State Hermitage Museum, St Petersburg, S-61⁴⁰

Typical Sasanian ewer with medallions on two sides containing images of the *Simorgh*. Between the medallions are sacred trees. A Sasanian floral design decorates the ewer and lid. MD

89 • *Senmurv* (NP *Simorgh*)

Iran • early 7th century CE
Moulded stucco • H: 16.5 cm; w: 20 cm; d: 7 cm
Vahid and Cathy Kooros Collection

This moulded stucco figure within a pearl-studded medallion is typical of the Sasanian period, when the motif is also found on silverware (Cat. 87) and stone reliefs and murals depicting contemporary textiles (at Taq-e Bostan, Iran, and Afrasiab, Sogdiana, respectively), but only rarely on seals. It is in keeping with the earlier composite creatures of Near Eastern art, such as the griffin or lion-griffin, but the hybrid form represented here has a canine head, forward-pointing ears, wings and a 'peacock' tail. Usually the front paws are clawed like a wolf's (although often referred to as leonine), but in this case the forepads are missing.

The fantastical beast is generally identified as the *senmurv*, a Middle Persian rendition of the Avestan *Saena meregha* (later known as *Simorgh*), the great Saena bird of Zoroastrian mythology (yt. 14.41). The Middle Persian Zoroastrian text *Vizidagiha i Zadspram* describes the bird as resting on the tree of all seeds that grows in the middle of the ocean: when the bird rises from the tree, the motion scatters the seeds into the water, whence they are caught up with the rains and showered back down onto the earth (*Vizidagiha i Zadspram* 8.3–4). The motif is found on textiles excavated in Central Asia and the Caucasus, and on metalware. It is also replicated on textiles produced within Byzantine and Islamic contexts. In Ilkhanid and Timurid manuscripts of the *Shahnameh*, illustrations of stories associated with the *Simorgh* depict her as similar to a Chinese phoenix (see also 403).[42] JR

88 • **Plate representing struggle of a lion and a bull**

Iran • 7th–8th century CE
Silver, with gilding • Diameter 21.8 cm
Found in 1903 on the Shinva river in Perm region (Russia)
The State Hermitage Museum, St Petersburg, S-40[41]

A lion tearing a bull, a typical subject of the Achaemenid and Sasanian periods, may symbolize the equinox. The background, characteristic of Sasanian silverwork, consists of a decorative tree dividing the surface of the plate into two parts. The tree grows from a chain of mountains. Below can be seen a duck and a fish. MD

COINS

ACHAEMENID AND PARTHIAN COINS

90 · Achaemenid coin (daric)
4th century BCE · Gold · Diameter: 1.5 cm; weight: 8.35 g
British Museum 1866, 1201.4099

This gold daric shows the Achaemenid Persian
king as a kneeling archer holding a bow and a spear.
His crenellated crown, long beard and long Persian
garb are similar to depictions of the Persian kings
on the reliefs of Persepolis. Darics were minted in
the western part of the Achaemenid Empire. VC

91 · Parthian coin (tetradrachm)
Minted at Seleucia on the Tigris, modern Iraq · 52–3 CE
Silver · Diameter: 2.7 cm; weight: 9.78 g
British Museum 1878, 0301.408

The Arsacid Parthian king Vologases/Valakhsh I
(r. 51–78 CE) wears a diadem with long ties. He is
associated in the later Zoroastrian tradition as the
king who gathered the dispersed remains of the
Avestan text that had been scattered as a result of
Alexander's conquest of the Achaemenid Persian
empire in 330 BCE. VC

92 · Parthian coin (tetradrachm)
Minted at Seleucia on the Tigris, modern Iraq · 52–3 CE
Silver · Diameter: 2.6 cm; weight: 11.33 g
British Museum 1848, 0803.74

The back of this coin of Vologases/Valakhsh I shows
the king receiving a diadem, a symbol of kingship,
from a standing goddess. He wears a short jacket and
baggy trousers. The inscription in Greek describes
him as 'Of the great Arsaces, king of kings'. Parthian
kings were given the dynastic name Arsaces after the
founder of the dynasty Arsaces I (c. 238–211 BCE). VC

93 • **Parthian coin (drachm)**

*c.*190 CE • Silver • Diameter: 2 cm; weight: 3.33 g

British Museum 1894, 0506.2283

The Arsacid Parthian king Osroes II (*c.* 190 CE)
with moustache and long beard wears a tall hat/
tiara adorned with pellets at the top. A wide-ridged
diadem is tied around the hat, ending at the back in a
bow and long parallel ties. Long ear flaps fall over the
cheeks. A plain torque is worn around the neck. VC

SASANIAN COINS

94 • **Sasanian drachm**

276–93 CE • Silver • Diameter: 2.7 cm; weight: 4.11 g

British Museum OR0030

Silver drachm of Bahram II (r. 276–93 CE) showing
the Sasanian king wearing a winged cap topped with
a globe and a diadem. A diadem is tied around the
cap ending in long ties above his long curls. His long
beard is tied into a knot and covered with silk. The
inscription on the front describes him as the 'Mazda
worshipping Lord Bahram, king of kings, of Iran
and non-Iran, whose origin is of the gods'. VC

95 • **Sasanian drachm**

224–41 CE • Silver • Diameter: 3 cm; weight: 4.28 g
Presented by J. F. W. de Salis in 1862

British Museum 1862, 1004.2

Silver drachm of Ardashir I (r. 224–41 CE). The
Sasanian king wears a cap with a diadem, and a
diadem is also tied around the covered ball of hair.
His hair and long beard are neatly coiffured with
rows of vertical curls. The inscription in Pahlavi
describes the ruler as 'The Mazda-worshipping
Lord Ardashir, king of kings of the Iranians,
whose lineage is of the gods'. VC

96 • Sasanian drachm
309–79 CE • Silver • Diameter: 2.8 cm; weight: 4.21 g
British Museum 1922, 0710.3

Silver drachm of Shapur II (r. 309–79 CE). The Sasanian king of kings, who is described as a Mazda worshipper, wears a crenellated crown with a diadem tied around it. A covered ball of hair is placed on top of his head. His curly hair is combed back and his long, twisted beard is covered with a material, possibly silk, so as not to expose facial hair according to the Zoroastrian tradition. VC

97 • Sasanian drachm
309–79 CE • Silver • Diameter: 2.9 cm; weight: 3.33 g
Donated by William Marsden, 1834
British Museum MAR.518

The back of this silver coin of Shapur II shows a Zoroastrian fire holder with two figures holding consecrated barsom sticks. On either side of the flames are royal crests or *nishan*, including a diadem, a symbol of kingship. A diadem is also tied around the altar shaft, ending in long ties on either side. The Pahlavi inscription to the right and left of the altar describes the fire as the 'fire of Shapur'. VC

98 • Sasanian drachm
Hamadan, Iran • Regnal year 37 (567 CE) 531–79 CE
Silver • Diameter: 3.2 cm; weight: 4.11 g
British Museum 1964, 0306.2

Silver drachm of Khosrow I (r. 531–79 CE), known as Khosrow Anushirvan (Khosrow of the Immortal Soul). The king wears a crenellated crown with a diadem, topped with a globe and diadem. Astral symbols of the moon crescent and star appear around the king's portrait on his shoulders, and moon crescents decorate the outer margin of the coin.

These are symbols of Ohrmazd's creations. A long vertical diadem tie flanking each shoulder symbolizes Khosrow's kingship. He wears earrings and a necklace with pendants. VC

99 • Sasanian drachm

Darabgird, Iran • Regnal year 26 (615 CE)
Silver • Diameter: 3.1 cm; weight: 4.17 g
British Museum 1981, 0109.8

Silver drachm of Khosrow II Parviz (the Victorious, r. 591–628 CE) showing the Sasanian king wearing an elaborate crenellated crown with two wings and topped with the crescent and star symbol. A star is placed behind the crown, and a moon crescent is on the king's left shoulder. Vertical diadem ties symbolizing kingship and glory appear behind the king's shoulders. The king's name appears on the right, and the phrase 'May his glory increase' appears behind his head. The wings of the crown symbolize the king's glory (khvarenah/farr). VC

100 • Sasanian drachm

Minted in Sistan, Iran • Regnal year 16 (637 CE)
Silver • Diameter: 3.2 cm; weight: 4.05 g
British Museum IOC.537

Yazdegerd III (r. 632–51 CE), the last Sasanian ruler, who was deposed by the Arabs in 651, is shown beardless, wearing an elaborate crenellated crown with wings and topped with a globe. The inscriptions are stylized, but the name of the king appears on the right and the phrase 'May his glory increase' can be seen on the left. He wears elaborate drop earrings and a necklace with three pendants. The Zoroastrian astral symbols, which appear on the outer margin, were adopted by the Muslim conquerors and became an important symbol of Islam after the collapse of the Sasanian Empire. VC

6 POST ARAB CONQUEST

Sarah Stewart with Ursula Sims-Williams,
Burzine Waghmar and Alexandra Buhler

In the centuries following the Arab conquest of Iran, Zoroastrianism was steadily replaced by Islam as the state religion. Those who were unwilling to convert were relegated to the margins of society, losing wealth and position, but retaining their religious rituals and practices, their language (which remained the language of Iran) and their fire temples, although many of these were eventually replaced by mosques. Zoroastrians, together with Christians, Sabeans and Jews, were granted *dhimmi* status by the Arab Muslim rulers, which meant that their religion was tolerated provided they paid the *jizya* or poll tax.

Conversion to Islam occurred unevenly across the former Sasanian Empire. The province of Pars (Arabic: Fars), for example, remained Zoroastrian until around the tenth century CE. The preceding century had witnessed a proliferation of religious literature in Middle Persian, reflecting the pressing need to dissuade Zoroastrians from conversion. During this period, most of the surviving Pahlavi literature was composed or revised, mostly by the Hudinan Peshobays, or 'Leaders of the Good Religion', who represented the community to the Muslim officials in various localities, including Baghdad. Texts such as the *Epistles of Manushchihr* (who came from a distinguished line of Hudinan Peshobays) and the *Dadestan i denig* ('Religious Judgements') reflect the preoccupations of both priests and laymen at the time – namely, the descent of evil upon the community, the appropriate penalty for the sin of conversion, the potential for relaxation of ritual and law during straitened circumstances (*Vizidagiha i Zadspram*) and the defence of the faith against Islam, Judaism and Christianity (*Shkand-gumanig Vizar*, 'Doubt-dispelling Exposition').[1]

THE REVELATIONS OF VIRAZ THE JUST

The instability of the early Islamic period is further reflected in the Pahlavi text of the *Arda Viraz Namag*. The story is set in the reign of the founder of the Sasanian Empire, Ardashir I (r. 224–41 CE), and describes how the Zoroastrian community priests selected the righteous Arda Viraz – 'Viraz the just', or Viraf as he is known in Persian (they are both possible readings of the Pahlavi spelling) – to visit the other world, returning with an account of the rewards and punishments in store. Although the story did not assume the form in which we know it until the ninth to tenth centuries CE, it can be regarded as part of a tradition of visionary accounts, the earliest documentary proof of which can be found in the third-century CE inscriptions of the Zoroastrian high priest Kirder in various locations near Persepolis (see page 15).[2] The story of Arda Viraz was retold several times in Persian prose and verse, as well as Gujarati. Interesting details in the Pahlavi version include a reference to the Zoroastrian practice of next-of-kin or *khvedodah* marriage, though this is omitted from the Persian versions. Many copies of this popular story survive, some of them including vivid illustrations, re-enforcing its underlying importance as a Zoroastrian pedagogic text.

فرو آویخته آنخوخ دیده

همی نالیده میزار بدلیبار

بیرسیدم زحالان سیه روز

نبردی گفت او فرمان غنوهر

هرا بخبر که از نوهر شنیده سر

کنون زنگوبه در سخنت قاهم

بیاله فراه و دربخبته فقاله

زبانش از قفا بیرون کشیده

عذاب وربع و باغه فراه وازار

کرد ارو کنا هست درس آموز

جوانش باز دادی این بزختر

بزردی یا سخت بدتر کردی

درمردی وقومی دیویدیم

اکر دیکازان یقطره کمتر

بدین زاری روان دیکر منبحو

کلیتیع در بکوتا خودجیه است

همیشه ره خلیع جیهانبو

سند اوزمل وکم کرد اوکسانز

چوبکه نشتم دکرجای رسیدم

کلکنجه زودمینیو ره او خره استر

همغروخبوب وروری سبه مکر

انخورالعقم المجرمش جیه بود در

سرولشم کفت او تاور جیهانبو

ترازوکج کروفت و سنک انز

جو بکارنی

چو بگذشتم دگر عقبای رسیدم
بر کفچه زود منجو برد او خر استر

همی رو زجوب و بروی سیه هکار در
اشنو الکفتم اینجرمش حیم بود در

سر وستم کفتا او قادر جهانبو
ترازو کج کرفت و سنک اثرا

در مردی وقوی می بودیم
اکر دیبر ازان یکقطره لمتر

بدین زاری روان دکر منجو
لکتیع در بکو تا خود جیم بود ست

همیشه ره روال خلیج جهانبو
ستد افزول وکم کرد او کساانز

زمال

preceding page and left
101 • Arda Viraf's vision of hell
Copyist: Peshotan Jiv Hirji Patvari
Navsari • 22 Shavval 1203 (16 July 1789) • Ink on paper
Provenance: Samuel Guise (1751–1811)
John Rylands Persian 41, ff. 47v–48r

102 • The revelations of Arda Viraf
India • 17th century • Ink on paper
Provenance: Thomas Hyde (1636–1703)
British Library, Reg.16.B.1, ff. 58v–59r

This copy of the *Arda Viraf Nameh* contains 60
illustrations, more than half of which depict the
gruesome punishments awaiting the souls of those
judged deficient at the Chinvat Bridge ('bridge of the
judge'). Punishments were to some extent tailored to
the crimes committed on earth; for example the man
who had butchered believers was punished by being
flayed alive, another who had overindulged and not
given food to the poor was starved until forced to eat
his own arms out of hunger. Punishments were meted
out by demonic creatures, mostly consisting of those
same evil scorpions, snakes and reptiles which good
Zoroastrians were encouraged to destroy.

In this opening, on folio 47v (preceding page),
sinners who neglected to wear the *kusti* (Cat. 184)
and were slack in matters of religious ritual are being
eaten by demonic animals, while on folio 48r (left), a
woman is hung upside down and her tongue is being
pulled from the back of her neck. Her crime was to
disobey her husband and argue with him. USW

This popular Persian poem, the *Arda Viraf Nameh*
('The Story of Arda Viraf') was composed in Iran at
the end of the thirteenth century by Zartosht Bahram
Pazhdu. Based on a Pahlavi original of the ninth/tenth
century, it describes Arda Viraf's journey through
heaven and hell and his return home afterwards.

This passage describes a garden in Paradise where
musicians play and people dance. On enquiring what
these fortunate souls did to earn such a reward, Arda
Viraf is told by his guides, the divinities Srosh and
Ardibihisht Amshasfand, that, while living, they killed
frogs, scorpions, snakes, ants and other evil creatures
(Persian: *khrastar*; Avestan: *khrafstar*) – one of the
most meritorious actions a good Zoroastrian could
perform.

Although this poem is in Persian, it has been
rendered here in both Persian and Avestan scripts,
reflecting a tradition of transcribing Zoroastrian
texts in a 'Zoroastrian' (i.e. Avestan) script. The
manuscript was acquired for the orientalist Thomas
Hyde who used it as a means of deciphering the
previously unknown Avestan script. USW

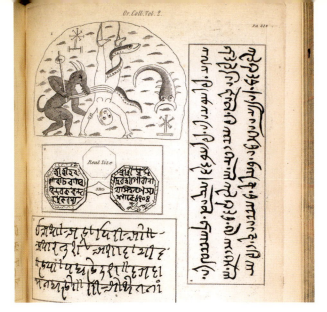

103 • An 18th-century facsimile of the *Arda Viraf Nameh*

London • 1798 • Printed book

British Library, SV 400, vol. 2 part 3, facing p. 318

When Samuel Guise (1751–1811), whose manuscripts feature prominently in this exhibition,[3] showed his collection to the Persian scholar William Ouseley (1767–1842), Ouseley published a partial catalogue in his new journal *Oriental Collections* including some of the earliest facsimile engravings of Zoroastrian manuscripts. The three texts illustrated here are the first four lines of the *Khordeh Avesta* in Gujarati script, a passage from a *Videvdad Sadeh* of 1759 (both these MSS are today in the British Library collections), and an illustration from the *Arda Viraf Nameh*: 'The soul of a woman who was disobedient to her husband suffering due punishment in the infernal regions of the Parsees' (see Cat. 101 for the original from which this engraving has been made). USW

VISIONARY JOURNEYS IN OTHER LITERARY TRADITIONS

The *Mi'raj Nameh* or ascent of the Prophet Muhammad

The *mi'raj* (lit. 'ladder', later 'ascent') is the celestial, nocturnal, apocalyptic sojourn under-taken miraculously by the Prophet Muhammad on his steed, Buraq, from Jerusalem through the seven heavens. Literary traditions of the *mi'raj* are obliquely referred to in the Qur'an (17:1, 53:4–8) and the term is not mentioned in the earliest literature.

An exceptionally produced *Mi'raj Nameh*, arguably one of the more celebrated illustrated Persian manuscripts, is the Paris manuscript shown here (Cats 104–106).

Just why such a sumptuous production was composed in Chaghatay (a Turkish dialect), and transcribed in Uyghur instead of Arabic script, remains inexplicable; however, it remains a truly significant work, modelled on features adopted from the Zoroastrian *Arda Viraz Namag*, and influenced by Jewish and Christian apocalypses, to bolster the glorification of the then Ummayad Jerusalem – Christ's ascension site – and the finality of Muhammad's apostleship.

right 104 • **Muhammad and the celestial cockerel**
overleaf 105 • **Doorway to hell**
overleaf 106 • **The ordeal of the adulteresses**

Original probably copied by Hari-Malik Bakshi of Herat in Arabic and Chaghatay in Uyghur script, with later annotations in Ottoman Turkish and New Persian.

possibly Herat • *c.* 1436–37

Bibliothèque nationale de France, Paris, Suppl. Turc 190 (f. 11r, f. 61v and f. 53r)

Muhammad, following his nocturnal sojourn (*isra*') from Mecca to Jerusalem, leaves the first stage of heaven, whereupon he observes a white cockerel (Pahlavi: *xros*, Persian: *xorus*, Chaghatay: *xoros*). His guide, Gabriel, informs Muhammad that 'this cockerel is an angel who keeps track of the hours of day and night' and its celestial cry at the hour of prayer glorifying God is heard and imitated by its terrestrial counterparts.[4] The cock assists Srosh, the Zoroastrian divinity of prayer and nocturnal protection during the *Ushahin gah* vigil between midnight and dawn (Vd. 18.15).[5] In Perso-Muslim tradition, demons and *jinn*s were fearful of it and regarded it as friendly to the Prophet and hostile to his enemies.[6] In 105 Gabriel introduces Malik, the 'gate-keeper of hell', and in 106, adulteresses suspended by their breasts and tortured for bearing 'illegitimate sons' and 'claiming that they were by their husbands' so as to inherit property unlawfully. BW

فى الأرض وراسه تحت العرش

رسول الله عدم سماية اول يه واصل اولدقده عرشك بر آق حور رزكورد يكه باشنى عرش آلنن ايا قلا روى بر يوز بنك باصل اول محمد

سهعمه وهيد هد سهد سهت سهقد بسهد سهه سههم تد سهم سههى بيه سهه

سهر سد وسهه سهه ستسهمه سهسر سهى ل لهيم سهقى سهد سرق سهقه تسهيقمه

سههمه ستير سهق عهيست عهيهت سهر عهمه ده سهم بر عهد سهمه ممه عهستد

ستقهى سهم سد سهمه سهت سسهل سسوق سهق سهوق سهشت دسهق سهد سد وه سهد

سسمهى وه سهسى هيد بر قست سه سسقى سعوفى سهد وههمه سهد هيو قسر سهد دسهق

ههدد بهو بر سهيه بهو عهيهددهى سهر سهد عهسدده يه سهد بهمه سيهه ه سد وسد ستسيقمه

سههمه دستير سهمر سبهقه هد ست تسهمد سهعمد سهه يه د سه سيهقط سيهد بهسهى بهستى

سهق ههمه وهمه ممه عهيست مهد سهمه بهسهمه ده بر تسهمد همهه ممه عهسدد سبهستى سههقممه

نار جهنم دفعة واحدة وكيف اخذت الهيبة للنبي صلى الله عليه وسلم
وكذلك لجبريل عليه السلام ۝

53

Dallaltro cinghio e dismoutam lontano,
che chomio odo qumei e nonmuerdo,
chosi giu ueggio euiente assegnann.

Altra risposta disse nonciendo
seno lostare chella dmanda onesta,
si te seguire chollopera tacendo.

Noi discendemo il ponte dalla testa
doue sagiungie chon lottaua ripa,
epoi mi fu labolgia manifesta.

Euidoi uentro terribile stipa
discepenti e dun diuersa mena
chella memoria il sangue ancbor ne scipa.

Epin nostri uanti libia chon sua rena
chese chelidori iaculi e pharee
pdnucie e cientri cd amphisilena.

Netante pistolençie nesi ree
mostro gia mai cotutta lethiopia
ne choncio che disopra almar rosee.

Tra questa cruda etristissima chopia
chorreuan gienti gnuite espauentate,
sança sperar priuso ocheuropia.

Con serpi lemati dietro auien leghate
quelle fichauan ple rem la choda,
el chapo. edcran dmançi agroppate.

Edecrco aduno chera diuo stra proda
sauento un serpcr cheimaffisse
lauuel chollo alle spalle fannoua.

Aeio, si tosto mai ne ço si scriffe
chimel sacctese e arse e ciemer tutto,
chonuenne che chaschando nuenisse.

Epoi chefu atterra si distructo,
la poluer siraccholse pse stessa,
enquel medesimo ritorno douicto.

Cbosi pli gran saui si chonfessi
chella finacie more e poi renascie,
quandal cinqueciententesimo anno apressa.

Left lower column:

Notandu est sup banc qualitate septi
me bulcie q de latrombs distinguib
magiis debent scire q aubiber p pena
figuiratur siue figuratiue ponitur
ab auctonbs cogitatoibs prius qua hoies
buit. Un qz latrones semp habet co
gitatone pdicam secu cupiditate fu
randi hic figuratiue ponit inter di
uersos e nulti spentes ad demostra
diu pdicti Latrones semp morantiur
cu puicto cogitationibs.

Et debent notare q culpa ista forma
die in hoiby in tribo modis, piuus mo
dus e q aliqui sut ex babitu latrone
tali modo q nuqua possiit se extrahe
re de pctis cogitatioiby. Scds mo d'
est q aliqui sut no arbitratu si cu
inuenit aliquod boni furare, e co
gitat in se si bu est accipere aut no
e sinaliter accipuit. Tercius mod'
est q aliqui sut no arbitrati adbuc
nec nuiqua cogitit furtu face s qn
accioit eis qd inueniat aliqu furtu e
to sine aliqua cogitatoe ipin funat
e postea se penetrunt.

Right top notes:

b. Libia est regio deserta e affituca
arenosa ac sterilis ita qr mebil
grigint qp uehemetia caloris. e
eni in torrda çona. sub equinoc
ali linea. e multis spetibus bu
bundat.

c. Sut noia spentium qui babi
dant inlibia. ut chelidon iaculi
aphisibena et c.

Divina Commedia

It is possible that the Prophet Muhammad's *mi'raj*, 'ascent' (Cats 104–106), may have been one of a wide range of sources upon which Dante Alighieri (*c.*1265–1321) drew for his *Divina Commedia*, which was translated into Castilian and then into Latin in the thirteenth century as the *Liber scale Machometi*. This tradition was itself based on Zoroastrian and Jewish sources such as the revelations of Arda Viraf (Cats 101 and 102).

107 · Dante's descent to hell

Original copied in Emilia or Padua, north Italy
2nd quarter of the 14th century
photograph of British Library Egerton 943, f 43v

This striking image, from a fourteenth-century Italian copy of Dante's *Divina Commedia*, describes Dante's crossing, with his guide Virgil, through the seventh ditch (*bolgia*) of the eighth circle of hell. Here they witness naked thieves pursued relentlessly by snakes. On the right, an identified thief, Vanni Fucci, is bitten between the shoulders by a fire-breathing serpent before being burned alive. The accompanying text is a Latin commentary. USW

An important consequence of the Arab conquest of Sasanian Iran was the adoption of Arabic script in place of Pahlavi script. The subsequent growth of the New Persian language, which was close to Middle Persian, was a further blow to the preservation of Zoroastrian heritage, but conversely also became a means for the transmission of the culture of pre-Islamic Iran via poetry and prose to the Iranian Muslim population, who were committed to the preservation of an Iranian national heritage.

The development of literature in New Persian included the genre of Persian epic, which had no counterpart in Arabic. Over the centuries, a compilation of myths, legends and historical data had been compiled by the Sasanian court into a chronicle, the *Khwaday Namag*, or 'Book of Kings'. This work contained a variety of material, including the history and traditions of past dynasties, both mythical and historical, Zoroastrian wisdom literature and legends of local heroes. Some of these legends – for example, those relating to Rostam, the prince of Sistan – have been passed down the centuries to modern times. Although no copies of the *Khwaday Namag* survive, it provided, through intermediate texts, a source for the epic poem by Abu'l-Qasem Ferdowsi, completed in 1009–10 CE. The form and subject matter of Ferdowsi's New Persian *Shahnameh* appears to have been influenced very little by Islamic ideas and to be strongly rooted in Iranian traditions. The heroic ages of the mythical Pishdadians and the legendary Kayanian dynasty afforded unlimited scope for the poet. While Ferdowsi would have drawn on ancient oral traditions, including the Avesta, for the earlier part of the epic, the later part reflected documents and records still in existence from the Sasanian period. Once the narrative entered the historical era of the Sasanian dynasty, much of the epic spirit was lost.

In the *Shahnameh*, the dualistic imagery of the kings and heroes of Iran perpetually at war with the Turanians is strongly reminiscent of the *Yashts*. However, unlike the *Yashts*, which are essentially hymns of praise, the purpose of the *Shahnameh* is to provide a chronology of events.

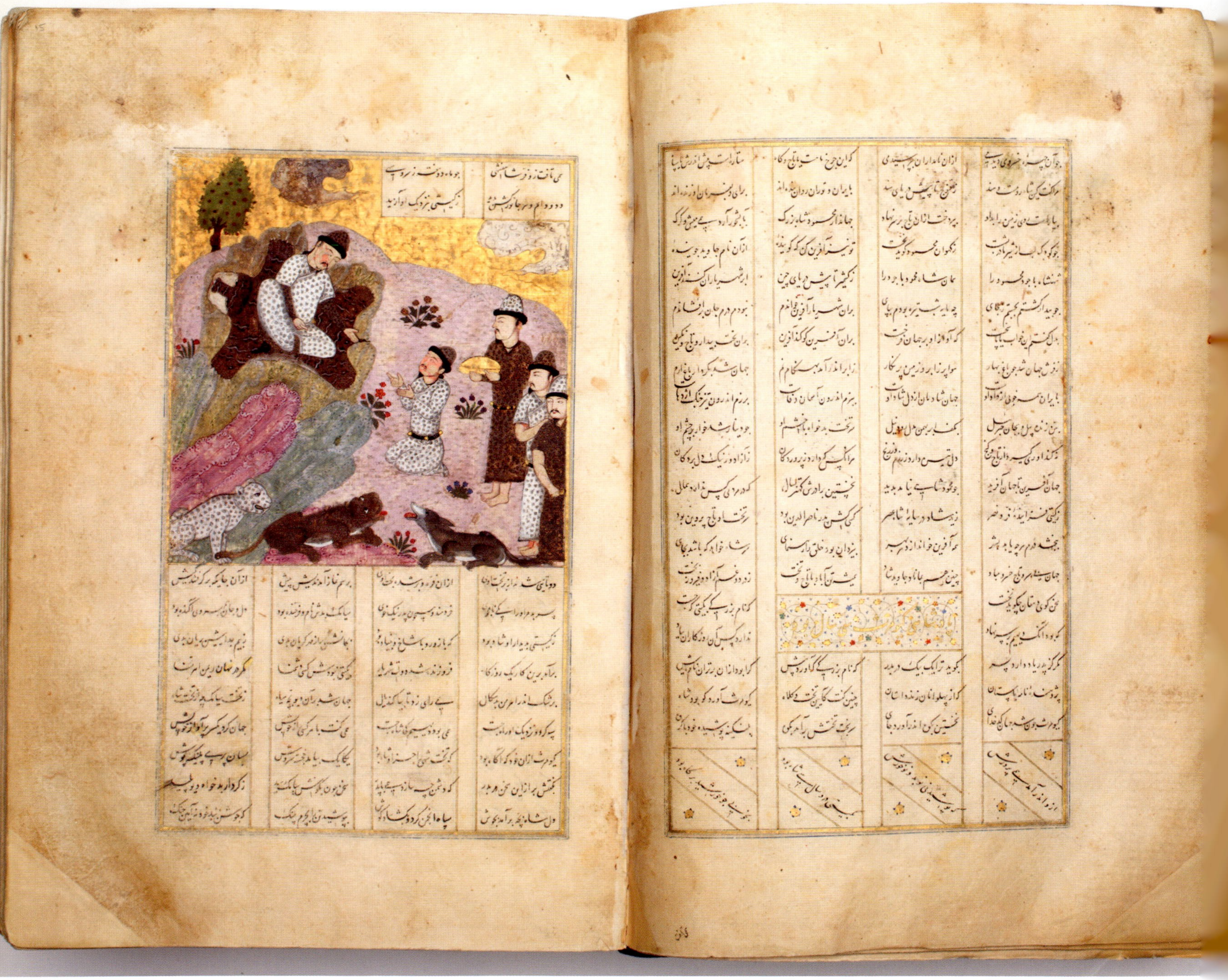

108 • The court of Gayomars

Copyist: Na'im al-Din al-Katib al-Shirazi
Iran, probably Shiraz
13 Ramadan 890 (24 September 1485)
Ink on dark cream burnished paper
The Nasser D. Khalili Collection of Islamic Art, MSS 713, ff. 14b–15a

This copy of Ferdowsi's *Shahnameh* was made for the Aqqoyunlu prince Baysunghur ibn Ya'qub, written in fine *nasta'liq* hand.

This painting shows the first man, Gayomars (Avestan: Gayo maretan, Middle Persian: Gayomard), dressed in leopard skin, holding court in the mountains. Animals are shown before him and it is said: 'The cattle and the diverse beasts of prey grew tame before him.'[7] In the Avesta (vd. XXII, 19:53), Ahura Mazda revealed the law to Zarathustra on top of a mountain, and Gayo maretan, the first man, is said to have ruled the Iranians from the top of a mountain. In the Pahlavi books, Gayomard was slain, his seed purified by the sun and preserved by Neryosangh, Ahura Mazda's messenger, and Spendarmad, guardian of the earth, until the birth of Mashya and Mashyanag, from whom generations of the human race appeared (*Bundahishn* XV: 1–6). At the time of the resurrection the bones of Gayomars will be the first to rise (XXX: 7). SS, FPM

109 • Brass bowl inlaid with scenes based on the *Shahnameh*

Artist: Turanshah • Iran • *c.*1351–2
Copper alloy engraved and overlaid in silver and gold
11.2 x 22.7 cm
Victoria and Albert Museum, London, Inv. no. 760–1889

The frieze shows six scenes of horsemen, loosely based on the Persian epic *Shahnameh*. In one scene, King Faridun is shown riding an ox, followed by a captive on foot. The snakes growing from the captive's shoulders identify him as the evil king Zahhak, whom Faridun overthrew. In the *Shahnameh*, Zahhak is the enemy from the Arab lands whom Ahriman kisses on both shoulders thereby causing two serpents to grow. Their daily diet must be the brains of two Iranian boys.

In the *Denkard*, Faridun attempts to cut off Zahhak's head, but this only increases the number of *khrafstras*, or noxious creatures, in the world. The *Bundahishn* describes how Ohrmazd advised Faridun to bind him, thereby restricting evil. In both the *Bundahishn* and *Bahman Yasht*, Zahhak is eventually slain by Kerespaspa, son of Thrita.[8] SS, FPM

left

110 • **Men worshipping at a fire altar and idol shrine**

*c.*1650–1700 • Purchased from Maggs Bros in 1949
Ink, opaque watercolour and gold on paper
20 x 13.10 cm (sheet)
British Museum 1949, 1210.0.7

With their hands held out in prayer, the four men in this painting demonstrate acts of worship associated with two different faiths. On the left, two men pray to a fire altar, most likely representing Zoroastrians. The right side of the composition, however, distinguished by an architectural framework suggestive of a shrine, is more difficult to interpret without an accompanying text. Identified as Europeans by their hats and dress, these two men appear to be worshipping an idol, once embellished in silver (now oxidized) and gold, distantly reminiscent of a seated Buddhist sculpture yet dressed in contemporary costume and crown.

It is possible that the painting, which was cropped and reformatted onto a gold-flecked page, once illustrated a copy of an Islamic cosmography belonging to the 'wonders-of-creation' genre first known to have been developed in thirteenth-century Iraq, Iran and Central Asia after the Mongol invasion.[9]
LA

above

111 • **Ilkhanid tile**

Iran, Shiz, Takht-e Suleyman • 15th century • Glazed tile
Mrs Fatema Soudavar Farmanfarmaian

A small (and rare) star tile from the Ilkhanid hunting lodge at Takht-e Suleyman. The motif shows the Iranian mythical bird, the *simorgh*, in sinicised form, in gold on a blue background. SS

The painting page shows Persian text in the manuscript cells surrounding the illustration.

112 • **The slaying of Iraj by his brother Tur**

Iran, Shiraz • *c.*1440–50
Provenance: H. P. Kraus Collection
Ink on dark cream lightly burnished paper
The Nasser D. Khalili Collection of Islamic Art, MSS 846v

This painting belongs to the early stages of the
Turkman School of Shiraz.[10] The scene of the crime
is a bed laid upon a carpet under a finely decorated
canopy. Tur's accomplice stands to the right, ready
to unsheath his sword.

Iraj and his two half-brothers, Tur and Salm, were
sons of the Iranian hero King Faridun (Avestan:
Thraetona), who belonged to the legendary Pishdadian dynasty of Iran. Faridun divided his realm
between his sons; Salm received the west (eastern
Roman Empire), Tur the east (Central Asia) and
Iraj the most coveted part, Iran. Unable to contain
their jealousy, the brothers conspired to murder Iraj.

The story in the *Shahnameh* draws on the heroes
and kings of the *Yashts* (particularly Yt. 13 and
Yt. 19) and evokes the parallel account contained
in the *Bundahishn* (31:7–11). It also marks the
beginning of endless battles between the Iranians
and Turanians,[11] echoing the time of 'mixture',
gumezishn, in Zoroastrian theology, which begins
with Ahriman's attack on the material creation. SS, FPM

113 • The *Simorgh* brings Zal to his father Sam from the mountain

Signed by Mo'in Mosavvir • Esfahan, Iran (Safavid) • 1660s
Ink on dark cream burnished paper
The Nasser D. Khalili Collection of Islamic Art, MSS 1070r

Zal and his father Sam were Saka princes of Zabulistan in Sistan. Born with hair the colour of moonlight, Zal was rejected by his father, abandoned in the mountains and left to die. The baby was noticed by the *Simorgh*, who carried him to her nest and reared him as her own, feeding him raw flesh instead of milk. When news of Zal's survival reached his father's ears, the old king, propelled by a prophetic dream, went in search of his son. Bidding farewell to Zal – 'let not thy heart forget to love thy nurse, for mine is breaking through my love of thee'[12] – the *Simorgh* returns Zal to his father. She gives him a feather that he can burn to summon her in time of need.

The illustration shows the joyousness of the occasion, with Zal riding in on the back of the *Simorgh*, holding on to her tail feathers for safety.[13] In the *Shahnameh*, Zal is attributed with the divine fortune, *farreh* (Avestan: *khvarenah*) in his campaigns against the Turanians and his bid to avenge the death of his grandfather, Iraj.[14] SS, FPM

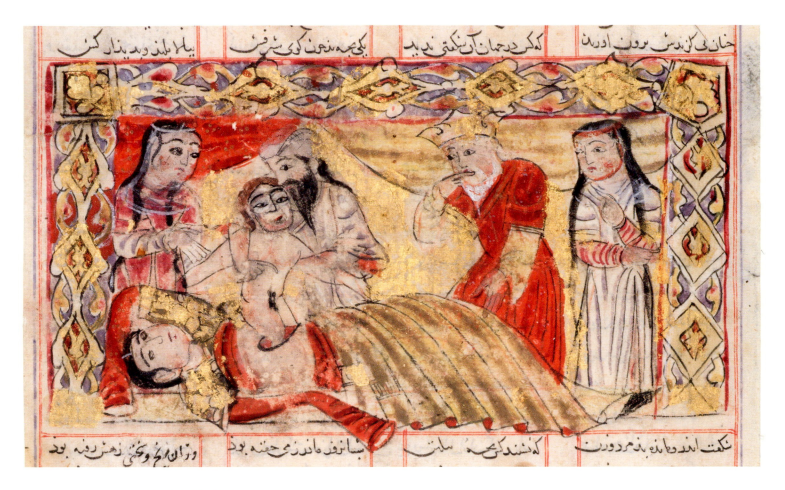

من كنت ندش بروس ادرن   لكنگردجهان آبریکتة ندبد   یکی جمه سخ کوی سرف   بلالا ملند ومدپذار كن

وزاروبم وتحن رهزردپه بود   بسانوف ماندزدمحبنه بود   کمشندکبحمه سلن   مکشندکپم پذمردوزن

114 • The birth of Rostam

A detached folio from the 'Stephens' *Shahnameh*
Iran, Shiraz • AH 753 (1352–3)
Provenance: H. P. Kraus Collection
Ink on dark cream burnished paper
The Nasser D. Khalili Collection of Islamic Art, MSS 920r

right

115 • Key Kavus's temporary ascent to heaven

Iran, probably Shiraz • *c.* 1600–20
Provenance: H. P. Kraus Collection
Ink on smooth cream lightly burnished paper
The Nasser D. Khalili Collection of Islamic Art, MSS 666

Zal fears that his wife, Rudabeh, will die in labour, and he burns a feather of the *Simorgh* to summon her. She instructs him as to how to perform a caesarean section. The painting shows a physician standing behind Rudabeh, who lies on a bed in the foreground of the picture.[15] Zal stands to the right, anxiously biting his finger.[16] SS, FPM

The painting depicts the Kayanian dynast Key Kavus (Avestan: Kavi Usan, Pahlavi: Kay Us) on a journey to conquer the heavens, having been persuaded by Ahriman that he could extend his rule beyond the earth. Four eagles chained to his throne carry it upwards in their endeavour to reach pieces of meat suspended on the ends of four spears.[17] In an apparent attempt to defy the heavenly world, Key Kavus aims his bow towards a divinity in the sky.[18]

In the Avesta, Key Kavus seeks rewards from the gods (yt. 5:45–7) and is accompanied by the *khvarenah* (*farreh*), or divine grace, which he loses as a result of his arrogance. His rule is marked by numerous battles against the Turanians and by episodes of repentance for various follies. In a typically Zoroastrian scene in the *Shahnameh*, Key Kavus goes to the fire temple with his grandson, the hero Key Khosrow, to make offerings and pray before the great fire temple of Azargushnasp for the successful capture and execution of the Turanian ruler Afrasiyab.[19] SS

پادشا بند کاوس بناز
سپاه و سوار کش در دمار
ورا دیدون کین کشتم کنار
خروشی بلم بر شهر برد
غم آمد جهان را زان کار بهر
همه دور جوشان و بکش کوی
یا شاه کاوس پر شرم شد
سری پرشرم دل سبکی دمش
فیری یزدان کین دمش
از انکشت سود او او شنید
جهانی بنوا و بکاوس کوی
تو کشی با آتش آتش بسوخت

زمره روز کیانیه همی بر کشیدا
یکسی سب و خود و پیاده وش مه
یکی شب بدیدگان جنون
کنا او ز آتش کی امه برون

116 • The fire ordeal of Siyavosh, son of Key Kavus
Iran • c.1600–20
Ink on smooth cream lightly burnished paper
The Nasser D. Khalili Collection of Islamic Art, MSS 452v

This painting shows Siyavosh, the son of Key Kavus, undergoing an ordeal by fire, to prove his innocence, following the accusation by his step-mother, Sudabeh, of violating her.[20] He urges his horse into the flames and re-emerges 'with rosy cheeks and smiles upon his lips'.[21]

The fiery ordeal took various forms in ancient Iran. The divinities presiding over it were Mithra and Rashnu ('one who judges'). In the Avesta, Rashnu is invoked to appear at the ordeal, where there is fire and *baresman* (*barsom*) – an indication that this was a religious ritual – boiling water and boiling ghee (YT. 12:5). Molten metal poured over a man's chest was another test of innocence and foreshadowed the eschatological vision of the Last Judgement, when all mankind will pass through a stream of molten metal. SS

overleaf
117 • Khosrow Parviz, rescued from Bahram Chubineh by the divinity Srosh
Iran, Shiraz • c.1485
Provenance: Hagop Kevorkian Collection;
H. P. Kraus Collection
Ink on smooth light-brown burnished paper
The Nasser D. Khalili Collection of Islamic Art, MSS 846

Khosrow Parviz, of Sasanian descent, and the Arsacid Bahram Chubin are rivals for the throne. Battles ensue between them, during one of which Khosrow Parviz is pursued up a blind canyon.[22] He prays to God, and the divinity Srosh (Avestan: Sraosha) appears, clad in green, to carry him to safety.[23] There follows a Zoroastrian scene in which a banquet is prepared by Khosrow Parviz and opened by a priest with a performance of the *barsom* ceremony.[24]

The illustration shows the hapless Bahram Chubin standing at the foot of the mountain, holding his mace and watching his enemy disappear.[25] SS

بدین جای بی چاره کی دوست گیر
کنو باشی پلاسم کیوان ویش
چو بیدار شو گشت خسرو دلیر

همه جامه سبز و خاک این نباش
بدید آمد ازراه فرخ سروش

هم اینک جواز کو بیند سروش
چو نزد یکی شد دست خود و کفت
ز یزدان پاک این نباش کفت

جواز پیش به جواه برد استشت
کسانی کاور دو بکد استشت
چو این سایان دور باش از خروش
برین سایان کبد زدشت سی
نباش زخم کس ن یار سا
جو دید ان جهان کار باکام او
نیا بد ازین بیچ تیزم رها
کراز تن نا بدیم جستن سری

فرشته بد وکت سروش
برین زود ایدرشسی می
چوتو کذار بر زمین پادشا
براش دل مرزه براذم او
اکرشم اید دم اثر ها
ندانم فرشته بد آن پا سی

بروکت خسروکه نام توچیت
توزین بس شوی بر جهان پادشا
کمن خون هرمز زاو کس پیچ
جوان دید بهرام خیره ماند
برین بخت خیره باید کرت
سی خواست از داد کرز یار

همی کت چندی وجندی کوچیست
نباش زنخم کبدان پا رسا
براکر که کشتن توکشتن بسیج
جهان آفرین رازدان جوا اند
بدآکنون که کنگ می بارست
تایا طوش ازان روی برکوشل

Following the invasions of the Seljuq Turks in the eleventh century and the Mongols thereafter, most of the surviving Zoroastrian literature was apparently destroyed, together with many fire temples, including the great fire of Karkoy in Sistan.[26] The two main priestly centres of Zoroastrianism were Yazd and Kerman, each with its Bahram fire and *Dastur Dasturan* or high priest. It was in these two cities that the remaining Zoroastrian population took refuge. In Kerman they were obliged to live outside the city walls, while Yazd had a *gabre mahalleh* or precinct for Zoroastrians. During the early Safavid period, a number of Zoroastrians were moved from Yazd and Kerman to work in the great court of Shah 'Abbas (r. 1587–1628), where they were employed as carpet-weavers, gardeners and grooms. Here they attracted the attention of European travellers, whose accounts depict the poverty and discrimination under which Zoroastrians lived. Conditions grew progressively worse for Zoroastrians in Isfahan under subsequent Safavid kings, and eventually they were given the option of death or conversion to Islam. Many died, but some fled to the city of Yazd and its surrounding villages.

118 & 119 • *Dakhma* objects

Collection: Alpaiwalla Museum

[above] Clockwise from top right: woven basket, spouted cup and earring, signet ring, finger ring, signet ring, bell, reels, spindle.
[below] Clockwise from top right: painted combs, wooden flute, wooden keys, dried fruit and twigs.

These objects were excavated by Jamshedji Maneckji Unvala from an old *dakhma* in Yazd in 1951. Normally, no personal belongings are left with the deceased in the *dakhma*. A severe outbreak of plague in the seventeenth century meant that infected items were relegated to the *dakhma* with the deceased. SS

120 • **Iranian Zoroastrian costume**
Yazd • early 20th century • Brocade, calico
Collection: Fereydoun Ave

The *kamiz* (see Cat. 124) is a loose upper garment that falls below the knee. It is stitched with alternating panels of red and green silk brocade and worn with a voluminous gathered trouser called the *shalvar*. A *kamiz* can be stitched with as many as 25 panels of silk, calico or thick cotton and is called *praneh-e tir o sikh*, the 'dress of arrow and thorn'. The *shalvar* is made from a variety of strips of silk joined by fine-running stitches referred to as *dandan-e mush*, 'the teeth of a mouse'. These display motifs from Zoroastrian myths, such as the three-legged ass, the *kar* fish or the Cypress tree.

The *makhnun*, or large scarf, is draped round the head, covering the shoulders and upper half of the body without concealing the face.[27] FPM

121-3 • Yazdi cloth
Yazd • early 20th century • Cotton
Collection: Fereydoun Ave

In nineteenth-century Iran there were a number of regulations governing the everyday lives of Zoroastrians. These were intended to marginalize and distinguish them from the majority Muslim population and included strict dress codes; Zoroastrian men were obliged to wear garments of yellow ochre or unbleached cloth. In Yazd and Kerman, Zoroastrians were not permitted to buy cloth by the yard. Shopkeepers would collect the strips of leftover fabric and leave them in bins outside their shops for Zoroastrians to buy. These were laboriously stitched together to make the *shalvar* and *kamiz* and were often embroidered with a variety of designs, including flowers, fish and geometric patterns.[28]

SS, FPM

From the mid to late nineteenth century – and mainly as a result of Parsi intervention – the condition of Zoroastrians in Iran began to improve. The establishment in Bombay of the Society for the Amelioration of the Conditions of the Zoroastrians in Persia and the work of its first emissary to Iran, Maneckji Limji Hataria, between 1854 and his death in 1890, resulted in the abolition of the *jizya* or poll tax. The internal governance of the community was structured through the establishment of *anjomans*, and the priesthood through the introduction of the Mobedan Council. As the Iranian Zoroastrian community began to prosper, and the Tehran population grew, wealth generated in both India and Iran was directed towards the establishment of schools and orphanages. By 1882, 12 Zoroastrian schools had been established in Iran.[29]

124
Zoroastrian lady in traditional dress

Collection:
Fereydoun Ave

125 • **Arbab Jamshid and his staff**
Tehran • *c.* 1903

Arbab Jamshid Jamshidian (1850–1932), seen here seated and wearing a scarf, was an influential Zoroastrian merchant and banker. By 1905 he employed over 100 Zoroastrians in Tehran alone and his company had offices across Iran as well as in Baghdad, Bombay, Calcutta and Paris. During the Constitutional Revolution (1906–11) prominent Zoroastrian merchants, including Jamshidian and members of the Jahanian merchant company, provided weapons and funds for the revolutionaries in the hope that a constitutional government would lead to greater rights for Zoroastrians. When the National Consultative Assembly (Majles) was established in 1906, Jamshidian was appointed as the first Zoroastrian representative.[30] AB

127 • **The Agency House in Tehran**
Tehran • *c.* 1904

In the early twentieth century, the majority of Zoroastrians in Iran lived in and around the towns of Yazd and Kerman, although the Zoroastrian population in Tehran was growing steadily, reaching 324 by 1903, and 500 by 1912. As in the nineteenth century, many Zoroastrians in Tehran worked as gardeners but some were now engaged in commercial activities. On the whole, greater tolerance was shown towards Zoroastrians in Tehran than to those living in the provinces.[32] AB

126 • **Zoroastrian schoolboys in Tehran**
Tehran • *c.* 1903

A group of Zoroastrian schoolboys with their teacher, Kayomars Vafadar (seated in the foreground), and some of the employees of Arbab Jamshid Jamshidian. In 1908 Jamshidian built the first formal Zoroastrian school house in Tehran which was called Jamshid Jam.[31] AB

128 • **Arbab Kaikhosro Shahrokh**
Tehran • *c.*1910

Arbab Kaikhosro Shahrokh (1874–1940) was born
in Kerman and educated in Tehran and Bombay.
He moved to Tehran in *c.*1905 where he worked for
Arbab Jamshid Jamshidian. In 1909 he succeeded
Jamshidian as the Zoroastrian representative in the
Majles, a position he held until 1940. Respected in the
Majles, Shahrokh used his position to champion the
rights of religious minorities. He was also involved
in community affairs, presiding over the Tehran
Zoroastrian Anjuman from 1909 until his death. He
was instrumental in the transition from the *dakhma*
system to burial amongst Zoroastrians in Iran.[33] AB

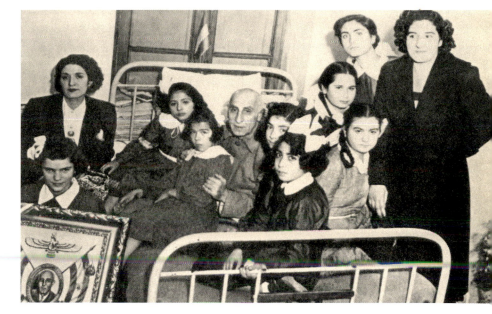

130
Prime Minister Mossadeq with Zartoshty children
*c.*1951

Conditions for the Zoroastrians in Iran improved
further during the Pahlavi monarchy (1925–79), in
part due to the extolling of the pre-Islamic period
and the secularization of society. This photograph
shows a group of Zoroastrians with Dr Mohammad
Mossadeq, the prime minister of Iran from 1951
until 1953. Many Zoroastrians were enraged by the
overthrow of Mossadeq in 1953, which was backed
by the British and the Americans.[35] AB

129 • **A house belonging to a rich Parsi (Persian)**
Tehran, Atabak Park • *c.*1908

Atabak Park was the summer palace of the grand
vizier Amin-al-soltan (also known by his title Atabak-e
A'zam) who was assassinated in August 1907. The
property was bought by Arbab Jamshid Jamshidian,
the Zoroastrian representative in the Majles at the
time. Jamshidian allowed the house to be used by
the Persian government and it was here that the
American Morgan Shuster, who had been appointed
treasurer-general by the Majles, stayed in 1911.[34] AB

7 JOURNEY AND SETTLEMENT

Sarah Stewart and Ursula Sims-Williams
with Alan Williams

Traditionally the history of Zoroastrianism in India begins, as related in the *Qesseh-ye Sanjan* (Cat. 134), with the story of Muslim persecution in Iran and the ensuing emigration that followed during the eighth to tenth centuries CE. However, our knowledge is largely dependent on texts which, in one way or another, look back on the past in a nostalgic manner characteristic of religious traditions. In reality, Iranians had spread eastwards along established trade routes well before the advent of Islam[1] and continued to settle long afterwards. That there were groups of 'Parsis' (*Parsiyan*) with diverse beliefs in north-west India is confirmed by the author Mobed Shah (Cat. 132) who recounts his meetings with them between 1630 and 1642. One of these, the Akhshi sect, a representative of which he met in Kashmir in 1631, even promoted next-of-kin marriages.[2] In the sixteenth century, the Mughal emperor Akbar's historiographer, Abu'l-Fazl, wrote that in his youth he had consulted with *mobeds* and sought to discover the secrets of the Zendavesta.[3] Zoroastrian motifs such as the *mobed* and the fire temple were incorporated into and became a normal component of Persian literary culture in the subcontinent which peaked between the sixteenth and nineteenth centuries.

overleaf
131 • Khosrow and Shirin visit a fire temple
India • 22 Muharram 1139 (19 September 1726)
Provenance: Nathaniel Bland (1803–65)
Ink on paper
British Library Or.2933, ff. 90v–91r

This painting, dating from the reign of the Mughal Emperor Muhammad Shah (r. 1719–48), depicts a scene from the twelfth-century poet Nizami's tale of Khosrow and Shirin, the romantic story of the Sasanian ruler Khosrow Parviz and his queen the Armenian princess Shirin. The scene illustrated here shows the couple with a *mobed*, about to worship at a fire temple.

Nizami's poems were amongst the most popular Persian works in India at this period. This unusual copy is an abridgement containing, according to the colophon, only 1522 verses out of the normal 6500. It includes 63 paintings, many of which depict subjects, such as this one, which are not normally found in other copies. USW

right
132 • A re-invention of pre-Islamic cosmology
India • 17th century • Ink on paper
Provenance: Richard Johnson (1753–1807)
British Library IO Islamic 746, ff. 15v–16r

Mobed Shah, the author of this popular seventeenth-century encyclopaedia, the *Dabestan-e Mazaheb* ('School of Religions'), came from a Zoroastrian background and offered a unique non-partisan account of the diverse religions of India.[4] His starting point was the religion of the Parsis (*Parsiyan*) or Iranians (*Iraniyan*), which he subdivided into 15 parts. A substantial section was devoted to the Zoroastrians and incorporated the texts of the *Arda Viraf Nameh* (Cats 101 and 102), and also the *Sad Dar* (Cat. 135).

The pages illustrated here come from an earlier part of the section on Parsis which was devoted to a description of the esoteric and syncretic beliefs of Azar Kayvan, a Zoroastrian high priest who emigrated from Fars to Gujarat during the reign of the Mughal Emperor Akbar (r. 1526–1605). Azar Kayvan presented a re-interpretation of pre-Islamic Iranian cosmology. This included worship of the seven planetary deities as illustrated here. On the right is a statue of Kayvan (Saturn) carved out of black stone, in human form, with an ape's head and a pig's tail, holding a sieve and a snake. On the left Hormazd (Jupiter), earthy coloured, with a vulture's head, wears a crown in the shape of a cock and a dragon's head and holds a turban and crystal ewer. USW

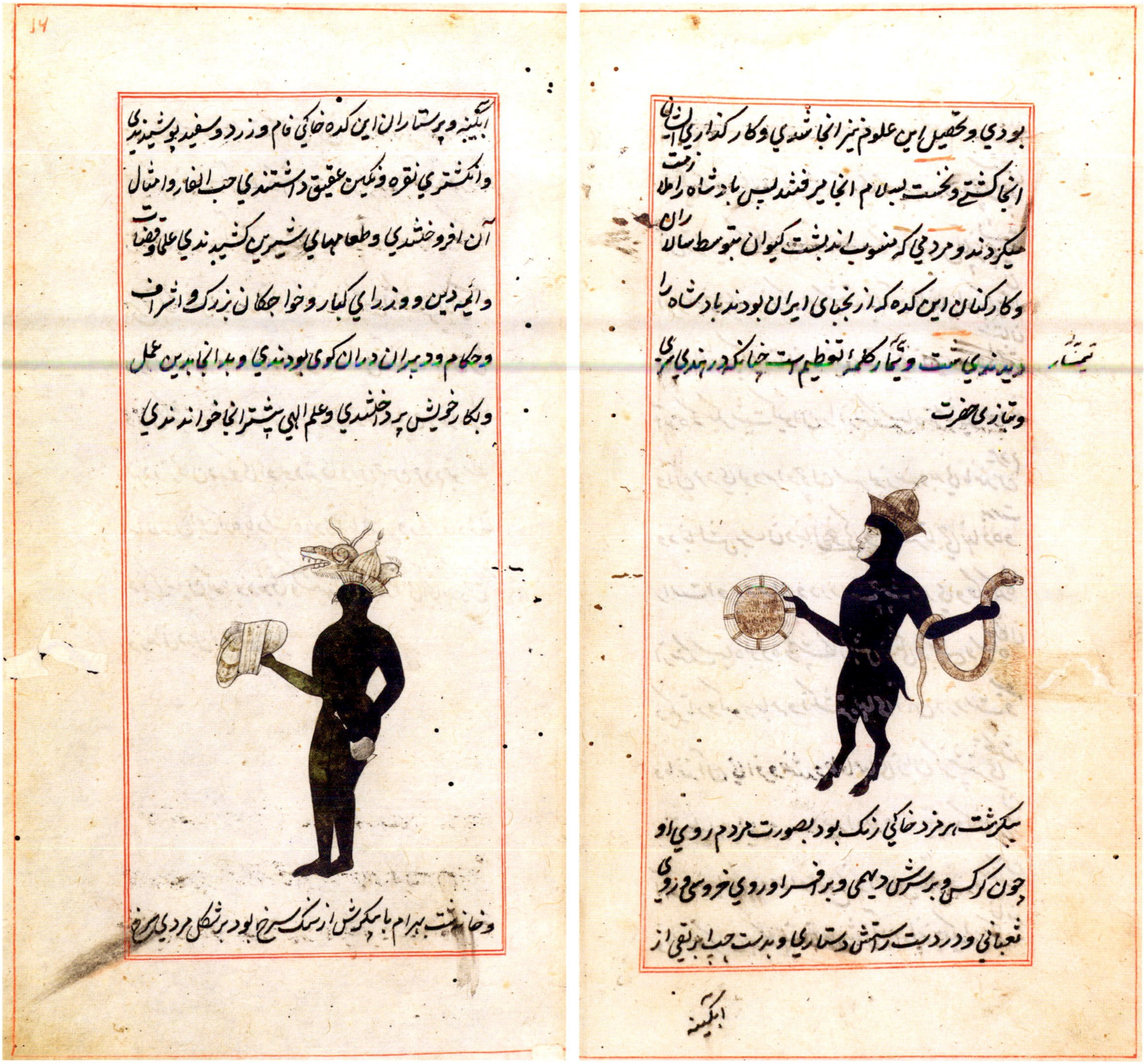

جوانی دارد بش زمستان بحول | به پیری تو سستی کرده فراموش

رفتن خسرو با آتشخانه و نشستن شیر بریه

چو خسرو رخت بست و شبر و بتخت | خو خسرور با آتشخانه اندرخت

که آتشخانه نه باشد جای خسرو | جهان آقا در زان بس نمی خسرو

زد و راه در سه را پاس سلست | نوشانوش می در کاس سست

که بر شیرین کسی بگذاشت مارا | در آن لحظی خیالی داشت باو

که آدر بندگی مستم آزاد | دل خسرو و نسرین آنجای شاد

کمنجی در جهان خرسند که بش | بدان نگذاشت اخری نندی کردش

دلش شاد و می خورد مس می کنی | شگرایب بیز فارغ رو بنو دی

کنجی شادی کنی می نبا رشید | که در دولت جبین بسیار یا بند

یکی کوهر دود دیگر که زا بست | و بکس برارو کار آرام داد

بدین شکلن زن خسرو سوزی | بدین افسانه خوش گشتی نش زمین

133 • The life of Zoroaster in Persian verse
India • 17th century • Ink on paper
Provenance: Thomas Hyde (1636–1703)
British Library Reg.16. B.8, ff. 9v–10r

The *Zaratosht Nameh*, a hagiographical portrayal of the life of Zoroaster, was written by Key Ka'us ebn Key Khosrow ebn Dara, in Rayy (Iran) in the thirteenth century as a deliberate attempt to keep the old traditions alive by writing about them in Persian verse. Subsequently copied by Zartosht ebn Bahram ebn Pazhdu (who is often understood to be the author) in Bizhanabad (near Jiruft, Kerman) in 1278, it became a favourite work in India and many copies exist, almost all, like the one shown here, based on a manuscript written by Khosrow Mavandad in the year 853 Yazdegerdi (1483 CE).[5]

Thomas Hyde's copy, shown here, dates from the seventeenth century and includes 59 blank spaces which were obviously intended to be illustrated. The pages on view describe the miraculous birth of Zoroaster, how he laughed at birth, how the jealous king of the sorcerers attempted to stab him but his hand withered, how he was struck with pain and anguish and writhed like a snake. These traditions are found in pre-Islamic Zoroastrian literature, but their presentation here owes much to Islamic literary conventions. USW

THE ARRIVAL IN GUJARAT

The port of Sanjan in Gujarat is thought to be the first major centre of Zoroastrianism in western India. Excavations have revealed a thriving seaport city which was occupied from the eighth to the thirteenth centuries CE. A brick and mud mortar *dakhma*, which can be dated to the tenth or eleventh century, is the earliest specifically Zoroastrian structure in India.[6]

The *Qesseh-ye Sanjan* (Cat. 134), though written down much later (1599), is unique in giving an account of the journey of Zoroastrians from their homeland in Iran to India in search of religious freedom. It can be regarded as perhaps the most important 'historic' narrative in Parsi Zoroastrian literature, though it is now seen as primarily mythical and poetic in form and content.[7]

The tradition of the *Qesseh-ye Sanjan* has it that the Zoroastrians initially settled in Sanjan, and thereafter established themselves along the seaport towns of Gujarat, spreading inland to rural areas. They lived as farmers, small-time merchants and liquor-traders, occupying a similar status to that of Muslims, existing on the periphery of Hindu society; through their economic activities, they would have maintained a place comparable to that of the Vaishiyas in the Hindu caste system.[8]

The Parsi settlers had brought with them no fixed code of law from Iran, and were subject to the jurisdiction of the ruling power. Civil and religious disputes which occurred within the community were settled by the priesthood. Traditional religious texts remained in currency in Persian (and Gujarati) translation, such as the *Sad Dar*, giving practical advice on matters legal and ethical which would have affected the community. Where agreement could not be reached, advice was sought from priests in Iran. Their correspondence (*rivayat*) from the fifteenth to the eighteenth centuries was recorded and

subsequently consulted as providing normative answers to questions of religious law, belief and ritual practice (Cat. 136). At the beginning of the eighteenth century, when disputes broke out between the Bhagaria and the Sanjana priesthoods, the local Hindu ruler was asked to intervene.

With respect to the priesthood, it seems that by the late thirteenth century, priests had divided Gujarat into five *panthaks* or parishes with a hereditary priesthood in each. Sanjan, which was the home of the only Atash Bahram, remained the foremost parish, followed by Navsari with its Bhagaria priest-hood,[9] and then the parishes of Godavara, Broach and Cambay. The origin of the first Atash Bahram is known from the account in the *Qesseh-ye Sanjan* alone, which mentions the donation of land by the local Hindu ruler, Jadi Rana, and describes the restrictions surrounding the ritual consecration of this first Atash Bahram outside Iran. The account refers to the ritual implements – the ritual sources and prerequisites of such an inauguration – as having been brought from Khorasan in north-east Iran, which suggests that they were brought overland, since a sacred fire could not, by religious law, have been transported by sea.

The author of the *Qesseh-ye Sanjan*, the high priest (*dastur*) Bahman Key Qobad of Navsari, completed his poem of 432 verse couplets in 1599 CE – the only date in the entire work. His story is based on 'the lore of priests and ancient sages' heard from 'a wise *dastur*' and encompasses the history of the Zoroastrian community from the days of Zoroaster up to the late fifteenth century.

The two pages illustrated cover 115 years, from the death of Yazdegerd: 'From that time forth Iran was smashed to pieces!', to the Zoroastrians' long sojourn in the mountains and their flight to Hormuz. There the *dastur* looks into his astrological tables and announces: 'At last our life is finished here', and they embark upon their sea journey to India. USW

The *Sad Dar* ('100 doors') came to be regarded as one of the most important Zoroastrian pedagogical texts, with several different versions existing in prose and verse. Intended for practical use, it gives compulsory rules on 100 topics which range from justifying instant death for sodomy to the treatment of good and evil animals, and the avoidance of different forms of pollution. This chapter lays down rules for wearing the *kusti* ('sacred girdle' see Cat. 184).[10]

This particular manuscript is a prose version written in the Persian language, but in Avestan script (right to left), together with a Gujarati translation (left to right, hence upside down). It was probably copied from a manuscript which was sent to India from Iran with the *Rivayat* of Kamdin Shapur in 1558, together with an illustrated *Arda Viraf Nameh*.[11] According to the colophon (which may in fact be copied from an earlier manuscript) the scribe was Padam Ram, the recipient of the above mentioned *Rivayat*. USW

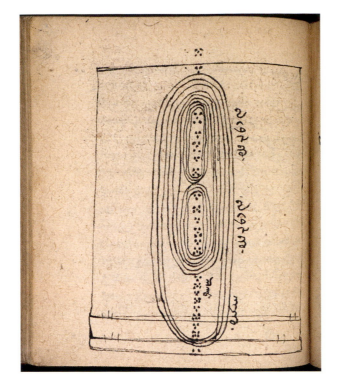

136 · *Rivayat* (questions and answers)
Copyist: Peshotan Faridun Homji
probably Navsari • *c.* 1651 • Ink on paper
Provenance: Samuel Guise (1751–1811)
British Library MSS Avestan 8, f. 81r

Although many Avestan and Pahlavi texts were translated into Gujarati and Sanskrit between the twelfth and fifteenth centuries, a need to maintain a knowledge of the old traditions embodied in the Avestan and Pahlavi texts led the Parsi priests to establish closer links with Zoroastrian communities in Iran. Letters were exchanged between the two communities consisting mostly of questions and answers on ritual practice, but sometimes also asking for copies of texts. These *Rivayat* (in the form of letters, often called 'questions and answers') date from between the fifteenth and the eighteenth centuries and were regarded as authoritative guides on ritual practice. Although the text is in Persian, they were sometimes, as in this example, written in Avestan script.

The section on display discusses the question as to how the *bagh-e bareshnom* (i.e. the 'garden' where the *bareshnom*, or nine-night purification ceremony, is administered) should be laid out together with a plan. The description includes quotations from the ninth chapter of the *Videvdad* (Cat. 18).[12] In the diagram the dots represent groups of five stones (originally these would have been dug pits) separated from each other by groups of three stones. The lines represent furrows enclosing the ritual space. USW

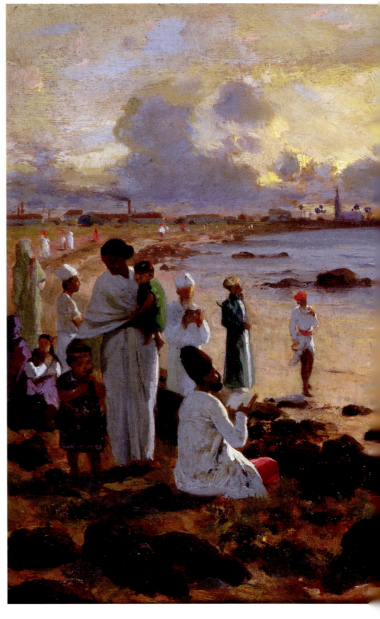

❀

By 1600 Navsari, Broach, Cambay and Surat had become established centres of merchant trade. The principal activities of these towns were shipbuilding, shipping, carpentry and weaving, and those engaged in these activities formed a distinct socio-economic group. From the early seventeenth century Parsis were drawn into the various foreign factories in Gujarat, particularly that of the English East India Company in Surat. By the end of the eighteenth century, the British had begun to assume military and political power in that town, and relations between them and the Parsis there deteriorated. This factor, together with the continued incursions of Maratha tribes, and a famine in 1790 which affected the whole of Gujarat, caused Parsis from Surat as well as other rural settlements and cities in Gujarat to begin migrating to Bombay.

137 • Parsis at prayer
Artist: Horace van Ruith (1839–1923)
Florence, 1900–20 • Oil painting on board • 20.5 x 43.5 cm
British Library F 593

Parsis at prayer, the shoreline of Bombay in the distance. The artist, Horace Van Ruith, was a professional painter who specialized in portraiture, landscapes and genre scenes in oil and watercolour. He visited Bombay some time between 1879 and 1884 where he is known to have established a studio. USW

of their Law inioyned to keepe the *Behedins* precepts, without violation, but also to fulfill these eleuen Precepts more, as particular to himselfe.

First, to know in what manner to pray to God, obseruing the rites prescribed in the *Zundauastaw*, for God is best pleased with that forme of prayer, that he hath giuen in his owne booke.

The second, to keepe his eyes from coueting or desiring any thing that is anothers, for God hath giuen euery man what he thinkes meete for him; and to desire that which is anothers, is not onely to dislike of Gods disposure of his owne gifts, but to chalenge to himselfe that which God hath denied him, and whereof hee seeth him vnworthie.

The third, to haue a care euer to speake the truth, for all truth commeth from God, and as it is most communicated to men of God, so they should most shew it in their wordsand Actions : but Lucifer is the Father of falshood, and whosoeuer vseth

it,

it, it may be a signe that the euill spirit is powerfull with such a one, the Herbood therefore shall shew himselfe to bee contrarie to him, by his speaking the truth, for all men must giue credite to his words.

The fourth, to bee knowne onely in his owne busynes, and not to enquire after the things of the world, it belonging onely to him to teach others what God would haue them doe. Therefore the Behedin or Lay man shall see that hee want nothing needfull, but shall affoord it him, and hee shall seeke nothing superfluous.

The fift, to learne the Zundauastaw by heart, that hee may be ready to teach it to the Behedin or Lay man, wheresoeuer he meeteth him, for from him must the people fetch their knowledge concerning God.

The sixt, to keepe himselfe pure and vndefiled from things polluting, as from the Carkeyses of the dead, or touching meates vncleane, for God is pure, whose seruant hee is, and it is expected hee should be such, abhorring the sight of all things that are

V   foule

The sixteenth century marked the beginning of established European settlements in western India, with the Portuguese conquest of Goa in 1510 and the establishment of the East India Company factory at Surat in 1612. Henry Lord, appointed chaplain in 1624, wrote the first substantial account of Zoroastrianism, *The Religion of the Persees*, published in 1630 (Cat. 138). Unlike previous published descriptions of Zoroastrianism, it was based on personal observation. In the introduction, he writes that he studied with a Zoroastrian priest and with the help of an English-speaking Parsi, 'I gained the knowledge of what hereafter I shall deliver, as it was compiled in a booke writ in the Persian Character, containing their Scripture, and in their owne language, called their ZUNDAVASTAVV.'

The sixteenth century was also a time of increased European awareness of Persian and Arabic sources. The first writer to combine a knowledge of these with contemporary travellers' personal accounts such as Henry Lord's in addition to the well-known classical sources was Thomas Hyde (1636–1703), Professor of Arabic and Hebrew at Oxford University and also translator to the King. His *History* (Cat. 139) represents a landmark in the understanding of Zoroastrianism in Europe and remained a standard work until Anquetil du Perron's translation *Le Zend-Avesta* (Cat. 140) was published in 1771 and much later became accepted as a genuine work.

138 • Henry Lord, *The Religion of the Persees*

London: F. Constable • 1630 • Printed book
Provenance: Mary Boyce collection
Ancient India and Iran Trust MB.a.1114. pp. 32–3

Henry Lord's account of Zoroastrianism dates from the early sixteenth century, and is roughly contemporary with Mobed's *Dabistan* (Cat. 132). His description of the early history of the Parsis in Gujarat is similar in some respects to that in the *Qesseh-ye Sanjan* (Cat. 134) and he describes the creation, the life of Zarathustra and Parsi rites and ceremonies in basically traditional terms.

Additionally he describes the five rules of the laymen (*behdin*) which included ever present shame, fear, thinking about whether an action was good or bad, praising God for the first creature to be seen every day, and facing the sun or moon when praying. The 11 rules of the priests (*herbad*) are shown here and these were followed by 13 more which the chief priest (*dastur*) had to obey. These involved maintaining the strictest purity, receiving and spending the tithe received from laymen for charitable purposes, a knowledge of the whole Avesta including the parts on astrology and medicine, and maintaining the sacred fire. USW

TAB.VI.
pag.305.

Ex Mausoleo Persepolitano Rex coram Igne et Sole quasi adoraturus
stans, cujus Anima ceu Icuncula in nube ad coelum ascensura cernitur.

Honoratissimo et Illustrissimo Viro IOHANNI DOMINO SOMMERS Baroni
de Evesham, omnium bonarum Literarum Possessori et Patrono, hanc Tabulam
summa Gratitudinis ergo lubens merito humiliter DDD Autor T. H.

139 · Thomas Hyde, *Historia religionis veterum Persarum* (History of the Persian Religion)

Oxonii: e Theatro Sheldoniano · 1700 · Printed book
Provenance: Mary Boyce Collection
Ancient India and Iran Trust, Mary Boyce Collection, p. 305

The polymath Thomas Hyde (1636–1703) was additionally an avid collector.[13] His collection of Zoroastrian manuscripts was the earliest in Europe and included copies of the *Zaratosht Nameh* (Cat. 133), the *Arda Viraf Nameh* (Cat. 102) and the poetic version of the *Sad Dar* ('100 rules'), of which he included a Latin translation in his *History*. He also owned copies of the *Yasna* (Cat. 17) and the *Khordeh Avesta* (Cat. 19). Although he never travelled to the East nor understood Avestan, he learned the script and was the first to create Avestan type for printing. This engraving of one of the royal Achaemenid tombs at Persepolis shows the king worshipping at a fire altar. USW

COMMENCEMENT DU VENDIDAD SADE.

Tom. I. Pag. 77.

B. F.

Calqué sur l'original de la Bibliotheque du Roi.

Ell.ᵉ Haussard Sculp.

140 · Anquetil du Perron *Le Zend-Avesta*

Paris: N. M. Tilliard · 1771 · Printed book
Provenance: H. W. Bailey Collection
Ancient India and Iran Trust, B8 A23, vol. I, pt. 2, p. 76

In 1754 the Frenchman Anquetil du Perron (1731–1805) was shown four leaves copied from a fragment of the *Videvdad Sadeh* brought in 1723 to the Bodleian Library, Oxford, by Richard Colbe. On the basis of this he determined to travel to Kerman or Gujarat to study and translate the Zoroastrian scriptures. After arriving in India in 1755, Anquetil du Perron eventually reached Surat in 1758 where he studied with Dastur Darab (whose library was subsequently purchased by Samuel Guise) and Dastur Ka'us. In 1761 he left India with a collection of 180 manuscripts which were deposited in the Bibliothèque du Roi (now the Bibliothèque nationale de France). Anquetil du Perron was the first European to attempt a translation of the Avesta, although it was many years before the full value of his work was realized. The page reproduced here is copied from the beginning of his manuscript of the *Videvdad Sadeh*. USW

8 PARSI SALON

Firoza Punthakey Mistree

The Parsis who began to settle in Bombay from the seventeenth century onwards came largely in search of work. In 1662 the Portuguese ceded Bombay to the English when Catherine of Braganza married Charles II, and six years later the East India Company (paying an annual rent of ten pounds) took over the seven islands of Bombay from the crown and established a factory there. This marked the decline of Surat, which until then had been the chief trading port, and resulted in the increasing importance of Bombay as a trading centre. The sacking of Surat in 1670 by the Maratha chief Shivaji brought an increasing number of Parsis to Bombay; three years later, the community established a Punchayat or five-member governing body that signified their permanent settlement in Bombay. By 1684 the East India Company had transferred its headquarters to the city, which meant that ships stopped there instead of at Surat, and all trade, including trade from the hinterland, was routed through Bombay.

The Parsis were largely traders, builders, farmers, craftsmen and weavers, who specialized in weaving fine cotton goods and silk brocade. Their close relationship with the British had been established while Surat had remained the headquarters of the East India Company. Rustom Maneck had been the chief broker for the company's factory and had accompanied its president to the court of Aurangzeb to help resolve a dispute between the English and the Nawab of Surat (Cat. 211). By the end of the seventeenth century, families such as Rustomji Dorabji, who built the walls of the Fort of Bombay, and the Hirji Vatcha Modi family, who erected the first Tower of Silence on Malabar Hill and a fire temple in Bombay, had developed a flourishing trading network. Among those who came from Gujarat were members of the Wadia family. They were employed to build the docks of Bombay and later became ship-builders and ship-owners.

141 • [left to right]
Hirjeebhoy Merwanjee Wadia (1817–83), Jehangeer Nowrojee Wadia (1821–66) and Dorabjee Muncherjee Nanjivohra
Artist: J. R. Jobins • 1842
painted from a photograph taken in 1840 • 74.9 x 66.7 cm
Collection: Hameed Haroon

On 29 March 1838, two young Parsi cousins, Hirjeebhoy Merwanjee Wadia and Jehangeer Nowrojee Wadia, left for England accompanied by their cousin Nanjivohra and two Parsi servants. They had been apprenticed at the Bombay docks and came to England to learn the art of ship-building at Chatham. Wadia family members built a number of ships for the British Admiralty, including the oldest surviving British warship, HMS *Trincomalee*, which was built in 1817.[1] FPM

❋

The arrival in China of two Parsis, Hirji and Mancherji Readymoney, in 1756 marked the beginning of what was to become an immensely lucrative trade with China. The primary products exported from India to China were cotton and opium, and by the early nineteenth century Parsis dominated both the China trade and the ship-building industry. Their success as entrepreneurs, according to some historians, helped to strengthen British imperialism and fortified the economies of both India and England.

The fast-moving clippers that sailed into Bombay harbour came laden with goods: the finest of tea, silk brocade and embroidered sari lengths, *garas*, lacquered furniture, curios, porcelain and portraits done by Chinese artists filled their holds. This merchandise was paid for by vast quantities of silver generated from the sale of opium.

A small but significant number of portraits of Parsis testify to their presence in China. These were painted in the ateliers of Chinese artists such as Lamqua (also called Guan Qiachang) and Sunqua, whose studio was in China Street, Canton. Henry Moses, the British artist who visited Jamsetjee Jejeebhoy's home in 1840, described walls hung with 'portraits of celebrated mandarins, well executed in water colours by Chinese artists'.[2]

right
142 • **Unidentified Parsi with fob watch**
Artist: Sunqua (active 1860–70)
Canton • post 1860 • Oil on canvas • 94 x 73.7 cm
Collection: Hameed Haroon

This portrait is by Sunqua, a nineteenth-century Chinese artist who specialized in portraiture and seascapes for export to the European market. His trade albums, covering Canton and Macao street life, were popular souvenirs, depicting hawkers, snake charmers, tea sellers and especially dogs. He had large studios in both Macao and Canton, where he trained a number of artists. The canvas bears his name in yellow paint on the side of the portrait where the canvas is folded and stapled over the stretched frame.[5] FPM

overleaf, left
143 • **Portrait of Framji Pestonjee Patuck (1800–40) and his son Kaikhushru Framji Patuck (1826–51)**
Canton • 1833 • Oil on canvas • 83.5 x 63.9 cm
Gift of S. Patuck
CSMVS, Mumbai: 24.4682

Framji Pestonjee Patuck started work in Canton in the firm of the most successful China trader of the time, Sir Jamsetjee Jejeebhoy. In 1837 he returned to India and invested in the cotton and opium trade. In the 1839 *Bombay Calendar and Almanac*, Framji's name appears as a ship-builder and owner. This evocative portrait depicts Framji and his son Kaikhushru while resident in what was known as the 'foreign concession', namely one of the 13 factories where non-Chinese traders were allowed to live. Father and son are depicted in traditional dress; to their right, a house fire used for daily worship burns in a silver fire vase. This is perhaps one of the finest ethnographic portrayals of Parsis in China.[3] FPM

overleaf, right
144 • **Framji Pestonjee Patuck (1800–40)**
Canton • 1835 • Oil on canvas • 83 x 63.8 cm
Gift of S. Patuck
CSMVS, Mumbai: 24.4681

This portrait of Framji Patuck, at the height of his success, is reminiscent of the nineteenth-century artist George Chinnery. The costume worn by the sitter, the shawl draped on the arm, the handlebar moustache and the glowing rouge-laden Chinner-esque cheeks closely resemble a painting of Jamsetjee Jejeebhoy, also presumed to be by Chinnery. It seems likely that both portraits are of the same person, either Jamsetjee Jejeebhoy or Framji Patuck.[4] FPM

146 · Ratan Dadabhoy Tata (1856–1926)
Artist: unknown • probably Shanghai • *c.* 1880–1910
Oil on canvas • 76.2 x 61 cm
Tata Central Archives, Poona

As with many Parsi merchants of the nineteenth century, Ratan Dadabhoy Tata started his professional life in Hong Kong, having been sent there by his father to manage the family firm Tata and Co. He opened branches in Kobe, New York and Paris, trading in rice, pearls and silk. When business in China declined, he worked for his uncle Jamsetji Tata in the newly established Empress Mills. He played a role in building India's first steel-manufacturing plant, Tata Iron and Steel, and helped to set up the Indian Institute of Science, which produced the first batch of locally trained Indian scientists.[7] FPM

❀

The development of the Bombay port and the railways, the invention of the telegraph in 1844 and the opening of the Suez Canal in 1869 all facilitated trade and contributed to the unprecedented wealth created by the China merchants, who not only continued to export large quantities of opium to China, despite sanctions against it, but also exported cotton to England during the shortage created by the exigencies of the American Civil War.

145 · Nusserwanji Ratan Tata (1822–86)
Artist: Attributed to the school of Pestonjee Bomanjee
c. 1860 • Oil on canvas • 106.7 x 81.3 cm
Tata Central Archives, Poona

Nusserwanji Tata, the doyen of the Tata family, started life as an ordained priest in Navsari, Gujarat. He moved to Bombay, set up the firm Nusserwanji and Kaliandas General Merchants and traded with China. In December 1859 he opened a branch in Hong Kong and, later, one in Shanghai. From China the firm exported tea, silk, camphor, cinnamon, copper, brass and Chinese gold. He was a commissariat contractor during the Abyssinian war, which made him a wealthy man. Men such as Nusserwanji Tata represented a new India in which aggressive entrepreneurs willing to take risks worked as commissioning agents.[6] FPM

147 • Engraving of Sir Jamsetjee Jejeebhoy (1783–1859)
Artist: John Smart, engraver: R. J. Lane
*c.*1850 • Engraving on paper • 42.5 x 30.9 cm
Royal Asiatic Society: RAS 089.009

148 • Dhunbai Jamsetji Tata (1861–71)
Artist: P. B. Hatte • 1906 • Oil on canvas • 69.2 x 59.1 cm
Collection: Hameed Haroon

Sir Jamsetjee Jejeebhoy worked with the British firm Jardine Matheson to corner much of the China trade going out of Bombay. To avoid paying the high freight rates imposed by ship-owners, he became an independent ship-owner and over time owned more than seven vessels, all fitted out as swift-moving opium clippers. He was a philanthropist, using his wealth to build hospitals, art schools, water wells, tanks and schools. He was knighted in 1842 and, in 1857, became the first Indian baronet. Portraits in his honour are displayed in Bombay, London and Hong Kong, the three cities that were at the centre of his business world.[8] FPM

This is a posthumous portrait of Dhunbai Tata, daughter of Jamsetji Tata, the leading industrialist of the nineteenth century. It was probably painted from a photograph taken of her after her *navjote* ceremony. Tata Central Archives in Poona records a number of identical photographs of her. Her jewellery immediately identifies her as a person of considerable wealth. FPM

Prosperity brought with it social changes. Travellers and missionaries visiting Bombay at the time commented on the lavish lifestyle of the Parsis. The most famous merchant was Sir Jamsetjee Jejeebhoy. His mansion, decorated in Chinese and European styles, was in sharp contrast to the sewage-laden back streets of Bombay and its poverty-stricken populace.

The fashion for having one's portrait painted was adopted by Parsis to mark their stay in China. Portraits were also commissioned as gifts for friends and families back in India. The art of portraiture became increasingly important during the eighteenth century, when European artists, encouraged by the East India Company, flourished in India. In Bombay, after the establishment of the Sir J.J. School of Art, portraiture became especially popular among the Parsis, who commissioned paintings to mark special events, such as initiation ceremonies, *navjote*s and to commemorate those who had died.

149 • *Navjote* portrait of an unidentified Parsi girl

Probably Canton • Late 19th century
Oil on canvas • 86.4 x 72.4 cm
Collection: Hameed Haroon

Portrait of a young Parsi girl in a yellow *tanchoi* brocade coatee. Her head is covered with a velvet cap, embroidered in *zari* work (stitched with gold or silver thread) and worn by Parsi children on special occasions, such as initiation ceremonies. FPM

✿

Bombay in the late nineteenth century was home to many stores selling furniture, furnishings, crockery, cutlery and silverware imported from England. British stores such as the Army and Navy, and Evans and Fraser, thrived in a city that prospered on money made in the opium and cotton trades. Ships carrying French porcelain, Bohemian glass and Italian statuary made their way to the Bombay port.

facing page
150 • 19th-century dining room of Jamsetji Tata

Bombay • Late 19th century
Tata Central Archives, Poona: Res-A08-015

In this view of Jamsetji Tata's dining room at Esplanade House, Bombay, a dining table is laid out in Western style with decorative objects typical of the home of a wealthy Parsi of the nineteenth century. A large portrait of his daughter-in-law, Lady Navajbai Tata, is visible (now in the CSMVS, Mumbai). FPM

top
151 • **Minton tea service**
Minton Factory, Staffordshire • *c.* 1810
Bone china, painted pattern no. 539
Private collection

This china tea service is in the 'New Oval' shape that was particularly popular during the early nineteenth century in England and, with its Chinese motifs, is typical of the kind of china that appealed to wealthy Parsis in India. FPM

right
152 • **Wooden cupboard with carving of Zarathustra**
Gujarat, India • 1880 • Rosewood • 212.5 x 108.2 x 46.2 cm
Alpaiwalla Museum

The cupboard, probably carved by a Mughal cabinet maker, is in two sections. The upper half has mirrors and the lower half the image of Zarathustra. Such pieces are found in Gujarat, where a large number of Parsis continue to live today. FPM

153 · **Bust of Jamsetji Nusserwanji Tata (1839–1904)**
Sculptor: Narayan Laxman Sonavadekar · 1984
Bronze · H: 64.5, w: 56, d: 36
Displayed at the 'Hanover Messe – 1984 – India'
Tata AG, Zug, Switzerland

A pioneer of industry, Jamsetji Nusserwanji Tata has been called 'the one-man planning commission of India'. A remarkable man for his time, he established several mills of his own and was one of the largest financiers of mills in Bombay. He also founded a hydroelectric power station and a steel-manufacturing factory. The diversity of Tata business interests globally today can be attributed to Jamsetji Tata's ability to grasp and understand the new, fast-changing period of enterprise and industrialization in India.[9]
FPM

❀

It was inevitable that close contacts with foreign cultures brought changes to the way that Parsis lived and in their perceptions of themselves. The early changes came in the sartorial styles they adopted from the British. Men's costumes were the first to undergo radical changes, and suits, waistcoats, bow ties and dressing gowns became fashionable. Some, such as Jamsetji Tata and his sons, were painted wearing Western clothes. The women seemed more conservative and continued to wear the sari, but their blouse styles were adapted to European fashions.

154
Portrait of Jamsetji Nusserwanji Tata (1839–1904)
Artist: Edwin Ward, RA • 1889
Oil on canvas • 168.91 x 144.78 cm
CSMVS, Mumbai: 33.72

Jamsetjee Tata is painted wearing a Parsi prayer
cap and an embroidered dressing gown. The latter
became fashionable among wealthy Parsis who,
by the end of the nineteenth century, had begun
to adopt Western modes of dress. FPM

155 • Dorab Jamsetji N. Tata (1859–1932)
Artist: M. F. Pithawalla • 1926
Oil on canvas • 132.1 x 101.6 cm
Tata Central Archives, Poona

Dorab Tata established the Tata Iron and Steel
works, Tata Power and several electricity-generating
companies. He diversified his business to include
insurance and the hotel industry, most notably the
famous Taj Hotel in Mumbai. His philanthropic
interests extended to institutions both in India and
abroad. Edward VII knighted Dorab Tata in 1910
for his contribution to industry in British India. FPM

156 • Ratan Jamsetji N. Tata (1871–1918)
Artist: Jehangir Lalkaka • 1938
Oil on canvas • 122 x 91.4 cm
Tata Central Archives, Poona

Ratan Jamsetji Tata was a property developer in Bombay and promoted several schemes for the reclamation of suburban land surrounding the city.

He was interested in education and endowed the Ratan Tata Foundation at the London School of Economics in order that the causes of poverty in countries like India could be studied. In his later years, he resided at York House, Twickenham, filling it with a spectacular collection of antiques and paintings, all of which were donated after his death by his wife Navajbai to the then Prince of Wales Museum (now CSMVS) in Bombay. FPM

157 • **Portrait of Lady Meherbai Dorab Tata (1879–1931) in court dress**

Artist: Sir John Lavery, RA • 19th century
Oil on canvas • 201.93 x 110.49 cm
CSMVS, Mumbai: 33.73

Lady Meherbai Tata was married to Jamsetji Tata's son, Dorab Tata. King George v made her Commander of the British Empire in 1919 for services during the war and for her work with women. She spoke out against child marriages and Indian indentured labour within the British colonies. Pictured in court dress, she is wearing a gold sari, white gloves and the 245-carat Jubilee diamond (named after the 60th anniversary of the coronation of Queen Victoria in 1897).[10] FPM

158 & 159 • **Dhunjibhoy Bomanjee and Lady Frainy Dhunjibhoy Bomanjee (b. 1894)**
Early 20th century • each photograph 46.5 x 36 cm
Collection: Zoroastrian Trust Funds of Europe

A naval contractor, Dhunjibhoy Bomanjee became one of the largest employers in western India.[11] During the latter part of his life, he lived with his wife Frainy in England[12] and was knighted in 1923. Both husband and wife were well known in British society and supported the war effort. Indeed their residence in Harrogate became a home to refugees during World War I. FPM

Although Parsi women were reluctant to embrace fully the English styles, they freely made use of *tanchoi* brocade and Chinese embroidered material to form a fashion that was wholly Parsi, wearing the embroidered lengths as *garas*, and making shawls and short jackets to wear over saris. Their children wore smock-like blouses and loose trousers also made from the embroidered cloth.

160 • **Children of the Tata family wearing traditional Parsi costume**
Late 19th century
Tata Central Archives, Poona: TF-A01-003

Parsi children in the nineteenth century were dressed traditionally in Chinese embroidered *jhablas* (smock-like dresses) and *ijars* (loose pyjamas) for festive occasions. FPM

161 • Sooni Tata, the French wife of Ratan D. Tata and Lady Meherbhai Tata, wife of Sir Dorab Tata
Early 20th century
Tata Central Archives, Poona: JJB-A17-036

By the late nineteenth century, photography had become the rage in India and studio portraits such as this were popular keepsakes. Sooni Tata (née Suzanne Brière) was a French woman whose marriage to Ratan D. Tata and subsequent initiation into the Zoroastrian faith in the early 1900s caused uproar among the largely traditional Parsi community. FPM

above right
162 • Jamsetji Nusserwanji Tata and his family
Early 20th century
Tata Central Archives, Poona: OFF-RES-A04-007

This is one of the few photographs of Jamsetji Tata with members of his immediate family. His daughter-in-law, Lady Navajbai Tata, served as a director of Tata Sons, the holding company, for over 40 years and was the first female trustee of the Bombay Parsi Punchayet. Seated (left to right) are Hirabai Tata (wife of Jamsetji N. Tata); Meherbai Tata (wife of Sir Dorab J. Tata); Jamsetji N. Tata (founder of the house of Tata); and Lady Navajbai Tata (wife of Sir Ratan Tata). Standing (left to right) are Sir Dorab Tata (eldest son of Jamsetji N. Tata) and Sir Ratan J. Tata (youngest son of Jamsetji N. Tata). FPM

163
Sir Ratan J. Tata and his wife, Lady Navajbai Tata
Early 20th century
Tata Central Archives, Poona: TF-RJT-E19-001

Exotic birds, flora and fauna were popular in twentieth-century Bombay. African Grey parrots, brought from the small Parsi settlement in Zanzibar, were popular pets. FPM

New textiles were introduced to India through the China trade. Parsi traders brought back embroidered lengths of fine translucent silk, which they called *garas*. They were short in length and so extra pieces of silk had to be attached to create the sari length required. The embroidery, usually of Chinese motifs, was done in white or cream twisted silk and covered the full *gara*. This was a new concept, and saris were soon sought after by Parsis who liked the contrast between the white embroidery and the deep maroon, red and purple silk background.

Another textile introduced by Parsi traders was the *tanchoi* fabric. The word is an amalgam of the three (*tan*) brothers from Surat who learned the art of weaving this brocade silk under their master Chhoi in China. The *tanchoi* became popular and formed part of a bride's trousseau.

164 • Black silk gara sari with *kanda papeta* design
Surat • early 20th century • Leno weave Chinese silk
Collection: Shernaz Engineer

A *gara* with two-toned dots on black silk is commonly known as a *kanda papeta* (onions and potatoes) because the pale peach and white twisted silk threads used to embroider the dots are similar in colour to onions and potatoes. The *gara* has a border embroidered with peacocks. The popularity of the peacock motif in Indian textiles suggests that the *gara* was embroidered in India. The position and shape of the flowers further indicate that it was probably embroidered in Surat, Gujarat.[13] FPM

165 • Red ghat (satin) gara embroidered with imperial knots

Early 1900s
Indian satin silk with Chinese-style embroidery
Collection: Shernaz Engineer

Gara saris with *khakho* (seed pearl) embroidery, also known as the imperial knot, became popular in India in the early 1900s. This *gara* sari is embroidered with flowers, vines, birds and Chinese pheasants in flight amidst a trail of lotus flowers and roses. The end corner of the *gara* has been left unembroidered, as it is this corner that is pinned at the waist. The top register of heavily embroidered *garas* is left plain so that when the sari is wrapped around, the folds can be tucked flat at the waist. FPM

166 • Deep pink gara sari on Chinese *sali* silk
India • 20th century • Embroidery on *sali* silk
Collection: Shernaz Engineer

right
**167 • Chinese *gara* embroidered
with a variety of birds and flowers**
China • 19th century • Silk embroidery on *sali* silk
Collection: Shernaz Engineer

The embroidery on this delicate *gara* sari has a gentle flow, giving the impression of constant movement. It depicts a typical Chinese scene with a couple surrounded by pavilions and bridges. Pavilions are used as secret trysts by lovers and afford shelter, since they are usually surrounded by foliage. In Chinese legend, as in Zoroastrianism, a bridge connects the physical world with the spiritual world. FPM

An unusual purple *gara* embroidered with peahens, peacocks, ducks, stalks, cranes, water-fowl, birds of paradise and parrots. The accuracy of the representation suggests that an artist who painted birds for a living had first sketched it on the sari length. The motif of the legendary Chinese fungus of immortality, a wish-fulfilling symbol, is interspersed among the embroidered birds and flowers. Large lotus leaves and lotus pods are scattered amidst the foliage. The sun rising from the waters appears as a single motif at one end of the *gara*. This striking *gara* with mirror-finish embroidery on the reverse has the embroidered pattern running vertically throughout the length of the sari, similar to a Chinese scroll. FPM

168 · *Sali* silk sari with gara embroidery
Surat, Gujarat • Late 19th century
Leno (gaj) silk embroidered with cream silk thread
Private collection

This *gara* was probably made as an engagement piece, as the auspicious shade of red, *kanku*, is traditional for Gujarati engagement saris. It displays the inter-cultural influences of Persian, Chinese, Indian and European designs that are combined in Parsi embroidery. It uses Persian trellis patterns drawn from ancient material culture with Indian peacocks and tiny endless knots, which are lucky in the Chinese tradition. It is edged with European-style scallops, creating an unusual border. SC

169 • *Tanchoi* sari
Early 20th century • Woven *tanchoi* silk
Private collection

This unusual *tanchoi* sari was probably woven in the
Joshi family workshop, Surat. It was ordered by the
Bhabha family but has never been worn. It combines
within its weave typical Chinese pagodas and architectural features together with tropical vegetation.
It also displays European figures, a scene at an inn
and a pattern consisting of dogs and the *gul-e-bulbul*
(a flowers-and-birds design) on the border. It is rare
to see a *tanchoi* with such patterns, which are more
commonly found on embroidered *garas*. SC

left
170 • Densely embroidered *gara*
China • Early 20th century
Silk with white floss thread embroidery
Private collection

Here the embroidery has been done in three registers
running parallel to each other across the width.
The top register has a floral design and the two larger
registers are mirror images with densely embroidered
roses, butterflies, leafy fronds and shrubs with
elegantly embroidered storks standing amidst
swirling waters and sacred fungus. FPM

above
171 • Purple stole with gara embroidery
Gujarat • Late 19th century • Silk thread embroidery on silk
Private collection

This stole is made from a *jhabla* piece since the
pattern is repeated in obverse and reverse. Children
wore *jhabla*s until their *navjote*. Several *jhabla*s
display symbols of protection or birds and animals
from Zoroastrian mythology. While the cock, the
bird of Srosh, is a very common pattern, here we
see the dog as a symbol of protection. Dogs play
an important role in Zoroastrian culture and are
accorded deep respect as guides both in this life
and the next. SC

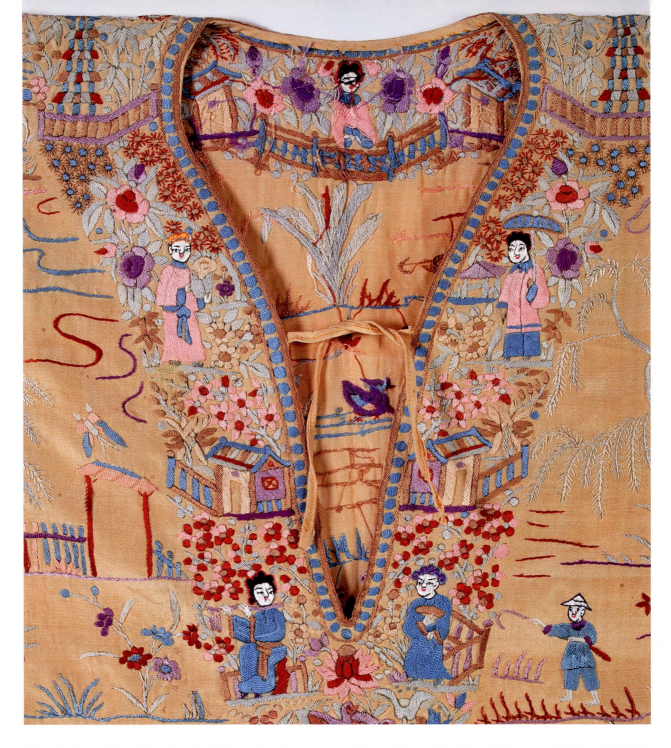

172 • *Jhabla* with multi-coloured silk embroidery
China • 20th century • Embroidered silk
Private collection

A smock-like dress made for a child is embroidered with Chinese motifs of flowing waters with swimming fish, overhanging fronds and bridges. A figure in a pavilion is shown selling silk to a customer. The *jhabla* is edged with a border and probably depicts a trading scene with a boatman coming into a harbour. The shoulder and neck area are embroidered with Chinese figures, flowers and pavilions. FPM

173 • **Single-diamond earring** *above*
174 • **Brooch-leaf with rubies** *right*
India • Early 1900s
Earring: Gold set with diamonds • 5.5 x 2.2 cm
Brooch: Gold set with rubies • 4.4 x 7.7 cm
Collection: Aban Marker Kabraji

Jewellery is greatly valued by Parsis both as an investment and as a symbol of wealth. The single earring for the left ear (Cat. 173) was adopted by Parsi women, who wore the sari draped over the head in such a way as to hide the right ear. Brooches were used by Parsi women to pin the folds of the sari gathered on the right shoulder. FPM

above right
175 • **Parsi lady in yellow sari**
Artist: unknown • Early 20th century
Oil on canvas • 95.3 x 80 cm
Collection: Hameed Haroon

The Parsi lady is wearing a single large diamond earring and a long-sleeved blouse. The small lace collar of the blouse and the lacy frill attached to her sleeves is inspired by English fashion. FPM

The publication in 1889 of a book by K. D. Kiash on the bas-reliefs and sculptures of ancient Iran, together with the increasing number of recitals of stories from the *Shanameh*, evoked nostalgia and a sense of longing for Iran. Thereafter, images of Persian kings and depictions of the rock carvings from Persepolis and other Zoroastrian sites began to appear on decorative metalware.

left
176 · Achaemenid gold rhyton, reproduction
Goldsmith: Zal Amrolia · Gold · 13.5 x 9.5 cm
Collection: Jal, Armin, Zar & Persis Amrolia

A modern reproduction of a gold rhyton found in Hamadan (Ecbatana) in the fifth century BCE, now in the National Museum, Tehran. FPM

right
177 · Gold bowl, Achaemenid
Goldsmith: Zal Amrolia · Silver · 12.06 x 22.64 cm
Collection: Jal, Armin, Zar & Persis Amrolia

A modern reproduction of a gold Achaemenid bowl found in Hamadan (Ecbatana), engraved with the name of the Persian king Xerxes I, *c.* fourth–fifth century BCE, now in the National Museum, Tehran. FPM

9 FIRE TEMPLE

Sarah Stewart and Firoza Punthakey Mistree

The cult of the temple fire grew out of the ritual tending of the ever-burning hearth fire, a custom that goes back to Indo-Iranian times when the fire in the home was kept alight for the duration of a man's lifetime. Acknowledged as the household divinity, the hearth fire received offerings of wood, incense and oblations of fat from the sacrificial animal. Fire is personified in the ancient Avestan prayer, the *Atash Niyayesh*, dedicated to this most esteemed of the seven creations:

> Fire gives command to all for whom he cooks the evening and the morning meal. From all he solicits a good offering, and a wished-for offering, and a devotional offering. [NY. 5.13][1]

Offerings to the two major elements of Zoroastrian ritual, fire and water, were performed as part of the priestly act of worship, the yasna, and took place in the open in a consecrated space. Oblations of fat were made to the fire while the ritual offering to water consisted of a mixture of milk and the juice from the pounded *haoma* plant. According to the ancient *Yashts*, hymns addressed to the divinities (*yazatas*) of the Zoroastrian and pre-Zoroastrian worlds, the divinities were invoked and invited to the sacrifice in order that rewards might be granted to the worshipper. The officiating priest held in his left hand a bunch of the grasses, *baresman* (Middle Persian: *barsom*), from those scattered under the sacrificial animal; in later Iranian tradition these were replaced by twigs. The *Atash Niyayesh* also refers to the priestly act of worship:

> Happiness may there be to that man,
> Who verily shall sacrifice unto Thee,
> With fuel in his hand, with the *Baresman* in his hand,
> With milk in his hand, with mortar in his hand. [NY. 5.7][2]

It is not known when an ever-burning fire first came to be permanently housed in a dedicated building. No remains of Achaemenid fire temples have been discovered, although seals from the period attest to the extension of the household or hearth fire to the king's dynastic fire, which was extinguished at the end of his reign. The introduction by Artaxerxes II (r. 405–358 BCE) of temples dedicated to the goddess Anahita/Anaitis are likely to have provided the template for an independent structure that housed a sacred fire. During the Parthian period the Greek authors Strabo and Pausanias both refer to ever-burning fires being tended by a *magus*, and the Persian epic *Vis u Ramin*, thought to refer to the Parthian ruling house, mentions offerings being made to the temple fire. The main change in usage from the domestic fire to the temple fire was that the latter was consecrated, regularly tended by priests and not put to practical use.[3]

The iconoclasm of the Sasanians resulted in the replacement of image shrines with temple fires in Iran (though not in Sogdiana). The importance of the king's dynastic fire is attested on the reverse of coins throughout the period starting with Ardashir I (r. 224–241 CE), whose later coin issues show a fire holder on the reverse with the legend, 'the fire of Ardashir'.[4] Royal inscriptions refer to the founding of many '*Atakhsh i Vahram*', or victory fires,[5] established by Sasanian monarchs from the time of Ardashir I. In his inscriptions the powerful high priest Kirder refers repeatedly to the fact that during his time 'religious services were multiplied in every province and place, and many Vahram fires were founded. And many a priest became joyful and prosperous'.[6]

We do not know when the two distinct forms of worship, veneration of the ever-burning fire and the priestly *yasna*, came to be performed within the fire temple complex. What is clear, however, is that no rituals other than those associated with the tending of the fire were performed inside the *gumbad*, or fire sanctuary. Sasanian fire temples evidently included a *yazishn-gah*, or 'place of worship', where such rituals could have been performed.[7]

After the Arab conquest of Iran the term *dar-e mehr* came to be used by Iranian Zoroastrians for the fire temple, alongside the older *atashkadeh*, or 'House of Fire'. Iranian priests writing to the Parsis in the fifteenth century advised that the 'priests' room for worship', *yazishn khaneh-ye dasturan*, should be 'around and near the fire-house'.[8] The Parsis used the term *dar-e mehr* for the place where rituals were performed. It seems that the *dar-e mehr* only became part of the temple complex, now referred to as the *agiary*, after the first *Atash Bahram* to be established on Indian soil found its final resting place in Udvada, where it remains today.

There are three grades of sacred fire: the *Atash Bahram*, consecrated from sixteen different fires as attested in the *Videvdad*, includes a fire kindled from lightning and can only be tended by a fully qualified priest; the lesser-grade *Atash Adaran* must also be served by a priest; and laymen may tend the third-grade *Dadgah* fire.

previous page
178 · Dastur Noshirwan Dastur Kaikhushru Behram Framroz (1822–97)
Artist: M. M. · Surat · 1 March 1898
Oil on canvas · 81 x 67 cm
Collection: Hameed Haroon

179 · Dastur Dinshah Jivanji Garda JP, high priest of the Kadimi sect of Zoroastrians of Surat (b. 1853)
Artist: Constancio · India · 1935
Oil on canvas · 138 x 112.5 cm (framed)
Collection: Hameed Haroon

Dastur Noshirwan came from a long line of Zoroastrian high priests who served the great Shehenshahi fire temple in Surat. His father, a Persian scholar, was in charge of the Sir Jamsetji Jejeebhoy School and trained his son in the performance of rituals and the study of Zoroastrianism. All rituals performed in the fire temple came under his ecclesiastical authority. Dastur Noshirwan also served as a delegate of the Parsi Matrimonial Court. FPM

Dastur Dinshah Jivanji Garda served as a high priest at the Dadyseth Atash Bahram in Bombay. He was appointed head priest of Vatcha Gandhi fire temple but continued to serve the sacred fire of the Dadyseth Atash Bahram. In 1911 he became Dastur of the Kadimi Anjoman of Bombay. Dastur Dinshah published a Kadimi *Yazishn* in 1916 and a Kadimi *Khordeh Avesta* in 1919. He was the President of the *Athornan Mandal*, a union of priests, and was one of the founding members of the Athornan Madressa, a seminary established in Bombay. FPM

180 • Manekji Navroji Sett fire temple, Mumbai

Front entrance replicated for the Everlasting Flame exhibition, SOAS
photograph: Noshir Gobhai

One of the oldest fire temples in Mumbai built by
Manekji Navroji Sett, the grandson of Rustam Manek,
broker to the Dutch, Portuguese and to the English
East India Company in the seventeenth century. The
façade of the fire temple was inspired by the Sasanian
site of Taq-e Bostan in Kermanshah, Iran, and began
a trend for fire temples to feature architectural motifs
from the Achaemenid and Sasanian periods. It is
served by the Bhagaria priests of Navsari, under
whose jurisdiction all the rituals in Mumbai are
undertaken. They authorize the presentation of the
main *varasya*, or sacred bull, that provides the ritual
urine (*gomez*) for the fire temples of Mumbai. FPM

When entering a fire temple, a Zoroastrian should be
in a state of ritual purity. A worshipper will perform
the *padyab-e kusti* while in the outer precincts of the
temple. This involves the ritual washing of the face
and hands, and sprinkling the feet with water, after
which the sacred cord is untied and re-tied while
prayers are recited. In fire temples in India an offering of sandalwood is always made; this is purchased
outside and placed on a tray at the entrance to the
fire chamber together with a donation for the priests,
which is put into a box. In Iran sandalwood is replaced
with sweet-smelling wood, and sticks of incense are
burned in the prayer hall. In all cases the head must
be covered; once inside the prayer hall, prayers are
recited facing the fire, which can be seen through
open grilles in the walls of the fire chamber. There is
no congregational worship in a fire temple; those who
visit may recite a short prayer and leave, while others
may stay longer. The prayer hall is generally devoid
of decoration; there are benches and chairs facing the
fire, and prayer books, *Khordeh Avesta*, are available
in Roman, Gujarati and Persian script.

181 • Silver filigree *ses*
India • 21st century • Silver
Collection: Bapsy Dastur

Ses, or tray, on which are placed: A. silver cone
containing sugar and representing the allegorical
Mount Hara, mountain of sweetness; B. rose-water
sprinkler; C. container for vermillion paste; D. silver
fish or leaf; E. *divo*, oil lamp.

On celebratory occasions such as a birthday or *navjote*
(initiation) the *ses* is garlanded and the appropriate
foods added to it, e.g. dry rice, dried dates, flowers
(in India these include coconut, turmeric sticks,
betel nut and betel leaves). FPM

182 • *Navjote* cap
Surat • early 20th century • Velvet with cotton lining
Private collection: Farokh Dubash

Purple velvet cap elaborately embroidered with birds
and flowers in silver-coloured metal thread. The
navjote (Ir. *sedreh pushi*) is a ceremony of initiation
into the faith. Usually performed between the ages
of seven and eleven (in Iran later, between 12 and 15)
a child is invested with the *sudreh* and *kusti* for which
they must have memorized the basic *kusti* prayers.
A ritual bath is taken before the ceremony as well
as the additional purification afforded by the sipping
of *nirang*, or consecrated bull's urine (a custom no
longer practised in Iran). A cause for celebration,
the ceremony is followed by an exchange of presents
after which the child will visit the fire temple. SS

183 • *Sudreh* (Ir. *sedreh*), sacred shirt
India • Muslin
Private collection: Shernaz Engineer

Zoroastrians wear an inner shirt of pure white cotton. A small pocket is stitched to the neckline in front to remind the wearer that he/she should be filling its emptiness with good deeds. FPM

184 • *Kusti*
India • Lamb's wool

Worn by men and women alike, the *kusti*, or sacred cord, is made of lamb's wool and woven on a hand loom. It consists of 72 threads, symbolizing the 72 *has* or sections of the *Yasna*. The 24 threads that make up each of the three tassels at the end of the *kusti* represent the 24 *kardehs* or sections of the *Visperad*. The *kusti* is passed three times around the waist, over the *sudreh*, and knotted in front and behind with a fourfold knot. A Zoroastrian should pray five times in 24 hours, standing in the presence of fire, a lamp, sun or moon. The basic prayer ritual involves untying and retying the *kusti*. As the wearer unties it, and so loses its protection, he recites the *Kemna Mazda* prayer; he reties it to the Middle Persian prayer known as *Ohrmazd Khoday*, followed by other short Avestan prayers.[9] SS

185 • Tying the *kusti*
Artist: M. F. Pithawalla • 1890
Oil on canvas • 76.2 x 55.8 cm (unframed)
Collection: Mrs Franey Irani

A Parsi Zoroastrian is usually initiated into the faith between the ages of seven and nine. During the ceremony, which is performed by an ordained priest, the child is vested with the *sudreh* and *kusti*. The painting shows a woman helping her child to tie the *kusti* in a typical Parsi setting with a picture of Zarathustra on the wall behind her. She is wearing the sari according to Parsi custom, with one side of her head completely covered and with an ornate embroidered *sudreh* visible over the skirt of the sari. FPM

186 · The *Khordeh Avesta* in Gujarati script: the earliest Parsi publication

Bandera, Mambai · 1167 (1798) · Printed book
Provenance: Thomas Grenville (1755–1846)
British Library G. 16737

The *Khordeh Avesta* ('Little Avesta') consists of a selection of prayers and devotional texts, *niyayesh*, *gah*, *yasht*, *baj* and *namaskar*, which function as a working prayer book for Zoroastrians. In this printed version, the Avestan language is written in Gujarati script which was much more widely accessible to the Parsis of India. The page illustrated here shows the beginning of the *Srosh Hadokht Yasht*, a hymn to the divinity Sraosha.

This book is the first work to be printed in a vernacular language without any direct European involvement and represents a landmark in publishing. Using a set of Gujarati types which they had especially created for the *Bombay Courier* newspaper in 1796, the two Parsi compositors, Behramjee Jejeebhoy and Nusserwanjee Cowasjee, published the prayer book in 1798 with the title *E kitaba Khurade Avasatani*. As Behramjee wrote in his English preface, 'we have thought ourselves bound to dedicate the first use of them to the purpose of our holy religion'. AH, USW

187 · *Lobandan* (incense burner)

India · German silver
Private collection: Firoza Punthakey-Mistree

The *loban* ceremony is performed by a woman, usually in the morning, and also at dusk. Traditionally embers from the hearth fire were put into an incense burner together with slivers of sandalwood and incense. It is taken from room to room in the house and across the thresholds of doorways. As well as protecting the household from evil, incense is thought to act as an insect repellent. FPM

❀

In the approaches to the prayer hall and in the main hall of the fire temple there are pictures of Zarathustra and paintings of benefactors to the temple, or to the community at large, as well as of priests who may have served there.

188 • Portrait of Zarathustra
India • late 20th century
Etched mirror work with a photograph of the face
placed on the reverse • 62.5 x 47.5 cm (framed)
Collection: Zoroastrian Trust Funds of Europe

Portraits of Zarathustra can be seen worldwide in fire temples and Zoroastrian homes. Although the religion is iconoclastic, such portraits came into frequent use after the rock sculpture depicting the Sasanian King Ardashir II standing beside the divinity Mithra at Taq-e Bostan (in Iran) was printed. The image of Mithra was taken to be that of Zarathustra. Subsequently Parsi artists recreated this image to suit modern tastes.[10] FPM

right
189 • Parsi lady in blue sari with fan
Artist: Aca Hosai, a Japanese artist (a.k.a. Kunisada III)
Late 19th century • Oil on canvas • 90 x 66 cm (framed)
Collection: Hameed Haroon

Before the Treaty of Kanagawa (1853–4), Japanese artists had seldom been exposed to foreigners. Foreigners were restricted to the area around Yokohama harbour, and aroused great interest amongst Japanese artists who began painting them after learning Western techniques of displaying light and shadows and the use of perspective.

The woman in this portrait is wearing a blue sari with an embroidered border, and holds a Japanese fan. One end of her sari is draped over her head under which a white *mathabana*, or muslin scarf, can be seen. Her rings, earrings and necklace indicate that she came from a well-to-do family and is likely to have been the wife of one of the few Parsi merchants engaged in trade with Japan.

The artist, Aca Hosai, was a specialist in woodcuts of Kabuki plays in 1880. FPM

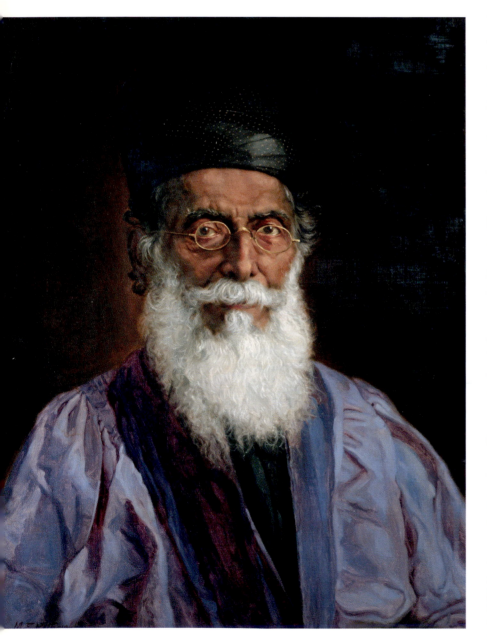

190 • **Kharshedji Rustamji Cama (1831–1909)**
Artist: M.F. Pithawala • Oil on canvas • 72 x 56 cm
Collection: Zoroastrian Trust Funds of Europe

Kharshedji Cama arrived in England in 1855 with Muncherji Cama and Dadabhai Naoroji to start the first Parsi firm in London and Liverpool. He had practised his skills as a trader while working in China for his uncle Ratanji Hormusji Cama, but his heart lay elsewhere. Disillusioned with the opium trade, Cama studied Zoroastrianism in Europe and returned to India to teach the religion as well as the Avestan and Pahlavi languages to lay Parsis. His early group of students became the first Parsi scholars to contribute to the study of Zoroastrianism in India. He was a friend of the Orientalist Martin Haug, who shaped his ideas about Zoroastrianism. FPM

right
191 • **Rustomjee Pestonjee Karkaria (1869–1919)**
Artist: M.F. Pithawalla • 1927
Oil on canvas • 126 x 103 cm (framed)
Collection: Hameed Haroon

Rustomjee Pestonjee Karkaria was Assistant Professor of English and History at St Xavier's College, Bombay. He became prominent in the literary world following his discovery and publication of Thomas Carlyle's lectures on European literature. He wrote on Indian history and politics.

He is wearing black-lacquered ceremonial headgear, *paghri*, which is of Indian origin. The shine of the *paghri* is obtained through a lacquering process, introduced by Chinese workers living in Bombay in the nineteenth century. The books on the shelf behind him and those kept on the table indicate his academic status. He is wearing a black *daglo*, a coat, with a white shirt and grey trousers. FPM

FIRE CHAMBER

The fire chamber of the *agiary* encloses the sacred space in which the ever-burning fire is housed. In ancient Iran the sacred fire was installed on a stone pillar, three-stepped at the top and bottom as depicted on the stone reliefs of Darius and his descendants at Persepolis.[11] This model is still in use in the fire temples and shrines in Yazd and its surrounding villages. The fire chamber itself is designed on the model of the *chahar taq*, or four arches forming a square chamber that supported a round dome resting on squinches. This feature distinguished many Sasanian religious buildings. Today this structure is simply referred to as *gumbad*, 'dome'.[12] Above it is a secondary roof, which acts as a special protective cover. Both dome and roof are punctured by flues to allow the smoke to escape.

193 • **Priest wearing *padam*
serving the fire in the fire chamber**

photograph: Noshir Mulla

192 • **Eighteenth-century fire temple, Baku**

photograph: Khojeste Mistree
courtesy of *A Zoroastrian Tapestry: Art Religion and Culture*

In use until 1900, this temple is a clear example of the *chahar taq*, a square chamber surmounted by a dome. SS

The fire chamber may only be entered by a serving priest, *boyvara*, (Iranian: *atashband*), who performs the *boy devi* ceremony (Iranian: *boy dadan*). This involves feeding the fire at the beginning of each of the five *Gahs*, or periods of the day with small logs (in Iran, dry wood and fragrant herbs). Priestly costume includes: white gloves and a nose-and-mouth mask, *padam*, to prevent pollution of the fire.

The fire vase is set on a stone table (which resembles in design the *chahar taq*). A concave metal hood, *taj*, or crown hangs over the fire. In the sanctum are two long-handled ladles for serving the fire and a vessel of water for the ritual washing of the stone table prior to the *boy* ceremony. A tripod containing a tray of sandalwood is kept near the fire and a niche in the wall contains bottles of *nirang*. Two bells hang in the opposite corners of the sanctum, one of which is rung during the fire service, depending on the watch of the day. FPM

above
194 · **Silver *toran* ('shield')**
photograph: Noshir Gobhai

A garland (*toran*) of small silver shields decorates the lintel of the fire chamber (Cat. 32). Each shield is engraved with the motif of the sun, moon, stars, trees and water to remind the worshipper of their duty to venerate these creations. FPM

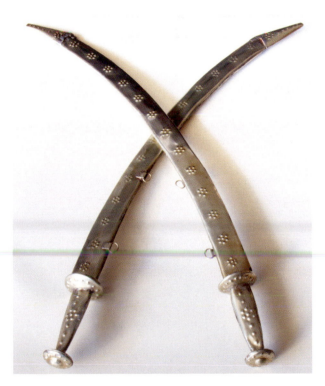

right
195 & 196 · **Bull-headed mace and two swords**
photographs: Noshir Mulla

The walls of the fire chamber are decorated with two crossed swords and a bull-headed mace (Cat. 73). This marks a tradition, first attested in post-Sasanian times, in which the procession of priests that accompanied a newly consecrated *Atash Bahram* to its sanctuary 'victoriously' carried swords and maces, which were then hung on the walls of the sanctuary. FPM

RITUAL PRECINCT

The 'inner' liturgical services of Zoroastrianism are performed in the ritual precinct, *urvis-gah* or *yazishn-gah*, which is situated within the complex of most fire temples. In the precinct are a number of designated spaces marked out with furrows, *pavi* (Iranian: *kash*), that can be consecrated and kept ritually pure for the duration of the ceremony. The major inner ceremony is the ritual recital and performance of the *Yasna* of 72 sections, which incorporates the Gathas, the hymns of Zarathustra, and may be dedicated to Ohrmazd or to a lesser divine being. It is usually celebrated between dawn and midday (the period known as *Havan Gah*) and is generally commissioned by a member of the laity, who may attend the service but does not have any role to play. While the immediate function of the Yasna is to bring blessings to the patron and to the souls of the departed, the wider objective is to preserve cosmic order and maintain the balance between the spiritual, *menog*, and material, or *getig*, worlds. Some scholars see the Yasna ceremony as fulfilling a more powerful role, namely to foreshadow the final Yasna that will bring about the renewal of the world at the end of limited time, that is, at *Frashegird*.[13] At the centre of the ceremony are ancient rituals which include the representation of all the good creations in the form of fire, water, plant life, animal products and the materials of the ritual implements (see chart of *Amesha Spentas*, page 239).

Whereas once there could be up to eight priests taking part in the Yasna, today in India there are only two: the *zot*, or officiating priest, and the *raspi*, or serving priest, both of whom must be fully qualified and have undergone the *barashnom*, an extensive purification ritual. In Iran the full Yasna is no longer performed but has been modified to reflect the lessening of formal priestly training and a decline in the number of hereditary priests.

The liturgy has been reduced to the *baj-e gahambar* and the recitation of the first 21 *has*, or sections, of the Yasna liturgy.

Prior to the commencement of the Yasna proper, the *raspi* will perform the preparatory *paragna* service after which he will be joined by the *zot* in the ritual precinct.

THE YASNA CEREMONY

The structure of the modern Yasna ceremony as performed in India.[14]

Preparation For The Yasna (*Paragna*)
1. Preparation of sacred water.
2. Preparation of *barsom*. These were originally twigs from a special tree, but in India metal wires are used. The *barsom* may originally have symbolized the vegetal nature, complementary to the water.
3. Preparation of the cord used to tie the *barsom*. It is made from a date palm leaf cut into six strands, which are braided and tied together and deposited in a vessel with sacred water.
4. Preparation of the plant. A shoot from a pomegranate is cut off and put into the vessel.
5. Preparation of the milk. A goat facing east (direction of the rising sun) is milked by a priest facing south (turning his back on the evil forces).
6. Preparation of the ghee.[15]
7. The bread (the solid offering).
8. Preparation of the *hom* (*parahom*). Branches of ephedra are washed in sacred water. A mortar is prepared by striking the walls, especially the northern side (direction of the evil forces), with the pestle. The *hom* is placed in the mortar with the pomegranate twigs and pounded, and water is added. The juice is then filtered through a net made of hairs from a sacred bull (now a metal ring with three, five, or seven hairs).

The Yasna

Y.1–2: Invitation of the deities.

Y.3–8: Offering of the bread, at the end of which the chief priest, the 'libator' (AV. *zaotar*, MP *zot*) consumes the bread and the ghee.

Y.9–11: Offering of the *haoma*, at the end of which the *zot* consumes the *parahom*.

Y.12: Libation of the waters, profession of faith.

Y.22–24: Beginning of the offering of the *hom* (*homast*).

Y.25–27: Preparation of the *hom*.

Y.27: Recitation of the *Ahunvar* (the *Ahuna Vairiya* prayer).

Y.28–53: Recitation of the Gathas, etc.

Y.54: Recitation of the fourth holy prayer, the *Airiyama ishiyo* prayer.

Y.54–55: Praise of the Gathas and the *Staota yesniya* texts.

Y.56–57: Praise of Srosh (AV. Sraosha), greatest fighter of the powers of darkness.

Y.58–61: Various prayers.

Y.62: Praise of the fire and offering of *hom* to the fire.

Y.63–69: Consecration of the waters. Water is mixed with the *hom* and milk, and is poured over the *barsom*.

Y.70–72: Conclusion: untying of the *barsom*. Some of the sacred water (*parahom*) is returned to the well. The rest of the *parahom* is drunk by the one who ordered the sacrifice or by one of the assistants.

right

197 • The 'place of the Yasna liturgy' (*yazishn/urvisgah*)

3.86 x 2.15 m

courtesy of Dasturji Dr Firoze M. Kotwal

The ritual area marked out with the furrows, *pavi*, and laid with the ritual implements, the fire vase and stone seat for the priest. SS

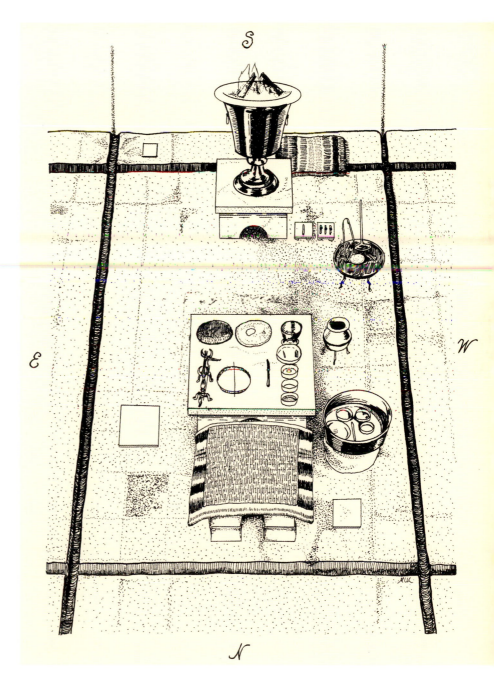

198 • **Ritual precinct at the Dadar Athornan Madressa, Mumbai**

photographs: Noshir Gobhai

The Yasna ceremony performed by the priests Ervad Asphandiar Dadachanji and Ervad Hormuz Dadachanji, courtesy of Principal Ervad Ramiyar Karanjia. The Dadar Athornan Madressa is one of the last training madressas for priests. Currently (2013) there are 24 boys, from priestly families, undergoing religious and ritual training. Most will be expected to work part-time as priests. SS

right (top)
***Hamazor*, handshake, before Yasna ceremony**
The *zot* and the *raspi* perform the ritual handshake before the Yasna ceremony commences. FPM

right (middle)
***Kusti* ritual prior to Yasna ceremony**
The *zot* and the *raspi* perform the *kusti* in preparation for the ceremony. FPM

right (bottom)
The *raspi* tends the ritual fire
The stone table, resembling a *chahar taq*, has the metal fire vase set on it. The fire, which is lit at the start of the Yasna ceremony and must not be allowed to go out, is tended at regular intervals by the *raspi*, who will use the ladle and tongs to feed the fire with sandalwood and incense. These are placed on a tripod (*esm-boy khvan*). FPM

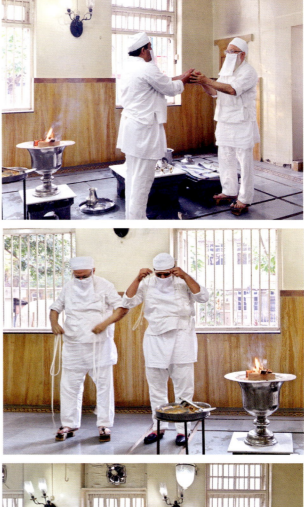

200 • Ritual table (*alat khvan*)

photograph: Noshir Gobhai

The ritual implements for the Yasna ceremony include: small metal saucers containing the sacred bull's hair tied to a ring (*varas fuliyan*); *hom* and pomegranate twigs (*hom-urvaram tashta*); mortar (*havan*) for pounding the *hom*; the sacred bread (*dron tashta*) with clarified butter; the inverted saucer covering a cup containing the *parahom* mixture; the *mah-ruy*, half-moon stands, holding the *barsom tays* and the saucer containing goat's milk (*jivam tashta*) on which is placed a metal wire used to libate the date-palm cord with the milk; the knife for cutting the date-palm leaf (*barsom-chin*). FPM

199 • Fire table (*atash-khvan*)

51 x 28 cm

photograph: Noshir Gobhai

With ritual fire burning in the fire vase, *afringanyu*. FPM

201 • Mortar (*havan*) and pestle (*abar-havan*)
photograph: Noshir Gobhai

The pomegranate and *hom* twigs are pounded together during the *parahom* ceremony. The *parahom* is prepared during the *paragna* service in which a mixture of consecrated water and juice obtained from pounding the *hom* and pomegranate twigs is mixed together. FPM

202 • Half-moon stands (*mah-ruy*)
photograph: Noshir Gobhai

Holding the *barsom tays*. The two stands are connected at the base with a metal wire, *tay*, and a bundle of metal wires *barsom tays* are placed on the top part of the half-moon stands, *mah-ruy*. These are tied together with a date-palm cord (*aivyahan*). The metal rods are a modern replacement for the grass that was strewn beneath the feet of the sacrificial animal, a handful of which was held by the priest during the sacrificial ritual. FPM

203 • Metal basin (*kundi*)
photograph: Noshir Gobhai

Containing: water; extra metal saucers; pestle (*abar-havan*); nine-holed saucer (*surakhdar tashta*). FPM

204 • Tripod
photograph: Noshir Gobhai

Holding sandalwood (*sukhur*) tray (*khvancha*), incense container (*loban*), tongs (*chipyo*) and ladle (*chamach*). FPM

205 • Water container on a tripod (*karasyo*)
photograph: Noshir Gobhai

Used by the *zot* to wash the ritual implements and the ritual table. FPM

206 • Container
photograph: Noshir Gobhai

For water for ablutions prior to the start of the Yasna ceremony. FPM

left
207 • Wooden platform slippers
photograph: Noshir Gobhai

As worn by the *zot*, and leather *mojris* as worn by the *raspi*. A Zoroastrian is not permitted to go barefoot during a ritual, as it breaks the ritual purity. FPM

below
208 • *Muktad* table
19th century • Brass with a marble top
and a portrait of Zarathustra embossed in silver
Collection: Firoza Punthakey Mistree. photograph: Noshir Gobhai

Muktad (Avestan: *Hamaspathmaedaya*) is the annual observance for the spirits of the departed, the *fravashis*, which are believed to return to earth during this ten-day period where they are welcomed with rituals, prayers and food offerings. In return, they bring their blessings to the living. FPM

209 • The ritual of the *Videvdad sadeh*

Copyist: Rostam Darab Framrozi Manuchehri
Karshaspazi Pavadi
Bombay • 1792 • Ink on paper • 29 x 25 cm
Provenance: Samuel Guise (1751–1811)
British Library MSS Avestan 5, ff. 38v–39r

Although today only two priests are required for the
Videvdad Sadeh liturgy, this diagram, dating from
the end of the eighteenth century, describes the full
ritual as it used to be. The chief priest (*zaotar*) calls
for seven assistants to help perform the ritual of
the sacred *haoma* plant. In this diagram the *zaotar*
stands at the northern (lower) end. He is assisted by:

1. The *havanan* who presses the *haoma*.
2. The *atrevakhsh* who feeds the fire.
3. The *fraberetar* who brings the necessary tools to
   the *zaotar*.
4. The *aberet* who brings the water for the ceremony.
5. The *asnatar* who washes the *haoma* and strains it.
6. The *raethwishkara* who mixes the *haoma* with milk.
7. The *sraoshavarez* who watches over the whole
   ceremony. USW

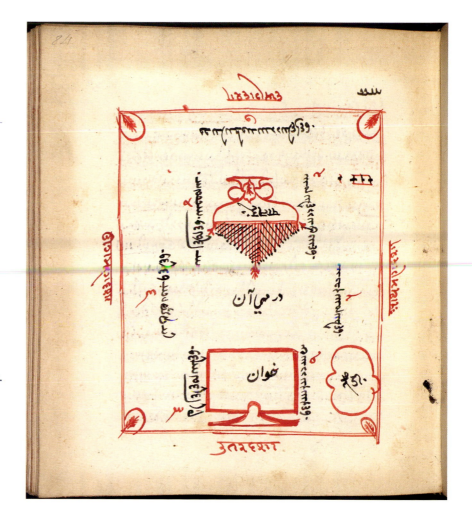

10 ZOROASTRIAN COMMUNITIES AROUND THE WORLD

Jenny Rose

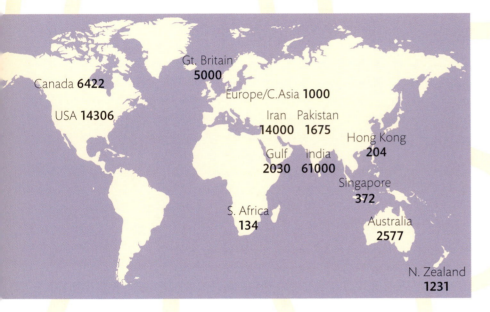

These figures, supplied largely by professional demographers or officials of local Zoroastrian organizations, and including the Iran Census data of 2011, indicate that the number of Zoroastrians in the 'homelands' of Iran, India and Pakistan have decreased considerably, but that the numbers in North America, New Zealand and Singapore have grown.[2]

EUROPE

The first Zoroastrian known to have visited England was Naoroji Rustomji Manek Sett, the youngest son of a Parsi agent-broker for the British East India Company in Surat. In April 1724, Naoroji arrived in London and brought a claim before the East India Company directors concerning moneys owed to his family by Company officials in Bombay. Somewhat surprisingly, Naoroji won his case and returned home a wealthy man. JR

Naoroji wears the red robe of honour given to him by the directors of the British East India Company after he had won his lawsuit – the first instance of an Indian bringing a case against the British. JR

According to Chinese histories of the Tang dynasty, members of the Persian court accompanied Yazdegerd III's son and heir, Peroz (d. *c.*679 CE), to China following the incursion of Arabs into Iran. The story of how Zoroastrianism was carried into China by Sogdian merchants has been told in section 3. Over a thousand years later Parsi traders and brokers acting as middlemen in sea trade with China began to settle in Canton, buying a plot of land for a Zoroastrian cemetery in 1847.[1]

Other Sasanian Zoroastrians sought refuge in settlements such as Sanjan and Bharuch, in northwestern India, where, it is thought, Sasanian merchants had previously established trading posts. India remains home to the largest number of Zoroastrians but in the past 200 years many Parsis have emigrated from the subcontinent to Sri Lanka, Singapore, Hong Kong, East and South Africa, Europe, North America and Australasia.

By the mid-nineteenth century, many Parsis were coming to Britain to pursue business interests or to further their professional training. One such figure was Kharshedji Rustamji Cama (1831–1909) (Cat. 190), who travelled to England on business and also attended classes relating to Zoroastrianism at several European universities.

A European association of Zoroastrians was founded in 1861, and is now known as the Zoroastrian Trust Funds of Europe (ZTFE). It is the oldest Zoroastrian organization in Europe, established primarily to manage funds to bury the dead, to establish a place of prayer, to help impoverished Zoroastrians throughout Europe, to create a library of Zoroastrian publications and to promote scholarship in the religion. The second president of the Association, Dadabhai Naoroji (1825–1917), became the first Asian MP in the British parliament, sitting from 1892 to 1895, following a term as President of the Indian National Congress. Naoroji took his oath of office as the Liberal MP for Finsbury Central with his hand on a copy of the Khordeh Avesta, the Zoroastrian prayer book (Cat. 186).

left

212 • **Dadabhai Naoroji (1825–1917) in the House of Commons**

Collection: Zoroastrian Trust Funds of Europe

The second Asian MP was another Parsi, Sir Muncherji Bhownagree (1851–1933), the Conservative representative for Bethnal Green North East from 1895 to 1905. He was followed by 'Comrade Sak' – Shapurji Saklatvalla (1874–1936) – Communist MP for Battersea North 1922–3 and 1924–9, who went to prison for supporting the General Strike of 1926. JR

213 • Shapurji Saklatvalla: Communist candidate

Collection: Zoroastrian Trust Funds of Europe

A paper of the by-election, Shettleston, June 1930. JR

214 • New Year's greetings from Iran

Collection: Zoroastrian Trust Funds of Europe

Nowruz greetings sent by Zoroastrians in Iran to Muncherjee Bhownagree in London. JR

In 1862, a Zoroastrian burial plot was procured in Brookwood Cemetery in Surrey. The transition from *dakhma* to burial required some rationalization in order to meet the requirements of Zoroastrian purity laws. This issue was partly addressed by the use of stone sarcophagi. Both Parsis and Iranian Zoroastrians are interred at Brookwood. The specifically Persian features of the cemetery were introduced by the Orientalist and polymath Sir George Birdwood. The three mausoleums of the Tata family stand in a row near the entrance of the site.

above

215 • Tata family mausoleums in Brookwood Cemetry

photograph: Bruce Benedict

Sir Dorabji and Lady Meherbai Tata's mausoleum is finely decorated in the Persian style with brick-glazed friezes depicting Median and Persian guards. To the right of it stands the mausoleum of Jamshedji Nusserwanji Tata, a philanthropist who became known as the 'Captain of Indian Industry'. Next to him is the mausoleum of Sir Ratan Tata (1871–1918), the Parsi financier and industrialist knighted in 1916, who assisted Gandhi in his struggle against racial discrimination in South Africa. He was also a patron of the arts and helped to establish both a Chair and the Department of Social Sciences at the London School of Economics. JR

ZTFE manages a registered place of worship in London, the Zoroastrian Centre, and has appointed legally authorized registrars to solemnize weddings and to issue certificates of marriages there. There are around 5,000 Zoroastrians living in the United Kingdom, and about 1,000 elsewhere throughout Europe.

216 • **The Zoroastrian Centre**
Harrow, London
photograph: Bruce Benedict

In 2008, the ZTFE moved its base from Zoroastrian House in West Hampstead to a converted Grade II listed art deco building. The new Zoroastrian Centre in Harrow has a meeting hall downstairs, a library and an upstairs prayer room with a fire that is lit for ceremonies. JR

❋

In recent years, the Zoroastrian presence in the United Kingdom has become more prominent in the media, with visits from various members of the royal family and the Archbishop of Canterbury to the Zoroastrian Centre, a Zoroastrian Member of the House of Lords, and the attendance of Zoroastrian representatives at the royal wedding, Lambeth Palace, and the Queen's Diamond Jubilee celebrations throughout 2012.

217 • **Her Majesty Queen Elizabeth II and delegates from the ZTFE**
Lambeth Palace • 15 February 2012
Clockwise from left: President Malcolm Deboo; Ervad Rustam Bhedwar; Vice President Paurushasp Jila
courtesy of Lambeth Palace/Picture Partnership

One of the first public engagements marking the Diamond Jubilee of Queen Elizabeth II took place at Lambeth Palace, when the Archbishop of Canterbury, Dr Rowan Williams, invited the leaders of Britain's main faith communities to meet Her Majesty the Queen and His Royal Highness Prince Philip. JR

218 & 219 • Mehraban and Faridoon Zartoshty
74 x 64 cm (framed)
Collection: Zoroastrian Trust Funds of Europe

Mehraban and Faridoon Zartoshty were Zoroastrian businessmen from the town of Yazd in Iran. Through their philanthropy and as a result of their interest in community affairs the Zartoshty brothers supported a number of community institutions and projects across the world. In 2011 they contributed to the founding of a Chair in Zoroastrian Studies at SOAS. SS

SRI LANKA

Sanskrit sources recall the visit of an influential *magus* who came from Persia to Sri Lanka in the fifth century CE and became the Sinhalese king's counsellor.[3] Iranians had been visiting the country since the time of the Achaemenids. The link lasted through the next millennium until, in the late sixteenth century, we have the first tangible evidence of both Parsi and Irani Zoroastrian merchants or sailors who had died on the island, and whose gravestones along the coastal areas face towards the rising or setting sun: 'The reason for that placement was mentioned on a gravestone as reflecting the deceased man's routine of "performing devotion (Sinhala: *puja*)to the sun."'[4]

By the mid-eighteenth century, many Parsis had emigrated from India to Sri Lanka as planters, merchants and agent-brokers, and their presence is well documented in British Ceylon from 1803 onwards.

above
220 • Nowruz Baug Prayer Hall
Colombo, Sri Lanka
courtesy of Jamsheed K. Choksy

The Zoroastrian prayer hall in Colombo was endowed in 1927 and is administered by the Sri Lanka Parsi Anjuman. After Ceylon became independent in 1947, about half the Parsi community chose to return to India and the rest became citizens of Sri Lanka. JR

PAKISTAN

Parsis settled in Karachi in the early nineteenth century, working as traders, opium shippers and suppliers of goods for the many ships which docked in the harbour. With its natural harbour, Karachi became a conduit for British goods sent to Delhi, Afghanistan, Samarkand, Khiva and Bokhara.

The town was divided into the Cantonment or white area, where only the English lived, and the native areas which comprised the old parts of Karachi. The Parsis lived on the borders of the old town and the Cantonment and were frequently approached by the English to carry out construction work for them. The next wave of Parsis came as commissariat agents to the British army and, with the arrival of General Napier in 1843, an increasing number of Parsis from Bombay, Surat and Navsari settled in Karachi.

221 · Garden party, 1904

courtesy of *A Zoroastrian Tapestry: Art, Religion and Culture*

The photograph is of a garden party held in honour of Framroze Edulji Punthakey, who was a founding member of the Parsi Karachi Anjoman, Deputy Collector of Income Tax and Additional Sessions Judge. His services to the citizens of Karachi during a plague and cholera epidemic were rewarded with a substantive grant of land.[5] FPM

NORTH AMERICA

A Parsi presence is first recorded in America in 1803 – in the form of a portrait of a Parsi merchant from Bombay, donated by a local sea captain to the recently founded East India Marine Society archive in Salem, Massachusetts. The painting was accompanied by a set of clothing given by its subject, Nusserwanji Maneckji Wadia, which was similar to the outfit he had worn for the sitting. Records indicate that several Parsis sailed to America in the 1860s, at least one to fight in the Civil War and another to take part in the Gold Rush.

The first Zoroastrian Association in North America was founded in 1929. The entrepreneur and philanthropist Mehraban Zartoshty (Cat. 218) came to New York from Iran in 1947 with his wife Paridokht. Thirty years later, their compatriots Arbab Rustam and Morvarid Guiv arrived and became instrumental in establishing *dar-e mehrs* throughout North America, to meet the needs of the growing number of Zoroastrians from both India and Iran.

In 1987 the Federation of Zoroastrian Associations of North America (FEZANA) registered as a non-profit, religious and charitable organization in the State of Illinois. FEZANA forms an overarching organization that gathers and disseminates material relating to the understanding, perpetuation and practice of the Zoroastrian religion. There are currently 26 Zoroastrian organizations and 11 small groups across North America that are affiliated to FEZANA.

222 · The first FEZANA Board Meeting, 1987

Executive officers left to right: Dolly Dastoor (secretary); Rohinton Rivetna (president); Homi Minocher Homji (VP); Framroze Patel (treasurer); Sabar Balsara (assistant secretary)

FEZANA sponsors an annual North American Youth Congress, and co-ordinates regional seminars with local Zoroastrian Associations. The *FEZANA Journal* functions as both a global community newsletter and an educational tool. JR

223 • San Jose *Dar-e Mehr*

California

courtesy of Rashna Wadia

This *dar-e mehr*, for the Zoroastrians in the San Francisco area, is located in the hills above San Jose. The land was donated by Arbab Rustam and Morvarid Guiv and the building funded by the Parsi and Iranian Zoroastrian communities. JR

224 • *Pir-e Sabz* celebration

Shanon Falls, Vancouver, Canada • June 2013

courtesy of Azita Dehmobed

Since 1999, in midsummer every year, members of the Zoroastrian Society of British Columbia (ZSBC), based in Vancouver, meet at a site in the mountains nearby. They are emulating their co-religionists in Iran who, at around the same time, make a 'pilgrimage' to the shrine of Pir-e Sabz in Yazd province, where they stay overnight in hilltop shelters next to the shrine. Both groups celebrate with similar prayers, food, music and dance. JR

HONG KONG AND SINGAPORE

Some of the early Zoroastrians to arrive in Hong Kong were Parsi businessmen who came from firms in Canton. Others came directly from Bombay, such as Dorabji Naoroji, who began as a baker, then owned several hotels, and eventually founded the Star Ferry that still runs between Hong Kong and the Chinese mainland.[6] Parsis played a role in both the planning committee and the board of directors of the Hong Kong and Shanghai Bank, formed in 1864.[7] The Incorporated Zoroastrian Charity Funds of Hong Kong, Canton and Macau were established in 1822.

225 • **Hong Kong University**

courtesy of A Zoroastrian Tapestry: Art, Religion and Culture

Established by Sir Hormusji Nowroji Modi in 1910, the university building was designed by Alfred Bryer and could take up to 500 undergraduates. Situated 200 feet above sea level it overlooks the harbour and the city of Victoria.[8] JR

✻

By the late 1820s, there was a sizeable enough Parsi population in Singapore to warrant the purchase of land for a cemetery. A numerically small but influential influx continued for the next century, during which period Parsis funded a library, a department store, a water company and a free English-language school.

226 • **Parsi Road, Singapore**

courtesy of FEZANA

Parsi Road, officially named in 1954, marks a section of Singapore's Central Business District associated with the early Parsi community that settled in the neighbourhood. It runs perpendicular to Mistri Road, named after a local Parsi philanthropist. JR

AUSTRALASIA

When, in 1956, Sri Lanka opted for Sinhala to become the official language of the country, many Parsis chose to migrate to Australia.[9] A few Parsis came directly from India in the late 1960s, including some married to Iranians.[10] The Australian Zoroastrian Association (AZA) began in Sydney in 1970, and now lists members originating from Iran, Pakistan, East Africa and Canada, as well as India. There is also a flourishing community in Melbourne, Victoria, where the World Parliament of Religions was held in 2009. The Melbourne community, which formally established the Zoroastrian Association of Victoria (ZAV) in 1978, has a predominantly Parsi constituency.[11]

In Auckland, New Zealand, the family building supply business of 'Shroff and Sons' has been in existence since 1877, first established by a Parsi businessman named Hormusjee Ratanjee Shroff, who apparently arrived with an MA degree from Oxford. The decades after the mid-1960s have seen an exponential rise in the Zoroastrian population in New Zealand – from less than 20 in 1986, to over 1,200 by 2012. The community now has two associations, both in Auckland.

above

227 • **Zoroastrians at the opening of the World Parliament of Religions**

Melbourne • 2009

courtesy of Arnavaz Chubb

A multi-generational Zoroastrian choir took the stage to chant the powerful Avestan prayers, the Ashem Vohu and the Yatha Ahu Vairyo. The recitation followed an orchestral performance of the opening movement of Richard Strauss's symphonic composition *Also Sprach Zarathustra*, which had been inspired by Friedrich Nietzsche's work of the same title. JR

THE PERSIAN GULF

The presence of Zoroastrians in Persian Gulf countries dates back to the development of the oil industry in the 1960s. In the last 30 years, the Zoroastrian population in the United Arab Emirates has ballooned, with an influx of highly educated professionals from India, Pakistan and Iran. The 2,000 or so Gulf Zoroastrians have no designated place of worship, but *mobeds* from within the communities will visit homes to perform *jashans* and other ceremonies.

above
228 • *Hamazori* at the Closing of the
9th World Zoroastrian Congress
Dubai • 2009
courtesy of Meher Bhesani

The 9th World Zoroastrian Congress took place in Dubai over four days at the end of 2009. It marked a first for the sizeable Zoroastrian population of the Persian Gulf region. The action of hand clasping by priests and laity, known as *hamazor*, is more than just an act of cheering at the successful completion of an event. It follows after a ritual or festive occasion and marks the transition from the sacred to the mundane. JR

EAST AND SOUTH AFRICA

In the 1870s several Parsi entrepreneurs from Bombay and towns in Gujarat moved to South Africa. More followed with their families between the turn of the century and the outbreak of the Second World War. Many of the Parsis in South Africa allied with Mahatma Gandhi to counteract the discrimination and restrictions imposed by the British. The apartheid laws of the subsequent government led many to emigrate, and, since then, the Zoroastrian population of South Africa has been steadily declining.

229 • **Sorabjee Rustomjee carries the ashes of Mahatma Gandhi, 1948**
courtesy of Sohrab Framrose Shapurjee

When M. K. Gandhi arrived as a lawyer for the Indian business community in Pretoria in 1874, he was helped by Rustomjee Jivanji Ghorkhodu. Rustomjee's son, Sorabjee, attended Gandhi's funeral in 1948, and brought back an urn containing some of the ashes to Mombasa, where a memorial service was held. JR

The earliest Parsi settler in the Sultanate of Zanzibar was a trader named Maneckji Mistry, a Wadia family member, who arrived from Surat some time in the mid-1840s. After establishing himself, Maneckji brought his wife and children over. Soon several other Parsi families followed. By the late nineteenth century, many Parsis were employed by the sultanate in the capacity of builders and carpenters as well as engineers or civil servants.

In contrast, not much is known about Parsis in Kenya at this time. By the early twentieth century, however, there were two main communities, one in Mombasa and the other in Nairobi. The former was famous in the 1930s for its Dramatic Society and its cricketers.[12] After Kenyan independence, numerous Parsis migrated to Britain, and some to India.

230 • Ratonji Dorabji Dinshaw Adenwalla
Zanzibar • late 19th century
Oil on canvas • 52 x 46 cm (unframed)
Collection: Rusi Dalal

The Adenwalla family was one of many families who settled in Zanzibar in the nineteenth century. The engraving on the painting, which was rescued from the Zanzibar fire temple, reads: 'Jehangir Hormuz & Co. Contractors and Agents Presented to Ratonji Dorabji Dinshaw'. FPM

231 • Hormusjee Cowasji Dinshaw Adenwalla Kt., OBE, MVO (1857–1939)
Artist: E. A. Tachakra • 1895
Oil on canvas • 56 x 47 cm (unframed)
Collection: Rusi Dalal

Educated at King's College, London, Hormusjee was apprenticed to James Barber and Son and then with Leopold Bin Fils & Gans, Paris. He is seen as the man who modernized Aden, which was governed as part of British India. He built schools, waterworks, a floating pontoon and organized the Aden Chamber of Commerce. His family established consecrated fire temples in Aden and Zanzibar – the only ones outside Iran and the subcontinent of India. FPM

THE SEVEN CREATIONS

Sarah Stewart

In Zoroastrianism the creation of the material world, alluded to in the Avesta and given coherent form in the Pahlavi literature, begins with six benevolent divine beings known as the Amesha Spentas, or 'Bounteous Immortals'. These were brought into existence through the creative energy of Spenta Mainyu, the Holy Spirit of Ahura Mazda, 'Wise Lord', with whom they formed a heptad. Together they created the world in a state of perfection. The *Amesha Spentas* are central to the doctrine of Zoroastrianism as they are linked not only to creation but also to priestly ritual, observances of the laity and the seven holy days of obligation. These days are possibly the legacy of ancient seasonal festivals refounded in honour of Ahura Mazda and the divinities created by him. The Amesha Spentas are believed to dwell each within their own creations while at the same time remaining aspects of God's nature.

232–234 • *Fire and Water 1–3*
Artist: Fereydoun Ave • 2008
Mixed media on canvas • 2.4 x 1 m
LAL Collection on loan to the Zoroastrian Cultural Center in Paris

THE SEVEN CREATIONS
TRANSLATED BY P. O. SKJÆRVØ[1]

[GBd. 1a: 1] When the Foul Spirit was undone and lying unconscious, as I wrote above, he lay stunned for 3000 years.

[2] During that inactivity of the Foul Spirit, Ohrmazd fashioned the creation into the world of the living …

[3] First he set in place the sky to keep back – some say it was the first; second the water, to strike the lie-demon of thirst; third the earth with all things with bones; fourth the plants, to help the beneficent cow; fifth the Bull/cow, to help the Righteous Man (i.e. Gayomard); sixth he set in place the Righteous Man, to strike and undo the Foul Spirit together with the demons.

[4] Next he set in place the fire as living cinder (*khwarg*) and attached to it the brilliance (*brah*) of the Endless Light. Thus it has a good form, as is the fire's wish. Next he set in place the wind in the form of a fifteen-year-old youth, to carry and uphold the water and plants, the Bull/cow and the Righteous Man, and everything else.

235 • Sky
Aahan • Artist: Mehran Zirak • 1998 • 67 x 25 x 3 cm

[GBd. 1a: 6] First he set in place the sky, light, visible, very far and in the shape of an egg, made of shining metal, that is, its essence was steel and male, and connected its top to the Endless Light [cf. 17:2]. He set in place the entire creation inside the sky, like a fortified camp, in which all the tools needed for the battle have been placed, or like a house in which everything is stored.

The foundation of the sky is as thick as it is long, as long as it is high, as high as it is deep; with uniform measure, like the helmet of a mace-bearing (soldier). It was endowed with thought, speech, and action and was aware, causing increase, and discriminating. Thus was the sky in the world of thought.

It received a firm fortification against the Foul Spirit, in order not to let him run back. Like a heroic soldier dressed in armor, so that he is saved from the battle without fear, thus the Sky in the world of thought upholds the sky (in this world).

To help the sky he established bliss, for by means of it he established bliss, for even now in the Mixture the creation is *in* bliss.

Water

[GBd. 1a: 7] Second, from the substance of the sky he fashioned water, which flowed as deep as when a man puts his hands on the earth and walks on hands and feet and the water reaches him to the stomach. To help it he gave it the wind, the rain, fog, mist, and snow.

above (1)
236 · **Earth**
from the *Earth* series · Artist: Fereydoun Ave · 2008
Collage and mixed media on paper · 51 x 34 cm

[Gbd. 1a: 8] Third, from the water he established the earth, round, with its passages reaching far into the distance, without depressions, without elevations, even, its length equal to its width, its width equal to its depth. He set it up in the middle of the sky.

[10] And he placed as substance in the earth the mountains, which afterward expanded and grew out of the earth. And to help the earth he established iron, copper, sulfur, borax, and all the hard essence of the earth, except …(?), for they are of opposite essence. That hard. The earth was fashioned like a man whose various garments are placed close to all parts of his body. Beneath this earth there stands water everywhere.

above (2)
237 · **Plant**
Evergreen · Artist: Fereydoun Ave · 2004
Mixed media on canvas · 2.03 x 1.04 m
LAL Collection on loan to the Zoroastrian Cultural Center in Paris

[Gbd. 1a: 11] Fourth he created the plants. First one grew up above the earth as high as a stride, without branches, bark, or thorns, moist and sweet. And it contained the power of all the plant species in its seed. And to help the plant he gave it water and fire, for every single species of plants has a drop of water at the end and a fire four fingers long before it. By that power it kept growing.

above (3)
238 · **Cattle**
Ta naghsh bebin 2i · Artist: Mehran Zirak · 2013

[Gbd. 1a: 12] Fifth, in Eranwez in the middle of the world on the shore of the good River Daiti where the middle of the world is, he fashioned the Bull placed alone: white, luminous, like a moon that measures three spears in height. And to help it he gave it water and plants, for during the Mixture it receives strength and growth from them.

above (4)
239 · **Man**
L'Accroupi · Artist: Bijan Saffari · 2000
Painted bronze · 23 x 6 x 5 cm

[Gbd. 1: 13] Sixth he fashioned Gayomard, luminous like the sun – he measured four spears in height, his width equal to his height – on the shore of the River Daiti, where the middle of the world is, Gayomard on the left, the Bull on the right …

To help him he gave him sleep, the relaxation of the creator. For Ohrmazd fashioned forth that sleep in the shape of a luminous tall young man of fifteen. And he fashioned Gayomard together with the Bull from the earth. And from the light and turquoise color of the sky he fashioned the semen of humans and cattle, as these two seeds are from fire, not from water. He put them in the bodies of Gayomard and the Bull, so that it would produce plenitude of people and cattle.

240 • Fire

Fire and Water 4 • Fereydoun Ave • 2008
Mixed media on canvas • 2.4 x 1 m
LAL Collection on loan to the Zoroastrian Cultural Center in Paris

[GBd. 3: 10] Then he filled fire into each creature that he fashioned, like a house-master who goes into the house and puts his clothes down neatly in the house.

[11] He ordered the Fire to serve men during the Assault, to make food, and strike away pain …

[12] And he appointed and positioned all the Amahrspands so as to take part in the battle of the creatures, so that when the Assault comes, each takes on his own opponent to fight, that is, no new command is needed.

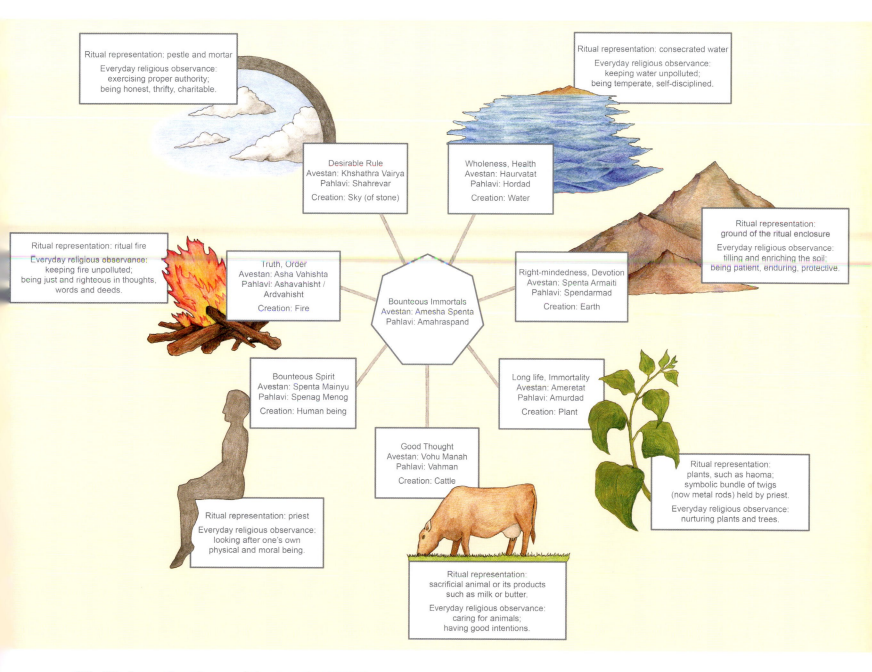

Ritual representation: pestle and mortar

Everyday religious observance: exercising proper authority; being honest, thrifty, charitable.

Ritual representation: consecrated water

Everyday religious observance: keeping water unpolluted; being temperate, self-disciplined.

Desirable Rule
Avestan: Khshathra Vairya
Pahlavi: Shahrevar

Creation: Sky (of stone)

Wholeness, Health
Avestan: Haurvatat
Pahlavi: Hordad

Creation: Water

Ritual representation: ground of the ritual enclosure

Everyday religious observance: tilling and enriching the soil; being patient, enduring, protective.

Ritual representation: ritual fire

Everyday religious observance: keeping fire unpolluted; being just and righteous in thoughts, words and deeds.

Truth, Order
Avestan: Asha Vahishta
Pahlavi: Ashavahisht / Ardvahisht

Creation: Fire

Bounteous Immortals
Avestan: Amesha Spenta
Pahlavi: Amahraspand

Right-mindedness, Devotion
Avestan: Spenta Armaiti
Pahlavi: Spendarmad

Creation: Earth

Bounteous Spirit
Avestan: Spenta Mainyu
Pahlavi: Spenag Menog

Creation: Human being

Long life, Immortality
Avestan: Ameretat
Pahlavi: Amurdad

Creation: Plant

Good Thought
Avestan: Vohu Manah
Pahlavi: Vahman

Creation: Cattle

Ritual representation: priest

Everyday religious observance: looking after one's own physical and moral being.

Ritual representation: plants, such as haoma; symbolic bundle of twigs (now metal rods) held by priest.

Everyday religious observance: nurturing plants and trees.

Ritual representation: sacrificial animal or its products such as milk or butter.

Everyday religious observance: caring for animals; having good intentions.

241 • **The Seven Creations and the *Amesha Spentas***

Artist: Alexandra Bühler with John Borsberry
commissioned for The Everlasting Flame exhibition 2013

NOTES TO THE CATALOGUE

ONE · **THE ANCIENT WORLD**
1. See Harper at al. (1992), nos 1–13.
2. 'Kaftari Ware', *Encyclopaedia Iranica* (www.iranicaonline.org/articles/kaftari-ware).
3. Spycket (1992), plates 150–5.
4. Woolley (1976), plate 88.
5. Information from Richard Dunbrill.
6. Spycket (1992), plates 141–55.
7. *Iranica Antiqua* xxviii (1993), plate 16b.
8. *Iranica Antiqua* xxviii (1993), plates 13–15.
9. Spycket (1992), plates 114–30.
10. Curtis (2005): 112.
11. Curtis (2000): 24, fig. 23.
12. Barnett (1962): 97, plate xlvi; Simpson (1997): 152–7; Middleton and Freestone: 28–30; Curtis (2000): 21, fig. 18.
13. Moorey (1974): 29–30, 48, pl. x. B. Simpson (2008): 188–9, cat. 188.
14. Curtis and Tallis (2012): 98, cat. 25.
15. Anthony (2007); Parpola (2002); Witzel (2003).

TWO · **SACRED TEXTS**
1. For a history of Samuel Guise's collection see Sims-Williams, U. (2009): 199–209.
2. Thomas Hyde's collection of Zoroastrian manuscripts is described in Sims-Williams, U. (2012): 173–94.
3. These leaves were recently identified by Professor P. O. Skjærvø (Harvard) as belonging to the missing first part of the manuscript TD4 (a) copied by Gobedshah Rostam Bundar, now in the K.R. Cama Oriental Institute, no. R-590, which also contains the *Dadistan i Denig*.
4. See Williams (1990): 7. *Revayat* is an Arabic/New Persian word meaning 'tradition', 'something handed from one to another', applied anachronistically by analogy to the New Persian *Revayats*. The full title was first coined by E.W. West (Geiger 1895: 104).

THREE · **THE SILK ROAD, CENTRAL ASIA AND CHINA**
1. Vaissière and Riboud (2003): 133–4.
2. Al'baum (1975); Vaissière and Compareti (2006); Grenet (2007): 9–19; Compareti (2009).
3. Sims-Williams, N. (2004b): 118; Sims-Williams, N. (1976): 46–8, with appendix by Gershevitch, I., pp. 75–82.
4. Sims-Williams, N. (2007): 136–7.
5. Naveh and Shaked (2005): 174–85.
6. Sims-Williams, N. (2004a): 248–9; Sims-Williams, N. (2005): 181–93.
7. Abdullaev and Berdimuradov (1991): 64–75.
8. Berdimuradov and Samibaev (1999): 46, figs. 92–93.
9. Belenitskii *et al* (1977) [1984]: 187–229; Shkoda (1985): 82–9; Shkoda (2009): 112.
10. Grenet and Zuang Guangda (1996): 175.
11. For a general account of funerary practices, see Grenet, this volume.
12. Rapoport and Lapirov-Skoblo (1963): 141–56, especially pp. 152–3; Rapoport (1971): 94, 96 and *passim*; Grenet (1984): 232–59;

Yagodin and Betts (2006); Snesarev (1969): 107–81.
13. Berdimuradov *et al* (2008): 137–42, pl. 1.
14. Ludmilla, V. (1983): 3: 46–9; Grenet (1986): 97–131, see especially pp. 101–4 and fig. 35.
15. Kastal'sky (1909): 1–36; Borisov (1940): 25–49; Stavisky (1961): 162–76; Grenet (1986): 106–107; Marshak (1995/96): 299–321.
16. Etsuko (2005): 257–78, see especially pp. 257–61.
17. Narshakhi (1954): 23.
18. Ibid.: 48.

FOUR · **THE JUDAEO-CHRISTIAN WORLD**
1. Margoliouth (1905): 53.
2. McKendrick *et al* (2011): 212–3.

FIVE · **IMPERIAL AND POST IMPERIAL IRAN**
1. See for example Boyce (1982): 6–12; J.R. Skjærvø (2005): 52–53; Hintze (1998): 139, 147–9; Curtis (2013): 18–22.
2. Ibid.
3. Barnett (1957): 62, pl. xx: 4; Mitchell (2000): 51, pl. xxi.b; Curtis and Tallis (2005): 71, cat. 28; British Museum (2009): 30.
4. Ouseley (1819): pl. xlv; Barnett (1957): 62, pl. xix: 2; Mitchell (2000): 50, 52, pl. xx.c; Curtis and Tallis (2005): 157, cat. 198.
5. Ouseley (1819), pl. xlv; Rogers (1929), fig. 23; Barnett (1957): 61, p. xix: 1; Mitchell (2000): 52, pl. xxii.b; Curtis and Tallis (2005): 72, cat. 29.
6. Perrot (2010), pl. 372; Harper et al. (1992), no. 159.
7. Curtis and Tallis (2005), nos 51–2; Harper et al. (1992), nos 155–6; Perrot (2010), pls 345–6.
8. Boyce (1982): 105.
9. Barnett (1960): 29–30, pl. vii.
10. Ibid.
11. British Museum (2009): 30.
12. Finkel (2013): 5, line 15.
13. Ibid.: 6–7.
14. Curtis (2013): 51–2.
15. In Isaiah 45.1, Yahweh refers to Cyrus as the 'anointed of Yahweh', a title formerly applied to the King of Israel. See Jones (1966): 1214.
16. Smith (1963): 419.
17. Jones (1966): 1214.
18. Kent (1953): 156.
19. Curtis and Tallis (2005): 79; Boyce (1982): 105–6; Schmidt (1939).
20. Sarkhosh Curtis (2007): 24.
21. Vanden Berghe and Schippmann (1985), fig. 1; Curtis and Tallis (2012), no. 127.
22. Nikitin (2000): 12–13.
23. Mithra refers to a word or act that is contractual. The Avestan Hymn to Mithra (*Yasht* 10), emphasizes Mithra's role as protector and sustainer of the one who keeps the contract. He is upholder of the principle of *asha* ('order', 'righteousness' and 'truth'), acting as judge in rooting out those who break the bond and smashing them with his mace (YT.10:28,80). In YT. 10, Mithra rises above Mount Hara and travels across the sky before the sun, surveying the entire material world from the mountaintops with 10,000 eyes (YT. 10:

13, 51, 82). Mithra is, therefore, ultimately linked with the sun, the greatest natural illumination for both the conceptual and corporeal worlds, which he protects from wrath, destruction and death (YT. 10.93).

24. Bivar (1969), pl. 28, NF 2; Gignoux (1976): 143.
25. Bivar (1969), pl. 6, BH 1; Harper (1985): 257; Simpson (2012): 83.
26. Warner and Warner 1 (1905):158.
27. Harper (1985): 256, pl. xiiib.
28. Bivar (1969): 5, BD 3.
29. Ibid.: p. 57, pl. 5, BD 4.
30. Ibid.: 57, pl. 5, BD 5; Lerner (1977): 38, pl. v, fig. 31; Gyselen (2006): 60–1; Freidenberg (2009), cat. 17: 36–7.
31. Dalton (1964): 55–7, pl. xxxii, cat. no. 202; Hughes and Hall (1979): 328, 330, table 1.
32. Brock and Ashbrook Harvey (1987): 73–6.
33. Wright (1872): 1079–83.
34. Dadoyan (2011): 22–5.
35. Zaehner (1955): 28–9.
36. Brunner (1979): 94–9; Harper (1978): 24; Russell (1987): 380, 393 n. 27; Simpson (2003): 347–75, at 366.
37. Daryaee (2012): 229–42, at 241–2; Harper (1978): 16.
38. Brunner (1979): 109–110, 112.
39. Harper (1978): 97–100.
40. Ibid.: 88, 113, 122, pl. 56.
41. Trever and Lukonin (1987): 118–19, 125, pl. 114.
42. Sotheby's catalogue, 8 October 2008 (see bibliography relating to senmurv motif).

SIX · POST ARAB CONQUEST

1. Boyce (1979): 154–5.
2. Skjærvø (2011): 608-628 (www.iranicaonline.org/articles/kartir).
3. Sims-Williams, U. (2009): 199–209.
4. Thackston (1994): 269; Séguy (1977); Gruber (2009): 197–202.
5. Kreyenbroek (1985) [1999]: 118, n. 38.
6. al-Jahiz (1965): 259; al-Qazvini: (1982): 434.
7. Ferdowsi (1905): 119.
8. Fischer (2004): 406, n. 25.
9. For the most recent scholarship on illustrated copies of these texts, see Berlekamp 2011.
10. For the episode illustrated, see Dabir-Siaghi (1956): 88, line 551.
11. Grube (1972): 89–91, no. 51; Brend and Melville (2010): 6.
12. Ferdowsi (1905): 247.
13. For the episode illustrated, see Dabir-Siaghi (1956): vol. I, VII, 129, line 199.
14. Brend and Melville 2010: 201; Sarkhosh Curtis (1993): 37.
15. For the episode illustrated, see Dabir-Siaghi (1956): 201–2, lines 1816–18.
16. Grube (1972): 68, no. 33.
17. For the episode illustrated, see Dabir-Siaghi (1956): vol. I, VII, 129, line 199 (translation: Ferdowsi (1905): 247).
18. Grube (1972): 168, 171, no. 149.
19. Brend and Melville (2010): 126; Boyce 1979: 104–5, 250; Skjærvø (2013): www.iranicaonline.org/articles/kayanian-v); Grube 1972: 171, no. 149; Fischer (2004): 87–8.
20. For the episode illustrated, see Dabir-Siaghi (1956): 484, line 550.
21. Ferdowsi (1906): 220.
22. For the episode illustrated, see Dabir-Siaghi (1956): 2360, lines 1987–8 (translation partly from Ferdowsi (1923): 299).
23. See Fischer (2004): 125 & n. 43. For the appearance of Srosh in dreams see Boyce (1989) [1975]: 86–7. In the Parthian epic *Vis u Ramin* see Davis: (2009): 263. For Srosh in Islamic times see Kreyenbroek (1985): 181, 183.
24. Modi (1995): 264.
25. Grube: (1972): 92, no. 51; Brend and Melville (2010): 77.
26. Boyce (1979): 162.
27. Punthakey Mistree (2002): 564–7.
28. Ibid.: 562–3.
29. Stewart (2012): 64–5.
30. Amighi (1990): 152; Choksy (2006): 149–150; Jackson (1906): 427; Mehr (2002): 298.
31. Amighi (1990): 152; Jackson and Williams (1906): 427.
32. Amighi (1990): 143, 148.
33. Amighi (1990): 162; Mehr (2002): 285, 287, 298; (Ringer) 2011: 187; Shahrokh and Writer (1994): 3–4, 20, 31; Stewart (2012): 69.
34. Calmard (1987): 878–890; Shuster (1912): 55.
35. Choksy (2006): 153–56.

SEVEN · JOURNEY AND SETTLEMENT

1. Mistree (2002): 411–33; Wink (1990): 48–51.
2. Shea and Jackson (1901): 115–6.
3. Abu'l-Fazl 'Allami (1939): 117.
4. Athar Ali (1999): 365–73; Behl (2010): 113–47.
5. Sheffield (2012).
6. Nanji and Dhalla (2007): 35–58.
7. See Williams, this volume, and Williams (2009).
8. See Kulke (1974): 238.
9. *Bhagaria* means 'sharer'; the Navsari priesthood was named in such a way because they divided the priestly work among them according to a strict rota or pattern. See Kotwal (1976): 26.
10. For edition of this chapter see Dhabhar (1909): 9.
11. Hodivala (1920): 309–10.
12. For a translation of this section see Dhabhar (1932): 360.
13. Sims-Williams, U. (2012).

EIGHT · PARSI SALON

1. Parsi Prakash, vol. 2: 137; Wadia (1964): 19; Darukhanawala (1939): 268.
2. Moses (1850): 256.
3. Godrej (2002): 641.
4. Ibid.: 640.
5. Crossman (1991): 130.
6. Harris (1958): 3–6.
7. Ibid.
8. Godrej (2002): 637.
9. Ibid.: 654.
10. Ibid.: 658.
11. Darukhanawala (1939): 4; Linklater (1961): 140.
12. Darukhanawala (1939): 94.
13. Shah and Vatsal (2010): 104.

NINE · FIRE TEMPLE

1. Dhalla (1908): 175.

2. Dhalla (1908): 155–7.

3. The Parthians, at about the same time they dropped the title 'philhellene', began to show fire holders on their bronze coins. See Sarkhosh Curtis (2007): 16–22.

4. For this and further discussion of fire altars on Sasanian coins, see Yamomoto 1981: 68–73.

5. Presumably developed from the Achaemenid 'victorious fire' carried before the Persian army when going to battle. See Boyce (1989) www.iranicaonline.org/articles/atas-fire.

6. From the inscription of Kirder on the Ka'ba-ye Zardosht. See Boyce (1984): 112.

7. The Armenian term *mehean*, probably denoting 'place of rites', came also to be used for 'temple', suggesting that this development goes back at least to Parthian times. See Boyce (1982): 228.

8. Boyce (1989): www.iranicaonline.org/articles/dar-e-mehr. A Zoroastrian term first recorded in the Persian *Rivayats* and Parsi-Gujarati writings.

9. Stewart (2007): 61–3.

10. Jackson (1938): 288–94.

11. See Boyce (1975b): 437.

12. Ibid.: 463–4.

13. See Shaked (2004): 336–7.

14. This table is based on the structure of the modern yasna ritual outlined by Oktor Prods Skjærvø in his *Introduction to Zoroastrianism*. See: www.fas.harvard.edu/~iranian/zoroastrianism/zoroastrianism1_intro.pdf (2006): 64.

15. This ceremony is not referred to in the yasna ritual described in Kotwal and Boyd (1991).

TEN · ZOROASTRIAN COMMUNITIES AROUND THE WORLD

1. This was one of the earliest internment sites outside British India in the modern period, established and maintained by the Parsi Anjuman of Hong Kong, Canton and Macao.

2. See www.fezana.org/files/demographics/zworld6Sep12.pdf.

3. Choksy (2007): 181–2.

4. Ibid.: 187. This practice appears to relate to the Zoroastrian belief that the soul rises to be judged as the rays of the sun alight on the earth at dawn on the fourth day after death.

5. Godrej and Punthakey Mistree (2002): 466.

6. Hinnells (2005): 173.

7. Ibid.: 174.

8. Godrej and Punthakey Mistree (2002): 461.

9. Choksy (2007): 194.

10. Hinnells (2005): 555.

11. Ibid.: 585.

12. Ibid.: 292–3.

THE SEVEN CREATIONS

1. Skjærvø (2011): 89–92, 93.

GLOSSARY

ab zohr • libation to the waters

aban • the waters; name of month

Adurbad-e Mahraspandan • high priest under the Sasanian king, Shapur II

afarganyu (PGuj; also *afrinagan*) • 'fire vase'

afrinagan • ceremony; a ceremony of blessing

agiary (PGuj) • fire temple

Ahuna Vairya/Ahunavar/Yatha ahu Vairyo
a sacred prayer that encapsulates the knowledge of the Avesta

Ahura Mazda (MP *Ohrmazd*) • the 'Wise Lord', the principal deity

Airyaman • divinity of 'friendship'

Ameretat • 'immortality'. One of the *Amesha Spentas*; name of month

Amesha Spentas • 'Life-giving Immortals'

Anahita • female divinity of the waters

Angra Mainyu (MP *Ahriman*) • the 'Destructive Force', antagonist of Spenta Mainyu in the Gathas and later of Ahura Mazda

anjuman association, 'community'

aramgah literally 'place of peace;' cemetery

Armaiti • 'Right-mindedness'. one of the *Amesha Spentas*

Asha • 'order', 'right', 'truth'. one of the seven *Amesha Spentas*

Asha vahishta (MP *Ardvahisht*; NP *Ardibihisht*) • 'Best Truth/Order'. One of the *Amesha Spentas*, associated with fire; name of a month

ashavan • one who follows *Asha*; a worshipper of Ahura Mazda

Ashem vohu • one of the three principal prayers of the faith

astodan • 'bone holder,' ossuary

Astvat ereta • 'he who embodies *Asha*.' The name of the final *saoshyant*

atashkadeh • ('house of fire') Iranian term for fire temple

Atash Adaran • second grade of ritual fire in fire temples

Atash Dadgah • third and lowest grade of fire, can be in a house or minor fire temple

Atash Bahram • highest grade of fire; name of 'cathedral' fire temple

Avesta • corpus of sacred texts of the Zoroastrians

Azhi Dahaka (NP *Zahhak*) • 'snake' or 'dragon Dahaka'. Evil King of Avestan and later myth

baj • a ritual for consecrating bread

baj-e gahambar • the liturgical service recited during the seasonal festivals

bareshnum • nine-night ritual of ablution and purification

baresman/barsom • the twigs or metal rods held by the priests in ritual

barsom tays • metal rods placed on the half-moon stands during in ritual

baug • a place where weddings or initiations are celebrated; a Parsi colony

behdin (MP *weh den*) • of the 'good religion' i.e. laity

Bhagaria • priests of Navsari, Gujarat, who agreed to share their earnings from ritual work

boyvara • a priest who serves the sacred fire five times a day

chahar taq • 'four arched' edifice within which stood a fire holder

chaharom • the rituals on the fourth day after death

Chinvat Peretu • 'crossing-place of the account-keeper,' the Chinvat bridge where the soul is judged at death

daena (MP *den*) • [religious] insight; religion; the conscience which appears before the soul on the third day after death before judgment at the Chinvat Bridge

daeva (OP *daiva*; NP *div*) • 'false/erroneous god; demon'

dakhma • site of exposure of the dead – 'tower of silence'

Darb-e Mihr • community prayer hall

Dar-e Mehr • 'Gate' or 'Court' of Mithra; a fire temple

dastur • highest rank of priest

divo • an oil lamp

drugvant (AV) • 'deceitful' one who follows the Lie.

dron (*darun*) • flat unleavened wheat bread consecrated by the priest

druj (AV) • deceit, chaos, confusion

Feridun (AV *Thraetaona*) • Iranian mythical hero

Frashokereti (MP *frashegird*) • 'the making wonderful/perfect' of the world; the renovation at the end of time

Fravardigan • ten day festival commemorating the *fravashis* in honour of the souls and spirits of the dead

fravashi • the 'pre-soul' that pre-exists and post-exists the individual, and is venerated as efficacious on behalf of the living

gah • one of the five divisions of the day

gahanbar • one of six seasonal festivals

gara • a silk sari originally from China with the ground fully embroidered with Chinese motifs.

garo.demana (MP *garodman*) • 'house of welcome/song'

Gathas • The Old Avestan poems of Zarathushtra

Gayo maretan (MP *Gayomard*; NP *Gayomars*) • the primal mortal

hamazor • a ritual handshake affirming spiritual unity

haoma (MP *hom*) • the ephedra plant pressed during the Yasna, and offered with milk and water as *ab zohr* at the end of the liturgy

Haurvatat • 'wholeness' or 'health'. One of the Amesha Spentas, associated with the waters; name of a month

herbad • 'religious teacher;' priest who has completed the first level of training (*navar*)

Indra • one of the main Indian deities

jashan • ceremony of praise or thanksgiving

jhabla • a smock like blouse with Chinese style gara embroidery worn by Parsi children

jizya • poll tax on non-Muslims

jud den/juddin • a non-Zoroastrian

Kayanian • the second mythological dynasty of Iranian kings

Keresaspa • ancient Iranian mythical hero

Kerdir • a powerful priest under several early Sasanian monarchs

Khordeh Avesta • prayer book

Khshathra Vairya • 'desired rule.' One of the *Amesha Spentas*

khvarenah (MP *khwarrah*; NP *farr*) • '[divine] fortune or glory'
kusti • woven cord of wool (usually lamb, but can be camel or goat hair) made of 72 threads; tied around the waist over the *sudreh* after initiation

leno • silk, a fine translucent gauze silk with lines found within the weave
loban • (PGuj) incense
lobandan • incense burner
lork (NP) • the festival food of seven kinds of dried fruits, dates, chickpeas and nuts, which are eaten at the end of the *gahanbar* prayers

madressa • a religious school
magu- (OP) • 'priest', 'Magi'
manthra • powerful word or prayer
Mihragan • a seasonal celebration in honour of *Mithra* held in the autumn
Mithra (MP *Mihr*) • 'bond'; male divinity of the contract; name of month
menog (MP) • 'conceptual' existence
mobedyar • lay helper to the priest, functions as priest in Iran
mowbed • (MP: NP *mobed*) • priest
Muktad • Parsi celebration before *Noruz* (equivalent to Iranian *Fravardigan*)

Nana • a goddess of Mesopotamian origin, worshipped by the Sogdians and Bactrians
nask • 'bundle:' refers to the 21 collections of Avestan texts
nasu (AV) • 'dead matter'
navjote (PGuj) • 'initiation'
nirang • consecrated bull's urine; a formulaic prayer
niyayish • hymns of praise to divinities
Noruz • 'New Day,' Zoroastrian New Year

Ohrmazd (MP) • Ahura Mazda

padan / padam (AV *paitidana*) • mouth covering worn by priest before the fire
padyab • washing of hands and face
panthak • (PGuj) jurisdiction of Parsi priest
parahom • a libation prepared during the Yasna ceremony
pavi • furrows made on the floor to mark a sacred space
Pazand • Middle Persian/Pahlavi texts transcribed into Avestan script
pheta • a stiff hat made of cloth and cardboard and worn by Parsis
Pishdadian • the first mythological dynasty of Iranian kings

Rashnu (NP *Rashn*) • divinity representing Justice
raspi • assistant priest
Revayats • correspondence sent from Iranian Zoroastrians to Parsis

between the fifteenth to eighteenth centuries
Rostam • an eastern Iranian heroic figure of the Shahnameh

saoshyant • 'one who will be strong'; also a posthumous son of Zarathustra who will appear before the Universal Judgement at the end of time
sedreh-pushi • Iranian Zoroastrian term for initiation
Shamash • a Mesopotamian deity also the sun god in Babylonia and Assyria
Simorgh (AV *Saena* bird; MP *Senmurv*) • a mythical phoenix-like bird of the Avesta and later myth
Spenta Armaiti (MP *Aspandarmud*; NP *Esfandarmoz*) see *Armaiti*, name of a month
Spenta Mainyu • 'beneficent inspiration/spirit.' One of the *Amesha Spentas*
Sraosha (MP *Srosh*) • 'readiness to listen'; a divinity associated with prayer
sudreh (NP *sedreh*) • white muslin shirt invested during initiation

Tanchoi • a silk brocade

varasyo • consecrated white bull
Videvdad / Vendidad • YAV. text
Vohu Manah (NP *Bahman*) • 'good thought.' One of the *Amesha Spentas*; name of a month

weh den (MP) • 'good religion'

Yasht • Young Avestan hymns to the *yazatas* 'divinities'
Yasna (AV) • 'worship, sacrifice, name of the central Zoroastrian ritual
yazata (MP *yazad*) • being 'worthy of worship', Zoroastrian divinity
Yazdegerdi • the Zoroastrian era which takes its name after the last Zoroastrian king Yazdegird III
yazishn • the Yasna ceremony
Yenghe Hatam • one of the three principal prayers of the faith

Zahhak (AV *Ahzi Dahaka*) • evil king in ancient Iranian myth and *Shahnameh*
zand • Pahlavi translation and exegesis of the Avesta
zaothra (MP *zohr*) • libation
zari • gold or silver metal thread used for embroidery
zot • chief priest

BIBLIOGRAPHY

NONSTANDARD REFERENCES

FO 248/852 (Foreign Office and Foreign and Commonwealth Office: Embassy and Consulates, Iran [formerly Persia]: General Correspondence from India, January–May 1905).

The Parsi (1905), 1: 2 (February): 49–50.

BOOKS AND JOURNALS.

Abdullaev, K. and A. Berdimuradov (1991), 'Novyi pamiatnik sogdiiskogo iskusstva', *Vestnik Drevnei Istorii*, issue 4: 64–75.

Abu'l-Fazl 'Allami (1939), *Akbarnāmah*, vol 3, trans. H. Beveridge (Calcutta - reprint).

Aijazuddin, F.S. (1979), *Sikh Portraits by European Artists* (London).

Al'baum, L.I. (1975), *Zhivopis Afrasiaba* (Tashkent).

Ali, M.A. (1999), 'Pursuing an Elusive Seeker of Universal Truth: The Identity and Environment of the Author of the "Dabistān-i Mazāhib"', *Journal of the Royal Asiatic Society* 9.3: 365–73.

Amighi, J.K. (1990), *The Zoroastrians of Iran: Conversion, Assimilation, or Persistence* (New York).

Andreas, F.C. and K. Barr (1933), *Bruchstückeeiner Pehlevi Übersetzung der Psalmen* (Berlin).

Anklesaria, B.T. (1964), *Vichitakiha-i Zatsparam* (Bombay).

Anklesaria, T.D. (1976), *The Datistan-i Dinik. Part I: Pursishn I–XL* (Pahlavi Codices and Iranian Researches 40, Shiraz).

Anthony, D.W. (2007), *The Horse, the Wheel and Language: How Bronze-Age Riders from the Eurasian Steppes Shaped the Modern World* (Princeton).

Assemani, S.E. (1748), *Acta Sanctorum Martyrum Orientalium et Occidentalium* (Rome), 2 vols.

Bailey, H.W. (1971), *Zoroastrian Problems in the Ninth-Century Books* (Oxford).

Barnett, R.D. (1957), 'Persepolis', *Iraq* 19.

— (1960), 'Ancient Oriental Goldwork', *British Museum Quarterly* 22.

— (1962), 'A Review of Acquisitions 1955–62 of Western Asiatic Antiquities (I)', *British Museum Quarterly* 26.

Bedjan, P. (1890–97), *Acta Martyrum et Sanctorum Syriace* (Leipzig), 7 vols.

Behl, A. (2010), 'Pages from the Book of Religions', in L.L. Patton and D.L. Haberman, eds, *Notes from a Mandala: Essays in the History of Indian Religions in Honor of Wendy Doniger* (Newark, DE): 113–47.

Belenitskii, A.M., et al. (1977), 'Raskopki drevnego Pendzhikenta v 1977g', *Arkheologicheskie Raboty v Tadzhikistane* 17: 187–229.

Bendezu-Sarmiento, J. and J. Lhuillier (2013), 'Sine sepulchro cultural complex of Transoxiana (between 1500 and the middle of the 1st millennium BC)', *Archäologische Mitteilungen aus Iran und Turan* 45 (forthcoming).

Berdimuradov, A.È. and M.K. Samibaev (1999), *Khram Dzhartepa* (Tashkent).

Berdimuradov, A.E., et al. (2012), 'A New Discovery of Stamped Ossuaries Near Shahr-i Sabz (Uzbekistan)', *Bulletin of the Asia Institute* 22: 137–42.

Berlekamp, P. (2011), *Wonder, Image, and Cosmos in Medieval Islam* (New Haven/London).

Bernshtam, A.N. (1952), *Istoriko-arkheologicheskie ocherki tsentral'nogo Tian'-Shania i Pamiro-Alaia* (Moscow).

Bivar, A.D.H. (1969), *Catalogue of the Western Asiatic Seals in the British Museum: Stamp Seals II: The Sassanian Dynasty* (London).

de Blois, F. (2012), 'A New Look at Mazdak', in T. Bernheimer and A. Silverstein, eds, *Late Antiquity: Eastern Perspectives* (Exeter): 13–24.

Borisov, A.I. (1940), 'Kistolkovaniyu izobrazhenii na biianaimanskikh ossuarii', *Trudy Otdela Vostoka Èrmitazha* 2 (Leningrad): 25–49.

Boroffka, N. and L. Swerçkow (2007), 'The Jaz Culture: New Research from Uzbekistan', *Miras* 1.

Boroffka, N. and S. Hansen, eds (2010), *Archäologische Forschungen in Kasachstan, Tadschikistan, Turkmenistan und Usbekistan* (Berlin).

Boyce, M. (1969), 'Maneckji Limji Hataria in Iran', in *The K.R. Cama Oriental Institute Golden Jubilee Volume* (Bombay): 19–31.

— (1975a), *A History of Zoroastrianism* (Leiden), vol. 1.

— (1975b), 'On the Zoroastrian Temple Cult of Fire', *Journal of the American Oriental Society*: 454–65.

— (1977), *A Persian Stronghold of Zoroastrianism* (Oxford).

— (1979), *Zoroastrians: Their Religious Beliefs and Practices* (London).

— (1982), *A History of Zoroastrianism* (Leiden), vol. 2.

— (1984), *Textual Sources for the Study of Zoroastrianism* (Manchester).

— (1989), 'Atash', *Encyclopædia Iranica* 3 (London and New York): 3.

— (1993), 'Dar-e Mehr', *Encyclopædia Iranica* 6 (Costa Mesa, California).

Boyce, M. and F. Kotwal (2006), 'Irānšāh', in *Encyclopædia Iranica* 13 (Costa Mesa, California): 531–3.

Brend, B. and C. Melville (2010), *Epic of the Persian Kings: The Art of Ferdowsi's* Shahnameh (Cambridge).

British Museum (2009), *Treasures: The World's Cultures from the British Museum* (Victoria).

Brock, S.P. and S. Ashbrook Harvey (1987), *Holy Women of the Syrian Orient* (Berkeley/London).

Brunner, C.J. (1979), *Sasanian Stamp Seals in the Metropolitan Museum of Art* (New York).

Bulliet, R.W. (2009), *Cotton, Climate, and Camels: A Moment in World History* (2009).

Burton, R.F. (1877), *Sind Revisited*, vol. 1 (London).

Calmard, J. (1987), 'Atābak-e A'dam, Amīn-al-soltān: Grand Vizier under the Last Three Qajar Kings', *Encyclopædia Iranica* 2 (London and New York).

Cereti, C.G. (1995), *The Zand ī Wahman Yasn: A Zoroastrian Apocalypse* (Rome).

Chavannes, E. (1903), *Documents sur les Tou-kiue (Turcs) occidentaux* (St Petersburg; reprint Paris, 1973).

Choksy, J.K. (1997) *Conflict and Cooperation. Zoroastrian Subalterns and Muslim Elites in Medieval Iranian Society* (New York).

— (2006), 'Despite Shahs and Mollas: Minority Sociopolitics in Premodern and Modern Iran', *Journal of Asian History* 40.2: 149–50.

— (2007), 'Iranians and Indians in Sri Lanka', in J. Hinnells and A. Williams, eds, *Parsis in India and the Diaspora* (London/New York).

Cohen, A. (1986), 'Iranian Jewry and the Educational Endeavors of the Alliance Israélite Universelle', *Jewish Social Studies* 48: 15–44.

Compareti, M. (2009), *Samarcanda centro del mondo: Proposte di lettura del ciclo pittorico di Afrāsyāb* (Milano-Udine).

Crone, P. (1991), 'Kavad's Heresy and Mazdak's Revolt', *Iran* 29: 21–42.

— (2012), *The Nativist Prophets of Early Islamic Iran: Rural Revolt and Local Zoroastrianism* (Cambridge).

Crossman, C.L. (1991). *The Decorative Arts of the China Trade: Paintings, Furnishings, and Exotic Curiosities* (Suffolk).

Curtis J. (2000), *Ancient Persia* (London).

— (2005), 'Iron Age Iran and the Transition to the Achaemenid period' in V. Sarkhosh Curtis and S. Stewart, eds, *The Idea of Iran: Birth of the Persian Empire*, vol 1 (London): 112–31.

— (2013), *The Cyrus Cylinder and Ancient Persia: A New Beginning for the Middle East* (London).

Curtis, J. and N. Tallis, eds (2005), *Forgotten Empire: The World of Ancient Persia* (London).

— (2012), *The Horse: From Arabia to Royal Ascot* (London).

Dabir-Siaghi, M. (1956), *Shahnameh* (Tehran).

Dadoyan, S.B. (2011), *The Armenians in the Medieval Islamic World*, vol. I (New Brunswick).

Dalton, O.M. (1964), *The Treasure of the Oxus with Other Examples of Early Oriental Metalwork* (London).

Dandamayev, M.A. (1999), 'Achaemenid Imperial Policies and Provincial Governments', *Iranica Antiqua* 34.

Darukhanawala, H.D. (1939), *Parsi Lustre on Indian Soil*, vol. 1 (Bombay).

Daryaee, T. (2012), 'Food, Purity and Pollution: Zoroastrian Views on the Eating Habits of Others', *Iranian Studies* 45.2 (March).

Davis, D., trans. and ed. (2009), *Vis and Ramin* (London/New York).

Dhabhar, B.N. (1909), *Saddar Nasr and Saddar Bundehesh* (Bombay).

— (1912), *Namakiha i Manushchihar: The Epistles of Manushchihar* (Bombay).

— (1932), *The Persian Rivayats of Hormazyar Framarz and Others: Their Version with Introduction and Notes* (Bombay).

Dhalla, M.N. (1908), *The Nyaishes or Zoroastrian Litanies* (New York).

Donner, H. (1986), 'Geschichte des Volkes Israel und seiner Nachbarn in Grundzügen, Part 2: Von der Königszeitbiszu Alexander dem Großen', *Grundrissezum Alten Testament* 4.2: 370–81.

Downing, C.T. (1838), *The Fan-qui in China, in 1836–7*, vols 1-3 (London).

Edwardes, S.M. (1910), *The Gazetteer of Bombay City and Island* (Bombay), vol. 3.

Etsuko, K. (2005), 'Quelques remarques sur des monuments funéraires de Sogdiens en Chine', *Studia Iranica* 34: 257–78.

Ferdowsi, Abu'l-Qasem, vol. 1 (1905), vol. 2 (1906), vol. 8 (1923), *The Shahnama*, ed. and transl. A.G. Warner and E. Warner, (London).

Finkel, I. (2013), *The Cyrus Cylinder* (London).

Fischer, M. (2004), *Mute Dreams, Blind Owls, and Dispersed Knowledges: Persian Poesis in the Transnational Circuitry* (Durham/London).

Friedenberg, D.M. (2009), *Sasanian Jewry and Its Culture: A Lexicon of Jewish and Related Seals* (Urbana).

Geiger, W., et al. (1895), *Grundriss der iranischen Philologie* (Strassburg).

Gignoux, P. (1976), 'Cachets Sassanides du British Museum', *Acta Iranica* 12 (Troisième Série V).

— (1983), 'Die religiöse Administration in sasanidischer Zeit: ein Überblick', in H. Koch and D.N. MacKenzie, eds, *Kunst, Kultur und Geschichte der Achämenidenzeit und ihr Fortleben* (Berlin): 253–66.

Gignoux, P. and A. Tafazzoli, transl. (1993), *Anthologie de Zādspram* (Leuven).

Gnoli, G. (1989), 'Avestan Geography', in E. Yarshater, ed., *Encyclopædia Iranica* 3 (London and New York): 44–7.

Godrej, P. and F. Punthakey Mistree (2002), *A Zoroastrian Tapestry: Art, Religion and Culture* (Usmanpura, India).

Godrej, P. (2002), 'Faces from the Mists of Time: Parsi Portraits of Western India (1750–1900), in: Godrej and Punthakey Mistree (2002).

Grenet, F. (1984), *Les pratiques funéraires dans l'Asie centrale sédentaire de la conquête grecque à l'islamisation* (Paris).

— (1986), 'L'art zoroastrien en Sogdiane: Études d'iconographie funéraire', *Mesopotamia* 21.

— (1990), 'Burial ii. Remnants of Burial in Ancient Iran', *Encyclopædia Iranica* 4, (London and New York): 560.

— (2007a), 'Religious Diversity among Sogdian Merchants in Sixth-Century China: Zoroastrianism, Buddhism, Manichaeism, and Hinduism', *Comparative Studies of South Asia, Africa and the Middle East* 27: 463–78.

— (2007), 'The 7th Century "Ambassadors' Painting" at Samarkand', in K. Yamauchi et al., eds, *Mural Paintings of the Silk Road: Cultural Exchanges Between East and West* (London): 9–19.

— (2012), 'Mary Boyce's Legacy for the Archaeologists', *Bulletin of the Asia Institute* 22: 29–46.

Grenet, F. and B. Marshak (1998), 'Le mythe de Nana dans l'art de la Sogdiane', *Arts Asiatiques* 53.

Grenet, F. and Zhang Guangda (1996), 'The Last Refuge of the Sogdian Religion: Dunhuang in the Ninth and Tenth Centuries', *Bulletin of the Asia Institute* 10: 175–86.

Grube, E.J. (1972), *Islamic Paintings from the 11th to the 18th Century in the Collection of Hans J. Kraus* (New York).

Grüber, C. (2009), 'Die Timuridische Handschrift *Himmelfahrt des Propheten Muhammad (Mi'rāj-Nāmeh)*', in A. Çoruh and H. Budde, *Taswir: Islamische Bildwelten und Moderne* (Berlin): 197–202.

Guandan, P. (1984), 'Jews in Ancient China: A Historical Survey', in S. Shapiro, ed., *Jews in Old China: Studies by Chinese Scholars* (New York): 46–102.

Gyselen, R. (2006), 'Chrétiens en terre d'Iran: implantation et acculturation', *Studia Iranica*, 33 (85a).

Hale, W.E. (1986), *Ásura in Early Vedic Religion* (Delhi).

Harper, P.O. (1978), *The Royal Hunter: Art of the Sasanian Empire* (New York).

— (1985), 'The Ox-Headed Mace in Pre-Islamic Iran', *Acta Iranica* 24 (1).

Harper, P.O. et al. (1992), *The Royal City of Susa: Ancient Near Eastern Treasures in the Louvre* (New York).

Harris, F. (1958), *Jamsetji Nusserwanji Tata (A Chronicle of His Life)* (Bombay).

Henkelman, W.F.M. (2008), *The Other Gods Who Are: Studies in Elamite-Iranian Acculturation based on the Persepolis Fortification Texts* (Leiden).

Hiebert, F.T. (1998), 'Central Asians on the Iranian Plateau: A Model for Indo-Iranian Expansionism', in V.H. Mair, ed., *The Bronze Age and Early Iron Age Peoples of Eastern Central Asia,* vol. 1 (Washington, D.C.): 148–61.

Hinnells, J.R. (2005), *The Zoroastrian Diaspora* (Oxford).

Hintze, Almut (1998), 'The Migrations of the Indo-Iranians and the Iranian Sound-Change s > h.', in W. Meid, ed, *Sprache und Kultur der Indogermanen* (Innsbruck): 139-153.

— (2000), 'Frašō.kərəti', in E. Yarshater, ed., *Encyclopaedia Iranica* 10 (Costa Mesa, California): 190–2.

— (2007), *A Zoroastrian Liturgy* (Wiesbaden).

— (2009a), 'Avestan Literature', in R.E. Emmerick and M. Macuch, eds, *The Literature of Pre-Islamic Iran* (London): 1–71.

— (2009b), 'The Cow that Came from the Moon', *Bulletin of the Asia Institute* 19: 58–61.

— (2013a), 'Perceptions of the Yasna Haptaŋhāiti', in E. Pirart and X. Tremblay, eds, *Questions zoroastriennes II: le sort des Gâthâs* (Leuven, forthcoming): 53–73.

— (2013b), 'Zarathustra's Time and Homeland: Textual Perspectives', in M. Stausberg and Y. Vevaina, eds, *Blackwell Companion to the Study of Zoroastrianism* (Oxford, forthcoming).

— (2013c), 'Monotheism the Zoroastrian Way', *Journal of the Royal Asiatic Society* 23 (forthcoming).

— (2013d), *Change and Continuity in the Zoroastrian Tradition* (London): 32–5.

Hinz, W. (1987), 'Elams Übergang ins Perserreich', in Ph. Gignoux, ed., *Transition Periods in Iranian History* (Louvain).

Hodivala, S.H. (1920), *Studies in Parsi History* (Bombay).

Howard-Johnston, J. (2010), *Witnesses to a World Crisis: Historians and Histories of the Middle East in the Seventh Century* (Oxford).

Hughes, M.J. and J.A. Hall (1979), 'X-Ray Fluorescence Analyses of Late Roman and Sassanian Silver Plate', *Journal of Archaeological Science* 6.4 (December).

Humbach, H and P. Ichaporia (1994), *The Heritage of Zarathushtra: A New Translation of his Gāthās* (Heidelberg).

Jaafari-Dehaghi, M. (1998), *Dādestān ī dēnīg. Part I* (Studia Iranica Cahier 20, Leuven).

Jackson, A.V.W. (1906), *Persia Past and Present: A Book of Travel and Research* (New York).

— (1938), *Zoroaster: The Prophet of Ancient Iran* (New York [1898]).

al-Jahiz (1965), *Kitab al-hayawan*, vol. 2 (Cairo).

Jaradi, P.M. (2011), *Parsi Portraits from the Studio of Raja Ravi Varma* (Mumbai): 17–18.

Jejeebhoy, J. (1849), letter, dated 7 May, to D. Jardine in London – Sir J. J. correspondence, 1 January 1849–12 December 1849.

Joisten-Pruschke, A. (2008), *Das religiöse Leben der Juden von Elephantine in der Achämenidenzeit* (Wiesbaden).

— (forthcoming [a]), *Die Städte der babylonischen Kultur im Sasanidenreich.*

— (forthcoming [b]), *Religions and Religious Conditions of the Sasanian Period with Special Reference to Zoroastrianism, Judaism and Christianity.*

Jones, Alexander, ed. (1966), *The Jerusalem Bible* (London).

Jong, A. de (1997), *Traditions of the Magi* (Leiden).

— (2009), 'The Culture of Writing and the Use of the Avesta in Sasanian Iran', in E. Pirart and X. Tremblay, eds, *Zarathushtra entre l'Inde et l'Iran* (Beiträge zur Iranistik 30, Wiesbaden): 27–41.

Josephson, J. (2003), 'The "Sitz im Leben" of the Seventh Book of the *Dēnkard*', in C.G. Cereti, M. Maggio and E. Provasi, eds, *Religious Themes and Texts of pre-Islamic Iran and Central Asia* (Wiesbaden).

Kanga, M.F. (1975), 'Sitīkar nāmak i Manushchihr Gōšnjamān. A Critical Study', in *Monumentum H.S. Nyberg I, Acta Iranica* 4 (Leiden).

Kashani, N.B. and T. Stoellner, eds (2011), 'Water and Caves in Ancient Iranian Religion: Aspects of Archaeology, Cultural History and Religion', *Archäologische Mitteilungenaus Iran* 43 (Berlin): 1–168.

Kastal'sky, B.N. (1909), 'Biya-naimanskie ossuarii', *Protokoly turkestanskogo kruzhka liubitelei arkheologii* 13 (Tashkent): 1–36.

Kellens, J. (1989), 'Avestique', in R. Schmitt, ed., *Compendium Linguarum Iranicarum* (Wiesbaden).

Kennedy, H. (2004), *The Court of the Caliphs: The Rise and Fall of Islam's Greatest Dynasty* (London).

Kent, R. (1953), *Old Persian: Grammar, Texts, Lexicon* (New Haven).

Kiash, K.D. (1889), *Sculpted Figures of Zoroaster, Ardeshir Babejan and Shapoor I – Takhat-i-Bostan Ancient Persian Sculptures: On the Monuments, Buildings, Bas-Reliefs Rock Inscriptions &c...* (Bombay).

Kottsieper, I. (2002), 'Die Religions politik der Achämeniden und die Juden von Elephantine', in R.G. Kratz, ed., *Religion und Religions kontakteim Zeitalter der Achämeniden* (Gütersloh): 150–78.

Kotwal, F.M. (1976), 'The Authenticity of the Parsi Priestly Tradition', *Journal of the K.R. Cama Oriental Institute* (Bombay).

Kotwal, F.M. and P.G. Kreyenbroek (2003), *The Hērbedestān and Nērangestān*, vols 1–3 (1992, 1995, 2003).

Krauss, W. (2005), 'Chinese Influence on Early Modern Indonesian Art? Hou Qua: A Chinese Painter in 19th-Century Java', *Archipel* 69.

Kreyenbroek, P.G. (1985), *Sraoša in the Zoroastrian tradition* (Bombay).

— (1987), 'The Dādestān ī dēnīg on Priests', *Indo-Iranian Journal* 30: 185–208.

— (1993), 'Cosmogony and Cosmology. I. In Zoroastrianism/Mazdāism', in E. Yarshater, ed., *Encyclopaedia Iranica* 6 (Costa Mesa, California).

— (1994), 'On the Concept of Spiritual Authority in Zoroastrianism', *Jerusalem Studies in Arabic and Islam* 17: 1–15.

— (1996), 'The Zoroastrian Tradition from an Oralist's Point of View', in H.J.M. Desai and H.N. Modi, eds, *K. R. Cama Oriental Institute: Second International Congress Proceedings* (Bombay).

— (2008), 'On the Construction of Zoroastrianism in Western Iran', in C. A. Bromberg, ed., *Bulletin of the Asia Institute*, New Series 22.

— (2010), 'Zoroastrianism under the Achaemenians: A Non-Essentialist Approach', in J. Curtis and S. Simpson, eds, *The World of Achaemenid Persia: History, Art and Society in the Ancient Near East* (London/New York).

— (2011), 'Some Remarks on Water and Caves in Pre-Islamic Iranian Religion', in Kashani and Stoellner (2011): 157–63.

Kulke, E. (1974), *The Parsees in India: A Minority Agent as Agent of Social Change* (Munich).

Kuz'mina, E.E. (2007), *The Origin of the Indo-Iranians* (Leiden/Boston): 413–20.

Lerner, J.A. (1977), *Christian Seals of the Sasanian Period* 44 (Istanbul).

— (2005), *Aspects of Assimilation: The Funerary Practices and Furnishings of Central Asians in China*, Sino-Platonic Papers 168 (Philadelphia).

Levy-Rubin, M. (2011), *Non-Muslims in the Early Islamic Empire: From Surrender to Coexistence* (Cambridge).

Lewellyn-Jones, R., ed. (2008), 'Introduction', in *Portraits in Princely India 1700–1947* (Mumbai).

Lhuillier, J. (2013), 'Les cultures "à céramique modelée peinte" en Asie Centrale', in *Iranica Antiqua* 48: 129–32.

Liesering, E. (1933), *Untersuchung zur Christenverfolgung des Kaisers Decius* (Würzburg).

Linklater, E. (1961), *Cities of Enchantment* (Edinburgh/London).

Livshits, V.A. (2008), *Sogdiiskaia epigrafika Srednei Azii i Semirech'ia* (St Petersburg).

Lubotsky, A. (2001), 'The Indo-Iranian Substratum', in C. Carpelan et al., eds, *Early Contacts between Uralic and Indo-European* (Helsinki).

Ludmilla V. Pavchinskaia, 'Ossuarii iz Mullakurgana', *Obshchestvennye nauki v Uzbekistane* (1983.3): 46–9.

Lyonnet, B. (1993), 'Central Asia, the Indo-Aryans and the Iranians', in A. Parpola and P. Koskikallio, eds, *South Asian Archaeology* 1 (Helsinki).

Macuch, M. (2008), 'Pahlavi Literature', in R.E. Emmerick and M. Macuch, eds, *The Literature of Pre-Islamic Iran*: 116–96.

Malcolm, N. (1905), *Five Years in a Persian Town* (London).

Mallory, J.P. (1989), *In search of the Indo-Europeans language, archaeology and myth* (London).

— (2002), 'Archaeological Models and Asian Indo-Europeans', in N. Sims-Williams, ed., *Indo-Iranian Languages and Peoples* (Oxford).

Mallory, J.P. and D.Q. Adams (2006), *The Oxford Introduction to the Proto-Indo-European World* (Oxford).

Margoliouth, G. (1905), *Catalogue of the Hebrew and Samaritan Manuscripts in the British Museum*, part 2 (London).

Marshak, B.I. (1995/96), 'On the Iconography of Ossuaries from Biya-Naiman', *Silk Road Art and Archeology* 4: 299–321.

— (2001), 'La thématique sogdienne dans l'art de la Chine de la seconde moitié du VIᵉ siècle', *Comptes Rendus de l'Académie des Inscriptions et Belles-lettres*: 227–64.

McKendrick, S. et al. (2011), *Royal Manuscripts: The Genius of Illumination* (London).

Mehr, F. (2002), 'Zoroastrians in Twentieth Century Iran', in Godrej and Punthakey Mistree (2002).

Menasce, J. de (1973), *Le troisième livre du Dēnkart* (Paris).

Middleton, A. and I. Freestone (1997), 'Inside View', *Ceramic Review* 166.

Mistree, K. (2002), 'Parsi Arrival and Early Settlements in India' in Godrej and Punthakey Mistree (2002).

Mitchell, T. (2000), 'The Persepolis Sculptures in the British Museum', *Iran* 38.

Modi, J.J. (1903), 'The Parsees at the Court of Akbar and Dastur Meherji Rana', *Journal of the Bombay Branch of the Royal Asiatic Society* 21 (57): 69–245.

— (1995), *The Religious Customs and Ceremonies of the Parsis* (Bombay).

Molé, M. (1993), *Dēnkard*, transl. as *La légende de Zoroastre selon les texts pehlevis* (Paris).

Monier-Williams, M. (1891), *Modern India and the Indians, Being a Series of Impressions, Notes and Essays* (London).

Moorey, P.R.S. (1974), *Ancient Bronzes from Luristan* (London).

Moses, H. (1850). *Sketches of India: with notes on the seasons, scenery, and society of Bombay, Elephanta, and Salsette* (London).

Muller, M. ed. (1980), *Sacred Books of the East*, vol. IV, part 1 (Delhi [reprint]).

Munshi, S. and S. Stewart, *Daily Observances: A Paradigm*, in: Godrej and Punthakey Mistree (2002).

Nanji, R. and H. Dhalla (2007), 'The Landing of the Zoroastrians at Sanjan: The Archaeological Evidence', in J.R. Hinnells and A.Williams, eds, *Parsis in India and the Diaspora* (London): 35–58.

al-Narshakhi, Muhammad ibn Ja'far (1954), *The History of Bukhara: Translated from a Persian Abridgment of the Arabic Original by Narshakhī*, trans. R.N. Frye (Cambridge, MA).

Naveh, J. and S. Shaked (2005), *Aramaic Documents from Ancient Bactria (Fourth Century BCE) from the Khalili Collections* (London): 174–85.

Neusner, J. (1969), *A History of the Jews in Babylonia* (Leiden), vol. 1.

Nikitin, A.B. (2000), 'Mitra iz Uruka', in *Ermitadjniya Chteniya 1995–1999 godov: Pamyati V.G. Lukonin (21.I.1932-10-IX.1984).*

Oelsner, J. (1986), *Materialien zur babylonischen Gesellschaft und Kultur in hellenistischer Zeit* (Budapest).

— (2002), '"Sieistgefallen, sieistgefallen, Babylon, die große Stadt." Vom Endeeiner Kultur', *Sitzungsberichte der Sächsischen Akademie der Wissenschaftenzu Leipzig*, Bd. 138, Heft 1.

Oppenheimer, A. (1983), *Babylonia Judaica in the Talmudic Period* (Wiesbaden).

Ouseley, Sir William (1819-23), *Travels in Various Countries of the East; More Particularly Persia* (London). 3vols.

Palsetia, J.S. (2001), *The Parsis of India: Preservation of Identity in Bombay City* (Leiden).

Parpola, A. (2002), 'From the Dialects of Old Indo-Aryan to Proto-Indo-Aryan and Proto-Iranian', in N. Sims-Williams, ed., *Indo-Iranian Languages and Peoples* (Oxford University Press).

Patel, B.B. (1878), *Parsi Prakash*, vol. 2 (Bombay).

Patel, B.B. and R. Barjorji, eds. (1891), *Parsi Prakash, being a Record of Important Events in the Growth of the Parsi Community in Western India* (Bombay), vol. 1.

Pavchinskaia, L.V. (1983), 'Ossuarii iz Mullakurgana', *Obshchestvennye nauki v Uzbekistane*, issue 3.

Perrot, J., ed. (2010), *Le Palais de Darius à Suse* (Paris).

Pilgrim, C. von (1998), 'Textzeugnis und archäologischer Befund: Zur Topographie von Elephantine in der 27.Dynastie', in H.

Guksch and D. Polz, eds, *Stationen, Festschrift Rainer Stadelmann* (Mainz): 485–97.

— (1999), 'Der Tempel des Jahwe', *Mitteilungen des Deutschen Archäologischen Instituts Kairo* 55: 141–5.

Pourshariati, P. (2008), *Decline and Fall of the Sasanian Empire: The Sasanian–Parthian Confederacy and the Arab Conquest of Iran* (London).

Punthakey Mistree, F. (2002) 'Hues of Madder, Pomegranite and Saffron: Traditional Costumes of Yazd', in Godrej and Punthakey Mistree (2002).

al-Qazvini (1982), 'Aja'ib *al-makhluqat* (Tehran).

Rapoport, I.A. (1971), *Iz istorii religii drevnego Khorezma. Ossuarii* (Moscow).

Rapoport, I.A. and M.S. Lapirov-Skoblo (1963), 'Raskopki dvortsovogo zdaniia na gorodishche Kalaly-gyr I v 1958 g.', *Materialy Khorezmskoi Arkheologo-ètnograficheskoi Èkspeditisii v 1958–1961 gg* (Moscow).

Razmjou, S. (2004), 'The Lan Ceremony and other Ritual Ceremonies in the Achaemenid Period: The Persepolis Fortification Tablets', *Iran* 42: 103–17.

Rezania, K. (2012), 'Mazdakism and the Canonisation of Pahlavi Translations of the Avestan Texts', in A. Cantera, ed., *The Transmission of the Avesta* (Wiesbaden).

Riboud, P. (2003), 'Le cheval sans cavalier dans l'art funéraire sogdien en Chine: à la recherche des sources d'un thème composite', *Arts Asiatiques* 58: 148–61.

— (2012), 'Bird-Priests in Central Asian Tombs of 6th-Century China and their Significance in the Funerary Realm', *Bulletin of the Asia Institute* 21: 1–23.

Ringer, M. (2011), *Pious Citizens: Reforming Zoroastrianism in India and Iran* (New York).

Rogers, R.W. (1929), *A History of Ancient Persia from its Earliest Beginnings to the Death of Alexander the Great* (New York).

Rose, J. (2011), *Zoroastrianism: An Introduction* (London).

Rtveladze, E.V. (1997), 'K istorii evreev-iudaistov v Srednei Azii (domusul'manskii period)', *Verovaniia i kul'ty domusul'manskoi Srednei Azii* (Moscow): 46–50.

Russell, J. (1987), *Zoroastrianism in Armenia* (Cambridge, MA).

Sachau, E. (1907–14), *Syrische Rechtsbücher* (Berlin), vols 1–3.

— (1919), 'Zur Ausbreitung des Christentums in Asien', *Abhandlungen der Preussischen Akademie der Wissenschaften*, Phil.-Hist. Kl.1 (Berlin).

— (2005), *The Chronology of Ancient Nations: An English version of the Arabic text of the Athâr-ul-bâkiya of Albîrûnî* (Lexington [1879]).

Saeki, P.Y. (1916), *The Nestorian Documents in China* (London).

— (1951), *The Nestorian Documents and Relics in China* (Tokyo).

Sarkhosh Curtis, V. (2007), 'The Iranian Revival in the Parthian Period', in V. Sarkhosh Curtis and S. Stewart, eds, *The Idea of Iran: The Age of the Parthians*, vol 2 (London).

— (1993), *Persian Myths* (London).

Schmermbeck, B. (2008), *Persische zarathustrische monāğāt: Edition, Übersetzung, Tradition und Analyse* (Göttinger Orientforschungen Iranica, N.F. 3, Wiesbaden).

Schmidt, E. (1939), *The Treasury of Persepolis and Other Discoveries in the Homeland of the Achaemenians*, Oriental Institute of the University of Chicago, Oriental Institute Communications 21 (Chicago).

Schwartz, M. (1990), 'Viiamburas and Kafirs', *Bulletin of the Asia Institute* 4: 251–5.

Séguy, M.-R. (1977), *The Miraculous Journey of Mahomet: Mirâj nâmeh, Bibliothèque Nationale, Paris (Manuscript Supplément Turc 190)*, trans. R. Peaver (London/New York).

Shah, S. and T. Vastal (2010), *Peonies and Pagodas: Embroidered Parsi Textiles: TAPI Collection* (Surat, India).

Shahrokh, S. and R. Writer, eds (1994), *The Memoirs of Keikhosrow Shahrokh* (New York/Ontario).

Shaked, S. (1984), 'From Iran to Islam: Notes on Some Themes in Transmission', *Jerusalem Studies in Arabic and Islam* 4 (Jerusalem).

— (1994), *Dualism in Transformation: Varieties of Religion in Sasanian Iran* (London).

— (2004), 'The Yasna Ritual in Pahlavi Literature', *Zoroastrian Rituals in Context* (Leiden).

Shastri, K.M. ('Nariman') (1918), *Dastur Meherji-Rana and the Emperor Akbar: Being a Complete Collection of the Editorials and Contributions Relating to this Controversy Conducted in the Parsi Press* (Bombay).

Shea, D. and A.V.W. Jackson (1901), eds, *The Dabistān: Or, School of Manners: The Religious Beliefs, Observances, Philosophic Opinions and Social Customs of the Nations of the East* (Washington).

Sheffield, D.J. (2012), *In the Path of the Prophet: Medieval and Early Modern Narratives of the Life of Zarathustra in Islamic Iran and Western India*, DPhil thesis, Harvard, available at nrs.harvard.edu.

Sheng, A. (2005), 'From Stone to Silk: Intercultural Transformation of Funerary Furnishings among Eastern Asian Peoples Around 475–650 CE', in É. de la Vaissière and É. Trombert, eds, *Les sogdiens en chine* (Paris): 141–89.

Shkoda, V.G. (1985), 'Ob odnoi gruppe sredneaziatskikh altarei ognia 5–8 vv', in *Khudozhestvennye pamiatniki i problemy kul'tury vostoka* (Leningrad): 82–9.

— (2009), *Pendzhikentskie khramy i problemy religii Sogda (v–viii vv.)* (St Petersburg).

Shuster, W.M. (1912), *The Strangling of Persia* (London).

Simpson, S.-J. (1997), 'Early Iron Age Rural Ceramic Traditions in Iran', in I. Freestone and D. Gaimster, eds, *Pottery in the Making* (London).

— (2003), 'From Mesopotamia to Merv: Reconstructing Patterns of Consumption in Sasanian Households', in T. Potts, M. Roaf and D. Stein, eds, *Culture Through Objects* (Oxford).

— (2008), *Bronzes du Luristan: Enigmes de l'Iran ancient: IIIe-1er millenaire av. J.C.*, ed. N. Engel (Paris).

— (2012), *Afghanistan: A Cultural History* (London).

Sims-Williams, N. (1976), 'The Sogdian Fragments of the British Library', *Indo-Iranian Journal* 18: 46–8, with appendix by I. Gershevitch: 75–82.

— (1998), 'The Iranian Languages', in A.G. Ramat and P. Ramat, eds, *The Indo-European Languages* (London/New York).

— (2004a), 'A Fourth-Century Abandoned Wife', in S. Whitfield, ed., *The Silk Road: Trade, Travel, War and Faith* (London): 248–9.

— (2004b), 'Zarathushtra Fragment', in S. Whitfield, ed, *The Silk Road: Trade, Travel, War and Faith* (London): 118.

— (2005), 'Towards a New Edition of the Sogdian Ancient Letters: Ancient Letter 1', in É. de la Vaissière and É. Trombert, eds, *Les sogdiens en chine* (Paris): 181–93.

— (2007), *Bactrian Documents from Northern Afghanistan II: Letters and Buddhist Texts* (London): 136–7.

— (2012), *Bactrian Documents from Northern Afghanistan I: Legal and Economic Documents*, rev. edn (London).

Sims-Williams, U. (2009), 'The Strange Story of Samuel Guise: An 18th-Century Collection of Zoroastrian Manuscripts', *Bulletin of the Asia Institute* 19: 199–209.

— (2012), 'Zoroastrian Manuscripts in the British Library, London', in A. Cantera, ed., *The Transmission of the Avesta* (Wiesbaden): 173–94.

Skjærvø, P.O. (2002), 'Praise and Blame in the Avesta: The Poet-Sacrificer and His Duties', in *Studies in Honour of Shaul Shaked* I, *Jerusalem studies in Arabic and Islam* 26 (Jerusalem): 29–67.

— (2007), 'The Importance of Orality for the Study of Old Iranian Literature and Myth', *Nāme-ye Irān-e Bāstān* 5: 1–23.

— (2011a), 'KARTIR', in *Encyclopaedia Iranica* 15.6 (Costa Mesa, California): 608–28

— (2011b), The Spirit of Zoroastrianism (New Haven and London).

Smith, Morton (1963), 'II Isaiah and the Persians', *Journal of the American Oriental Society* 83: 415–21.

Snesarev, G.P. (1969), *Relikty domusul'manskikh verovanii i obriadov u Uzbekov Khorezma* (Moscow): 107–81.

Spycket, A. (1992), *Les Figurines de Suse* (Paris).

Stade, K. (1926), *Der Politiker Diokletian und die letzte große Christenverfolgung* (Wiesbaden).

Stausberg, M. (2002), *Die Religion Zarathushtras. Geschichte – Gegenwart – Rituale I* (Stuttgart).

— (2009), 'Hell in Zoroastrian History', *Numen* 56.

Stavisky, B.Y. (1961), 'Ossuarii iz Biya-naimana', *Trudy Gosudarstvennogo Ėrmitazha* 5 (Leningrad): 162–76.

Stewart, S. (2007), 'Parsi Prayer and Song in India', in J. Hinnells and A. Williams, eds, *Parsis in India and the Diaspora* (London).

— (2012), 'The Politics of Zoroastrian Philanthropy and the Case of Qasr-e Firuzeh', *Iranian Studies* 45.1: 59–80.

Thackston, W., transl. (1994), 'The Paris Mi'rājnāma', *Journal of Turkish Studies* 18.

Thampi, M. (2005), *Indians in China 1800–1949* (New Delhi).

Trever, K.V. and V.G. Lukonin (1987), *Sasanidskoe serebro: sobranie Gosudarstvennogo Ėrmitazha: khudozhestvennaia kul'tura Irana III–VIII vekov* (Moscow).

Tsadik, D. (2007), *Between Foreigners and Shi'is: Nineteenth-Century Iran and its Jewish Minority* (Stanford).

Unvala, M.R. (1922), *Dârâb Hormazyâr's Rivâyat*, 2 vols (Bombay).

Vahman, F. (1986), *Ardā Wirāz Nāmag, The Iranian 'Divina Comedia'* (London/Malmö).

Vahman, F. and G. Asatrian (2002), *Notes on the Language and Ethnography of the Zoroastrians of Yazd* (Copenhagen).

Vaissière, É. de la and Matteo Compareti, eds (2006), *Royal Naurūz in Samarkand* (Pisa/Rome).

Vaissière, É. de la and Pénélope Riboud (2003), 'Les livres des Sogdiens

(avec une note additionnelle part Frantz Grenet)', *Studia Iranica* 32: 127–136.

Vanden Berghe, L and K. Schippmann (1985), *Les Reliefs Rupestres d'Elymaide (Iran) de l'Epoque Parthe* (Gent).

Varfolomeev, V. and V. Evdokimov (2013), 'Die Andronovo-Kulturen', in T. Stöllner and Z. Samasev, eds, *Unbekanntes Kasachstan – Archäologie im Herzen Asiens*, vol. 2 (Bochum).

Vitalone, M. (1996), *The Persian Revāyat 'Ithoter': Zoroastrian Rituals in the Eighteenth Century* (Naples).

Wadia, R.A. (1964), *Scions of Lowjee Wadia* (Bombay).

Walker, J.T. (2006), *The Legend of Mar Qardagh: Narrative and Christian Heroism in Late Antique Iraq* (Berkeley).

West, E.W (1882), *Pahlavi Texts II* (Sacred Books of the East 18, Oxford).

Williams, A.V. (1990), *The Pahlavi Rivayat Accompanying the Dadestan i Denig, Part II: Translation, Commentary and Pahlavi Text* (Copenhagen).

— (2009), *The Zoroastrian Myth of Migration from Iran and Settlement in the India Diaspora: Text, Translation and Analysis of the 16th Century Qesse-ye Sanjān, 'The Story of Sanjan'* (Leiden).

— (2012), 'The Replacement of Zoroastrian Iran: A New Reading of the Persian Qesse-ye Sanjan of Bahman Key Kobad Sanjana (1599)', *Bulletin of the Asia Institute*, n.s. 22: 79–93.

Wink, A. (1990), *Al-Hind: The Making of the Indo-Islamic World, Vol. 1: Early Medieval India and the Expansion of Islam, 7th–11th Centuries* (Leiden).

Witzel, M. (2003), 'Linguistic Evidence for Cultural Exchange in Prehistoric Western Central Asia', *Sino-Platonic Papers* 129.

Woolley, C.L. (1976), *Ur Excavations* VII (London).

Wright, W. (1872), *Catalogue of Syriac Manuscripts in the British Museum 3* (London).

Yagodin, V.N. and A.V.G. Betts (2006), *Ancient Khorezm* (n.p.).

Yamomoto, Y. (1981), 'The Zoroastrian Temple Cult of Fire in Archaeology and Literature (II)', *Orient* VII: 68–73.

Yarshater, E. (1998), 'The Persian Presence in the Islamic World', in R.G. Hovannisian and G. Sabagh, eds, *The Persian Presence in the Islamic World* (Cambridge).

Zaehner, R.C. (1955), *Zurvan: A Zoroastrian Dilemma* (Oxford).

Zimma, B.M. (1941), *Issyk-Kul'skiye zhertvenniki* (Frunze).

LENDERS TO THE EXHIBITION

Nasser D. Khalili Collection • Cats 29–30, 82–3, 84–86, 108, 112–117

LAL Collection • Cats 234, 239

Private Collection • Cats 28, 151, 168–9, 171

Afrasiab Museum, Samarkand • Cat. 36

Jal, Armin, Zar and Persis Amrolia • Cats 176, 177

Ancient India & Iran Trust, Cambridge • Cats 138–140

Fereydoun Avc • Cats 120–4, 232-4, 236–7, 240

British Library, London • Cats 15–22, 27, 31, 46–7, 54–7, 79–80, 102–3, 107, 127,
129, 131–7, 186, 209

British Museum, London • Cats 7, 10–13, 51, 58–60, 63–6, 69, 70–7, 90–100, 110

Chhatrapati Shivaji Maharaj Vastu Sangrahalaya Museum (CSMVS), Mumbai
Cats 14, 143–4, 154, 157

Bapsy Dastur • Cat. 181

Rusi Dalal • Cats 230–1

Farokh and Jean Dubash • Cat. 182

Shernaz Engineer • Cats 164–7, 183

Fatema Soudavar Farmanfarmaian • Cat. 111

FD Alpaiwalla Museum, Mumbai • Cats 1–6, 8–9, 61–2, 68, 78, 118–9, 152

Hameed Haroon • Cats 141–2, 148–9, 175, 178–9, 189, 191

Heatherwick Studios, London • Cat. 23

Almut Hintze • Cats 48–9

Institute of Archaeology Samarkand • Cats 26,32–3,35

Franey Irani • Cat. 185

Janet Rady Fine Art, London • Cat. 24

John Rylands Library, University of Manchester • Cats 81, 101

Aban Marker Kabraji • Cats 173–4

Hutoxi Kandawalla • Cats 170, 172

Farrokh K. Kavarana • Cat. 153

Vahid and Cathy Kooros • Cat. 89

Firoza Punthakey Mistree • Cat. 184

Khojeste Mistree • Cats 194–5

Royal Asiatic Society of Great Britain and Ireland • Cats 45, 147

Rossi & Rossi, London • Cat. 24

Bijan Saffari • Cat. 239

The State Hermitage Museum, St Petersburg • Cats 34, 37–41,
43–4, 87–8

Tata Central Archives • Cats 145–6, 150, 155–6, 160–3

Victoria & Albert Museum, London • Cats 42, 109

Warburg Institute, London • Cat. 53

Wellcome Institute Library, London • Cat. 52

Mehran Zirak • Cat. 238

Zoroastrian Trust Funds of Europe, London • Cats 158–9, 188, 190,
212–4, 218–9

PICTURE CREDITS

Frontispiece, Cats 141–2, 148–9, 175, 178–9, 189, 191
© Arif Mahmood – Whitestar Photo Archives (Pvt) Ltd.

Figs 1, 2, 25; Cats 7, 10–13, 51, 58–60, 63–6, 69, 70–77, 90–100, 110
© The Trustees of the British Museum, London

Fig. 3 • © Deutsches Archäologisches Institut, Eurasien – Abteilung, Berlin

Fig. 4 • Courtesy of Dastur Dr K. M. JamaspAsa

Figs 5, 6, 7 • © Mieke Kreyenbroek

Figs 8, 15 • © F. Grenet, F. Ory

Figs 10, 12, 13 • © F. Grenet

Fig. 14 • © Yang Junkai

Fig. 19; Cats 81, 101 • Reproduced by courtesy of the University Librarian and Director, The John Rylands Library, The University of Manchester

Fig. 20 • © John Bugge

Figs 21–2 • © Sarah Stewart

Fig. 23; Cats 215–6 • Courtesy of Bruce Benedict

Fig. 24 • © Freer Gallery of Art and Arthur M. Sackler Gallery Archives, Smithsonian Institution, Washington, D.C.

Fig. 26; Cats 15–22, 27, 31, 46–7, 54–7, 79, 80, 102–3, 107, 127, 129, 131–7, 186, 209 • © The British Library Board, London

Figs 27, 31, 35; Cats 425, 434, 443 • © A Zoroastrian Tapestry: Art, Religion and Culture

Fig. 29 • © Dr Ruksana Nanji

Fig. 32 • Courtesy of Phillips Antiques, Mumbai

Figs 33, 36; Cats 184, 187, 194, 195–208, 210 • © Noshir Gobhai

Fig. 34; Cats 145–6, 150, 155–6, 160–3 • © Tata Central Archives

Cats 1–6, 8–9, 61–2, 68, 78, 118–9, 152 • © FD Alpaiwalla Museum, Mumbai

Cats 14, 143, 144, 154, 157 • © Trustees, Chhatrapati Shivaji Maharaj Vastu Sangrahalaya, Mumbai

Cat. 23 • © Heatherwick Studio, London

Cat. 24 • Courtesy of Janet Rady Fine Art, London and Rossi & Rossi, London

Cat. 25 • © Bombay Parsi Punchayet

Cats 26, 35–6 • © MAFOUZ de Sogdiane

Cat. 28 • Courtesy of Nicholas Sims-Williams

Cats 29, 30, 82–3, 84–86, 108, 112–117 • © Nour Foundation. Courtesy of the Khalili Family Trust

Cats 32–3 • © Institute of Archaeology of the Academy of Sciences of Uzbekistan

Cats 34, 37–41, 43–4 • © The State Hermitage Museum/ Aleksey Pakhomov

Cats 42, 109 • © Victoria and Albert Museum, London

Cats 45, 147 • © Royal Asiatic Society of Great Britain and Ireland

Cats 48–9, 89, 111, 120, 151, 158–9, 164–9, 171, 173–4, 176–7, 181–3, 188, 190, 212–4, 218–9, 230–1 • © Glenn Ratcliffe

Cat. 50 • © Vatican Museums and Galleries, Vatican Cit /Giraudon The Bridgeman Art Library

Cat. 52 • © Wellcome Library, London

Cat. 53 • © 2013 The Warburg Institute, London

Cat. 67 • © Morris Associates, London

Cats 87–8 • © The State Hermitage Museum/Vladimir Terebenin, Leonard Kheifets, Yuri Molodkovets

Cats 104–6 • © Bibliothèque nationale de France

Cats 121–4, 232–240 • © Mehran Zirak

Cats 138–40 • © Ancient India & Iran Trust

Cats 153, 170, 172, 185 • Private Collection

Cats 225, 193 • © Noshir Mulla, A Zoroastrian Tapestry: Art, Religion and Culture

Cat. 211 • Courtesy of Sanjeev Prabhu

Cat. 217 • Courtesy of Lambeth Palace/Picture Partnership

Cat. 220 • Courtesy of Jamsheed K. Choksy

Cat. 222, 226 • Courtesy of FEZANA

Cat. 223 • Courtesy of Rashna Wadia

Cat. 224 • Courtesy of Azita Dehmobed

Cat. 227 • Courtesy of Arnavaz Chubb

Cat. 228 • Courtesy of Meher Bhesani

Cat. 229 • Courtesy of Sohrab Framrose Shapurjee

Every effort has been made to seek permission to reproduce the images in this book. Any omissions are entirely unintentional, and requests for details should be addressed to the publishers.

ABBREVIATIONS

AV: Avestan

DD: *Dadistan i Denig*

DK: *Denkard*

GBD: Greater *Bundahishn*

MP: Middle Persian

NP: New Persian

NY: *Niyayish*

OP: Old Persian

PGuj: Persian Gujarati

QS: *Qesseh-ye Sanjan*

VD: *Videvdad*

Y: *Yasna*

YAV: Younger Avestan

YH: *Yasna Haptanghaiti*

YT: *Yasht*

INDEX

au temps dabraham
retgnoit zoroastres q̃
trouua les art encha
teresses nigromance et les aut
Item il trouua les sept art qui
sont di3 liberaulx gramaire lo
grque retgorique geometrie
arismetreque mustque 2 astro
nomie Et les escript en vng co
lombes desquelles les sept estoi
ent saram et les autres de ma
tiere de tuille contre les deluges
de feu et deaue Aristote dist si
comme helmians raconte que
zoroastres escript par xx fois C˜
uere De ce zoroastres est dit que
tantost quil fut ne3 il commenca
a rire Et ce raconte st augustin
ou vng̃ liure de la cite de dieu.

Hermes fut ne3 en egipte et a sa
par toutes terre iij xx xix ans.
Auec sin lxxx personnes de diuers
langaiges qui tousiours enor
toient ses gens de obeir a dieu
Et edifsia C xviij villes lesqlles
il remplist de toutes sciences Et
sut le premier qui trouua la scie
ce des estoilles Et estabsi a chñ
peuple soy partirent 2 conue
nables a leurs oppinions · Au
quel hermes ses roys ou temps
present de sors obeyrent 2 toute
leur terre Et les contraint a
garder sa loy de dieu a dire de
rite a despire se monde a garder
iustice Et commanda oroisons
et prieres estre faittes 2 a uuer
se samedy · Et a destruire ses

LIST OF DONORS FROM THE ZTFE

The Zoroastrian Trust Funds of Europe (ZTFE) wishes to acknowledge the following families (in alphabetical order) for their generous financial support to our appeal for funding *The Everlasting Flame: Zoroastrianism in History and Imagination*.

Zarthustra and Caroline Amrolia
Mahiar and Siloo Godrej Ardeshir
ZTFE Counsel Emeritus and Past Trustee Noshir and Kumi Avari
Freni and Katy Bajina
Mahiar and Armaity Bhathena
ZTFE Trustee Ervad Rustom and Amy Bhedwar
Godrej Bhumgara
ZTFE Patron Lord Karan and Lady Heather Bilimoria CBE DL and The Cobra Foundation
Gul Billimoria
Gav and Benaifer Buhariwala
Zarir and Shelialla Cama
Sarosh and Pearline Collector
Kaiyumars and Rozy Contractor
Maharukh and Hoshedar Cooper
ZTFE Trustee and Past President Rusi and Roshan Dalal
Ervad Shahyan and Bapsy Dastur
ZTFE President Malcolm, Freddy and Roshan Minoo Deboo
Shernaz Engineer and Verity Education VIP's Ltd
Jamshid and Paridokht Falahati
Thrity Gazi
ZTFE Past President and Past Trustee Kersey, Silloo and Paoorooshasp Jasavala
Kairas and Aban Kabraji
Minoo and Nargis Kalifa
Darius and Aban Karkaria
Ervad Jal and Najoo Karkaria
Farokh and Jaloo Kateli
Rustom and Binny Kharegat
Dara and Freni Marchant
Betty Marchant-Appoo
Fariborz Mawandad
Jehangir Mehta and Perosha Tengra
ZTFE Past President Dorab and Shehnaz Mistry OBE
Jimmy and Shirin Mistry
ZTFE Past Trustee Firoze, Kerman and Rohinton Munshi
Phiroze and Roshan Munshi
Shahpur, Tehnaz and Hila Patell
ZTFE Past President Ervad Zal and Navaz Sethna
ZTFE Past President Shahrokh and Simin Shahrokh
Keki Sidhwa
Carlos and Gemma Trigo
Hoshang and Freny Writer
Sarosh Zaiwalla & Company Solicitors
Mehernosh and Shanaaz Billimoria
Gauver Surkari
Jimmy and Aban Suratia
Sheroo Amrolia

And other, anonymous, donors